The Dynamics of Human Aggression

THEORETICAL FOUNDATIONS, CLINICAL APPLICATIONS

by

Ana-María Rizzuto, M.D.
W. W. Meissner, S.J., M.D.
and
Dan H. Buie, M.D.

BRUNNER-ROUTLEDGE

New York and Hove

Published in 2004 by
Brunner-Routledge
29 West 35th Street
New York, NY 10001
www.brunner-routledge.com

Published in Great Britain by
Brunner-Routledge
27 Church Road
Hove, East Sussex
BN3 2FA
www.brunner-routledge.co.uk

Brunner-Routledge is an imprint of the Taylor & Francis Group.
Printed in the United States of America on acid-free paper.

Chapter 3 is adapted from Rizzuto, A.-M. (1999). "I Always Hurt the One I Love—and Like It": Sadism and a Revised Theory of Aggression. *Canadian Journal of Psychoanalysis* 7: 219- 244. Reprinted with permission.

Chapter 4 adapted from Buie, D. H., Meissner, W. W., & Rizzuto, A.-M. (1996). The role of aggression in sadomasochism. *Canadian Journal of Psychoanalysis* 4: 1–28. Reprinted with permission.

Chapter 8 is adapted from Meissner, S. J., W. W., Rizzuto, A.-M., Sashin, J., & Buie, D. H. (1987). A View of Aggression in Phobic States. *Psychoanalytic Quarterly* 56: 452–76. Reprinted with permission.

10 9 8 7 6 5 4 3 2 1

Library of Congress Cataloging-in-Publication Data

Rizzuto, Ana-María.
    The dynamics of human aggression : theoretical foundations, clinical applications / by Ana-María Rizzuto, W.W. Meissner, and Dan H. Buie.
        p. ; cm.
    Includes bibliographical references and index.
    ISBN 0-415-94591-7 (hardcover : alk. paper)
    1. Aggressiveness. 2. Psychoanalysis.
[DNLM: 1. Aggression--psychology. 2. Psychoanalytic Theory. WM 600 R627d 2003] I. Meissner, W. W. (William W.), 1931- II. Buie, Dan H. III. Title.

BF175.5.A36R59 2003
155.2'32--dc21

                                                        2003009528

Contents

Preface

The present work represents the efforts of three decades of thought, careful evaluation of extensive clinical material obtained through the analytic process as conducted by the authors, and correspondingly prolonged discussions regarding the nature of aggression and the role it plays in the analytic situation and process. Only gradually, slowly, laboriously—with countless steps of seeming progress forward in our understanding and ability to formulate our ideas in consensually resonant terms, followed all too often by new doubts, skepticism, and recurrent questioning of what we had once thought to have been settled and agreed upon—did we come to the common ground of theory and clinical application that we are presenting.

To keep our efforts in perspective, we realize that we are submitting a view of aggression and its role in the analytic process that is new, different, and challenging to the convictions and theoretical persuasions of the great majority of present-day analysts. The major focus of our revision is on the shift from a theory of aggression as drive to a concept of aggression as motive. This shift sacrifices nothing of the explanatory potential due to aggression, but removes the basis of explanation from an appeal to the drives to an appeal to motivating contexts and stimulus conditions. This shift calls for exposition on two fronts—the first theoretical, to justify its theoretical legitimacy, and the second clinical, to demonstrate the differences in clinical application between a view of aggression as motive and as drive. We have made the effort to accomplish both; however successfully remains to the judgment of the reader.

The spirit of our advocacy, therefore, cannot, should not, assume too much. Our confrontation with traditional and contemporary views of aggression and our proposal of a different model of aggression, along with a revision of its metapsychological underpinnings, calls for a degree of modesty, a sense that what we are proposing is tentative and to a significant degree exploratory and hypothetical. We have come to regard our approach as a new theory of aggression, but we wish to be specific about what is new and what is not. Other theorists, as we will discuss, have broken free of the classical view of aggression as rooted in hostility and destructiveness and have made room for a view of aggression as also potentially positive and constructive, as we do. Other theories too have abandoned the classical drive theory, as we do. In this respect our theory is not new. However, no other theory, in disparaging or disavowing the drive theory, has provided a workable metapsychological revision as we have tried to do. The essence of that revision is the separation of drive from motive, and the replacement of drive agency with the agency of the self.

In taking this fundamental step, we feel that our view is not only new but in a sense revolutionary. At the same time, the elements of our view have been previously published and scattered in the analytic literature for nearly a score of years. In the present work, we are drawing the pieces together and presenting a fully articulated theory that is not new to us but may be to potential readers. In similar terms, we have taken the bold step of questioning whether our theory provides a new paradigm. Without debating the issues of what we might mean by the term, our theory may qualify as such by reason of the fact that it reconstructs and realigns basic components of the psyche and its functioning, specifically the separation of drive from motive and the removal of agency from the drives, eliminating them from the psychic equation, and the recentering of agency in the self as synonymous with the human person.

In the course of our discussions with fellow analysts, we have encountered the view that our refashioning of the notion of aggression in distinction from the drive theory may be passé since the drive theory is already regarded by some as out-of-date and obsolete. And this may be the case for some theorists, but in our reading of current analytic literature we have not been able to escape the impression that the drive theory is alive and well, that it is reflected directly or indirectly on almost every page of analytic discourse, and not only among continental or English (especially kleinian) analysts, but very much among contemporary American analysts.[1] In consequence we felt impelled to argue, as convincingly as we are able, the cogency and clinical relevance of our perspective on aggression. But we are also aware that in presenting this material we are offering a proposal to our fellow analysts for their mature and thoughtful consideration, in the hope that our approach makes clinical sense to them and that the theoretical framework we argue carries a corresponding degree of persuasion.

It may be well, before we go any further, to caution our readers that our argument will remain within the confines of analytic theory and the analytic process. This is the area of our training, experience, and expertise. At the same time, we are well aware that the issues related to the understanding of aggression have broad implications for other areas of human endeavor and conflict. There is a good deal more to be said about aggression than we are able to encompass. There is a proliferation of studies of genetics, neurobiological processes, and emotional processes from empirical and nonanalytic sources; their importance and significance for the ultimate understanding of aggression cannot be underestimated, but they lie beyond our competence. By the same token, there are far-reaching implications of the understanding of aggression in social terms. To mention only one such concern, the problems of violence and so-called unneutralized aggression on so many levels and in so many areas of our society are pressing and even urgent issues that call for better understanding and more effective corrective intervention. Analysts have not ignored such problems (Twemlow, 2000), but there is room for much greater exploration and understanding. If these issues lie beyond the scope of our efforts, we would be persuaded at the same time that the theory of aggression we propose not only has potential application in these areas, but that it may offer a more advantageous basis for future integration with other nonanalytic approaches, both biological and sociological. We can hope that our view might stimulate experts in these other areas to take another look at aggression, especially in its destructive guises, as a powerful source of motivation underlying many of these socially disruptive manifestations.

---

[1]Hamilton's (1996) study of analytic theoretical attitudes gives some support to this perception.

Finally, we would also take this occasion to remember our friend and colleague Jerome I. Sashin, M.D., who was an important and intimate collaborator with us in the early years of our mutual endeavor. His contributions were major in helping us to fashion our thinking and are reflected in many dimensions of the thinking we are presenting in this volume. His untimely death in 1990 deprived us of the enriching collaboration of a valued and creative contributor. The present work is a tribute to our friendship and his memory.

Ana-María Rizzuto, M.D.
W. W. Meissner, S.J., M.D.
Dan H. Buie, M.D.

Section I

Toward a New View
of Aggression in Analysis

Chapter 1

Aggression in Psychoanalysis

FROM DRIVE TO MOTIVATIONAL THEORY

INTRODUCTION

In this work, we are seeking to advance a theory of aggression that we see as distinctly different from classical psychoanalytic approaches to and formulations regarding aggression and as proposing an understanding of aggression that diverges in important ways from currently extant theories of aggression. While the view of aggression we propose stands in opposition to classical drive theory, it remains consistent with certain core aspects of the classical paradigm. One of the core contributions Freud made to the understanding of human psychic functioning, in addition to the appreciation of unconscious mental functioning, was his appreciation of the centrality and pervasiveness of motivations operating at all levels of psychic functioning. Freud struggled to find ways of formulating and explaining these important motivational components of the human mind. He did so by adopting the drive theory that was prevailing in current German scientific circles. In so doing, as we would see it, he based his motivational theory in instinctual drives that incorporated not only motivational aspects but causative aspects as well. In other words, Freud's instinctual drives were not only sources of motivation but also active sources of causal

3

agency. In so doing he elided the distinction between motive and cause and combined them in a single source, making them for practical purposes synonymous.

Our approach takes a stand that is fundamentally distinct from this freudian paradigm. It might be risky or brash to suggest that we are advancing a new paradigm, since we hold staunchly to the basic freudian emphasis on the role of motives in psychic life, and most particularly the impact and expression of unconscious motives. There is nothing in the theoretical and clinical formulations we will offer in the course of this book that opposes or contradicts this profoundly meaningful freudian understanding. What we question is the theoretical underpinnings of the understanding of aggression. We will do so largely by clearly distinguishing cause from motive (chapter 5), reformulating aggression as a form of motivation and ascribing causality and agency to the person himself in the guise of the self-as-agent (chapter 4).

This shift in perspective and the corresponding metapsychological transformations may or may not correspond to concepts of a paradigm shift, but they are quite consistent with ideas of scientific progress. Although his ideas have not met with universal acceptance, the philosopher of science Kuhn (1970) spoke of scientific paradigms as "universally recognized scientific achievements that for a time provide model problems and solutions to a community of practitioners" (p. viii). Freud's drive theory certainly would qualify as such a dominating paradigm. Changes in paradigms in Kuhn's terms are normal processes in the transformation of knowledge requiring "rejection of one time-honored scientific theory in favor of another incompatible with it" (p. 6) and "the re-evaluation of prior fact" (p. 7). In fact-gathering, the process of articulating a new paradigm attempts to resolve ambiguities and find solutions to previously unattended problems (p. 27). This describes the tenor of our effort in this work.

Acceptance of any new theory depends on comparison with the preexisting paradigm and the judgment as to how well each responds to the problems it addresses. The paradigm change may call for "a reconstruction that changes some of the field's most elementary theoretical generalizations" (p. 85). Most important for practitioners of a particular discipline is that the paradigm they use provides them with a basis for interpreting the empirical data embedded in a constellation of beliefs, values, and techniques essentially shared by the members of their discipline's community. In psychoanalysis, interpretation of the meaning of aggression in the clinical situation and technical handling of aggressive material in the analytic process is currently contingent upon the present-day prevailing belief that aggression is a drive endowed with its own inherent energy constantly pressuring for discharge. The explanatory emphasis in our view of aggression, in contrast, falls on the meaning, contexts, circumstances, and patterns of developmental experience and the history of object relations that shape and give meaning to human motivations. Our view consequently dispenses with the drive concept as causal and shifts the emphasis to the role of aggression as motive.

In her closing scientific presentation on the theme of aggression at the 27th International Congress in Vienna, Anna Freud (1972) commented that even after surveying forty years of contributions to the study of aggression, the Congress had failed to remove "uncertainties concerning the status of aggression in the theory of drives" (p. 163). She concluded that the analytic world has remained, since Freud's 1920 description of the aggressive or destructive instinct, "divided into two factions, with convictions ranging from complete or even extreme commitment to Freud's dualistic theory of drives to an equally complete rejection of the assumption of a death instinct with aggression as its representative" (p. 170). In the three decades following the Vienna Congress, many authors have attempted to elaborate the psychoanalytic concept of aggression from several different angles, ranging from observational and developmental researchers to object relations theorists and self-psychologists and relational and intersubjective theorists. Aggression is conceived either as a primary aggressive destructive drive (Hartmann, Waelder, Kernberg), as a drive based reaction to frustration or unpleasure (Stone, Glasser, Parens, McDevitt, Stechler), as a drive-organized response to suffering from needed primary objects who fail to provide what the child needs from them (Spitz, Fairbairn, Guntrip, Winnicott), or as a drive related to the vicissitudes of narcisssistic needs (Kohut, Rochlin). Finally, other researchers (Parens, Lichtenberg) have classified several varieties of aggression serving different developmental and psychic needs. In none of these theories is there a clear distinction between external or internal aggressive actions and the affect experienced by the subject. For many theoreticians, starting with Freud and Klein, aggression is treated as synonymous with affects such as rage, hate, envy, revenge, and others.[1]

Lest anyone think that our theory has sprung full-blown from the head of Jove, we acknowledge our predecessors, not only in criticizing and diverging from a drive orientation, but in pointing the way to a motivational orientation. Some years ago, to cite only one example here, Greenspan (1975), in exploring the relevance of learning paradigms for enriching analytic theoretical and clinical resources, argued in favor of concepts of behavioral modification based on central representational contingencies, derived from the integration of situational (external) stimulus contingencies and incentive stimuli, in preference to stimulus-response reinforcement paradigms as potentially integrable with analytic perspectives. Stimuli, he argued, do not operate on the basis of extrinsic reinforcements or drive-need reduction, but rather they shift the emphasis from drive states to more complex and autonomous motivational states relatively independent of response contingencies, e.g., curiosity versus hunger. Such motivational states tend to reorganize certain selective situational stimuli as conditioned incentive-discriminative stimuli which in turn elicit and regulate behavioral response patterns. Approaches that recognize the operation of central motivational states and incentive stimuli may thus, he concluded, prove more amenable to integration with psychoanalytic theory. Our theory seeks to amplify and solidify this motivational perspective in relation to the role of aggression in the psychic economy.

There is no extant theory of aggression offering a unifying concept for understanding the wide-ranging variety of aggressive internal and external actions and behaviors and the variety of affects frequently experienced in conjunction with the aggressive moment. Consequently, it seems that psychoanalysis has reached a point in which a new understanding may be called for to solve the dilemmas besieging analytic clinicians and theoreticians alike. We would feel that the conditions of the field seem ripe for the emergence of such a new perspective on aggression. Subsequent to the Vienna Congress on aggression, we have had over three decades of "proliferation of theories" (Kuhn, 1970, p. 75), many of which have diligently accumulated facts in an effort to meet the challenge of unresolved ambiguities and unsolved or unattended problems, but we would regard the results as still unsatisfactory.

Our theory proposes that aggression is best conceptualized as the capacity of the mind to carry out any psychic or physical activity directed to overcoming any obstacle interfering with the completion of an intended internal or external action. The motive for aggressive activity is overcoming an obstacle in order to complete the action and achieve its intended goal. Affects experienced in the effort of attempting to overcome the obstacle are dependent on motivational sources related to the specific intended action and the obstacle(s) interfering with its goal-attainment.[2] This understanding of aggression advances a single concept to encompass all varieties of aggression from infantile to mature; it does not confuse aggressive motivation with the affects attendant on overcoming or failing to overcome an obstacle; it encompasses observable and inferential phenomena relevant for clinical conceptualization. It requires no postulation of aggression either as a primary drive or as reaction to frustration, object loss, narcissistic injury, or trauma. It does not call for the postulation of a specific aggressive energy. This conception sees aggression as a capacity of the mind, activated under appropriate stimulus conditions of encountering an obstacle that interferes with an intended internal or external action.

Acceptance of this theory requires revision of some of the field's basic theoretical generalizations. Our proposal requires review and revision of such fundamental subjects as the meaning of drive, energy, economic, and dynamic principles, the relation between affect and aggression, as well as some aspects of the theory of development and the nature of motivation in psychoanalytic theory. To help the reader with this difficult task, we have opted to start with some theoretical and clinical material, "the re-evaluation of prior fact," mentioned by Kuhn (1970, p. 7), in order to ask the relevant theoretical questions which we try to answer in the following chapters. We have selected only the main original authors, from Freud to contemporary writers, to probe the explicit and implicit theoretical assumptions, as well as omissions, found in their formulations. We hope that such detailed exercise may set the stage for better understanding of our arguments in the theoretical chapters.

FREUD

Freud's clinical depiction of aggression in his early case histories in 1909, following Alfred Adler's introduction of the aggressive instinct in 1908, described affects of hostility, rage, and antagonism, but did not present a theory of aggression. Freud (1909) declared, "I cannot bring myself to assume the existence of a special aggressive instinct alongside the familiar instincts of self-preservation and of sex, and on equal footing with them" (p. 140). His adoption of the term "aggressive drive" appeared only in 1920 in *Beyond the Pleasure Principle*, two years after the publication of his last case history, *From the History of an Infantile Neurosis* (Freud, 1918). In this last case history, Freud dealt almost exclusively with the vicissitudes of sexuality and the Oedipus complex. Freud referred to the anal-sadistic and oral organizations of the Wolfman's libido, but did not offer any theory about aggression or hostility. In short, Freud's clinical material does not help us much to understand his later theoretical thinking about the aggressive instinct. The case histories supply descriptions of hostile feelings and inclinations, but no more than that, reflecting the pervasive tendency to think of aggression in terms of related affects. Technically, Freud (1905a) had understood that the patient's resistance was connected to the transference and related hostile feelings and especially to the negative transference, but he offered no theory of aggression to explain these phenomena. Thus, to talk about the aggressive instinct in Freud is to talk about his work after 1920. To understand the clinical implications of Freud's conception of the aggressive drive, we are forced to examine his theoretical assertions and to try to draw our own clinical inferences from them since he provided no case material to illustrate them.

One place we can look is in Lecture XXXII of the *New Introductory Lectures in Psycho-Analysis* (Freud, 1933a): "In sadism and masochism we have before us two excellent examples of a mixture of the two classes of instinct, of Eros and aggressiveness; and we proceed to the hypothesis that this relation is a model one—that every instinctual impulse that we can examine consists of similar fusions or alloys of the two classes of instinct" (pp. 104–5). In reflecting on "the special problem of masochism," Freud states:

> If for a moment we leave its erotic components on one side, it affords us a guarantee of the existence of a trend of self-*destruction* as its aim. If it is true of the *destructive* instinct as well [as of libido] that the ego—but what we have in mind here is rather the id, the *whole person*—originally includes all the instinctual impulses, we are led to the view that masochism is older than sadism, and that sadism is the *destructive* instinct directed outwards, thus acquiring the characteristic of *aggressiveness*. . . . A certain amount of the original destructive instinct may still remain in the interior. It seems that we can only perceive it under two conditions: if it is combined with erotic instincts into masochism or if—with a greater or lesser erotic addition—it is directed against the external world as aggressiveness. And now we are struck by the

significance of the possibility that the *aggressiveness* may not be able to *find satisfaction* in the external world because it comes up against real obstacles. If this happens, it will perhaps retreat and increase the amount of self-destructiveness holding sway in the interior. . . . Impeded aggressiveness seems to involve a grave injury. It really seems as though it is necessary for us *to destroy* some other thing or person in order not to destroy ourselves, in order to guard against the impulsion of self-*destruction.* (p. 105, emphasis added)

He then applied these notions to superego formation during development:

There is no doubt that, when the super-ego was first instituted, in equipping that agency use was made of the *piece* of the child's *aggressiveness* towards his parents for which he was unable to effect *discharge* outwards on account of his erotic fixation as well as of external difficulties; and for that reason the severity of the super-ego need not simply correspond to the strictness of the upbringing. It is very possible that, when there are later occasions for suppressing aggressiveness, the instinct may take the same path that was opened to it at that decisive point of time. (p. 109, emphasis added)

The analysis of Freud's texts permits a systematic review of the concepts that are foundational for our proposed new paradigm. We will examine them systematically in all the examples presented in ensuing chapters.

AGENCY IN THE DRIVES

A central question here is: What or who is the agent of externally or internally directed aggressive actions? Freud refers in the quotation to the "whole person" as including "all the instinctual impulses." This reference to the total person is not to the person as agent but as container, as he explained in Appendix B of *The Ego and the Id* (Freud, 1923), where he says that "the 'ego-id' was originally the 'great reservoir of libido' in the sense of being a storage tank" (p. 65). Accordingly, agency is attributed to the instincts themselves, not to the whole person.

What kind of agency do instincts have in this theory? They are able to fuse with one another, but also to come apart, in which case "functioning will be most gravely affected by defusions of such a kind" (1933a, p. 105). The aggressive instinct itself thus becomes the agent of its own discharge to the external world, and in the case of the relationship and interaction with the parents discharges itself against them. This discharge is obligatory. If it cannot be effected against the parents because of the child's dependence and libidinal attachment to them, factors constituting a significant obstacle for such action, the drive must find another path of discharge in the internal world. This set of circumstances would "cause" it to "retreat and increase the amount of self-destructiveness holding sway in the interior" (1933a, p. 105).

This description highlights the compulsory nature of the agency of the aggressive instinct in its obligatory course of seeking discharge, whether externally or internally. The compulsory discharge tendency constitutes the characteristic "pressure" of an instinct, as Freud (1915) described in *Instincts and Their Vicissitudes*. This pressure "is the very essence" of an instinct understood as a "motor factor, the amount of force or the measure of demand of work which it represents" (p. 122). In this conception the pressure is "causative" of the amount of work necessary for discharge. Thus discharge is not effected by the agency of the whole person, but by the work of the instinct itself as a separate agency. The person involved in the aggressive action is, according to this description, no more than the theater, the *locus* in which causative discharge work is accomplished. Considerations of this kind prompted Moran (1993) to say that psychoanalysis does not have a concept of the person as a subject of its own actions.[3] The motivation of the subject carrying out the aggressive action, therefore, does not seem integrated with the causative urge of the aggressive instinct to find its compelling discharge.

ECONOMIC AND DYNAMIC FACTORS

The discharge of Freud's aggressive instinct is measured in energic terms: "the measure of the amount of work." This energic consideration, as all energic matters do, refers to the "causal" power of the force or work to complete its own course, not unlike a falling object that cannot elude the force of gravity in its downward course. The amount of aggressiveness not discharged externally must remain located in the "interior," causing self-destructiveness. This conception makes aggression appear as an energic substance measured by quantity. Similar considerations apply to libido. Two questions emerge here. If all the causality is in the drive itself, what is the role of the person who acts aggressively? In Freud's theory, the question does not come up. The causal power of the instinct effects its own discharge, or accumulation if discharge fails. The same can be said about fusion of the instincts. There is no indication in Freud that the subject, the person, is involved in prompting the instincts to fuse. Another vicissitude of the failure of aggression to discharge is the location of a certain amount of the destructive instinct in the agency of the superego, "causing" it to be harsh to its owner. Such structural localizing of aggressiveness has dynamic consequences by way of establishing a "path" for repeating this mode of locating undischarged aggressiveness in the superego. Once more the causative factor is located in the drive forcing the superego to execute its destructive aims.

We are arguing that Freud's theory of aggression presents a quasi-autonomous drive acting within the psyche to pressure and accomplish completion of its own inherent destructive discharge. It has no options, and gives the psyche no options. The impulse must be discharged. One might object that all these processes are unconsciously caused and may not require subjective participation of the individual carrying out the aggressive action. The objection loses its force, however, when it becomes clear that no aggressive external action can be carried out without conscious participation of the person who does it. This last point confronts us with the critical question: How do we integrate the causative power of an aggressive drive with the intentions and motives of the person acting consciously and intentionally in an aggressive mode? We will offer our attempt to answer this question in the following chapters concerning the theoretical foundations of aggression, specifically the economic, dynamic, and motivational perspectives related to the concept of the self-as-agent as source of all psychic actions, including those that are aggressively motivated (chapters 4 and 5), and as capable of experiencing the accompanying affects aroused in relation to execution of aggressive actions (chapter 6).

To anticipate the theoretical argument presented in forthcoming chapters, we argue that many contemporary psychoanalytic writers (Benjamin, 1995; Hoffman, 1996; Pollock and Slavin, 1988; Rustin, 1997; Schafer, 1976; Stern, 1985) and others have written about agency in psychic life. There is an essential difference between their conception of agency and ours. The agency they talk about is the subjective sense of agency that develops progressively in infancy and is an essential component of the transformational process resulting from analytic work. The concept of agency we are using in this study distinguishes between agency and subjectivity. Agency is attributed to the total person, conceptualized as the self-as-agent (Meissner, 1993), encompassing all actions of the self (conscious, preconscious, unconscious, voluntary, involuntary), while subjectivity is proper to the self-as-subject, namely that aspect of the self-as-agent involved in all conscious and preconscious mental actions (Meissner, 1999d, e). Self-as-agent and self-as-subject are identical and synonymous in regard to all conscious activity. but not in regard to unconscious activity in which some actions of the self-as-agent are beyond the scope of conscious subjectivity. The unconscious is the realm of the self-as-agent, not of the self-as-subject. Unconscious activity has no subject, only agency. Contemporary authors utilize a concept of agency that encompasses the subjective experience of the self-as-subject, including the awareness or *sense* of acting as the agent of psychical actions. In such instances, i.e., in conscious mental acts, it is the self-as-agent and the self-as-subject that serve as the source of action insofar as the self-as-subject *is* the self-as-agent in its conscious operation. The theoretic underpinnings for these distinctions are discussed further in the consideration of agency in chapter 4 and motivation in chapter 5.

Chapter 2

Other Theories

Psychoanalysis does not suffer from a lack of theories of aggression. While we regard the theory we are proposing as unique, it unavoidably shares some features with other approaches. We are divorcing out view of aggression from drive theory, but we are not alone in this. We take a further step, however, in proposing a revised meta-psychological underpinning and in reformulating the understanding of aggression in motivational terms. In this respect we feel that we have moved beyond merely distancing ourselves from drive considerations. To make the distinguishing features of our theory from other psychoanalytic approaches clearer, it may help to differentiate it from them as specifically as we can, especially from theories that in one way or another adumbrate or point toward the motivational perspective we are developing. Our discussion is limited to major positions, namely classical drive theories (Freud and Klein), more contemporary drive theories (Hartmann, Kernberg, Stone, Anna Freud, and Mitchell), then some of the object relations approaches (Fairbairn, Guntrip, and Winnicott), and finally some theories that seem to steer a path between drive- and object-orientations (Brenner, Loewald, and Kohut). We will also briefly consider perspectives added by recent neuropsychological findings. Our objective in undertaking this discussion is not refutation or rejection of any of these other views of aggression, but rather further clarification of our own approach by discriminating it from them.

CLASSICAL DRIVE THEORIES

Freud[1]

Early in his theorizing Freud did not have a theory of the aggressive drive and did not feel the need for one. Obviously, Freud was perfectly well aware of the many forms of aggressive behavior and hostility in the analytic situation, including resistance and ambivalence, as well as outside it. He had noticed the hostile intent of many jokes and parapraxes in everyday life. He was well aware of the hostile component of the Oedipus complex in addition to loving feelings and dependent needs.

His attempts to explain aggressive manifestations can be divided into three phases. As with Freud's other theoretical revisions, in each new phase he adds something new without discarding earlier affirmations. In the first phase (1905b), he saw aggression as a component of normal male sexuality striving to achieve its aim of union with a sexual object: "The sexuality of most male human beings contains an element of *aggressiveness*—a desire to subjugate; the biological significance of it seems to lie in the need for overcoming the resistance of the sexual object by means other than the process of wooing" (pp. 157–58, italics in original). Sadism was "an aggressive component of the sexual instinct which has become independent and exaggerated" (p. 158). Thus Freud's first conceptualization of aggression was as a force bolstering the sexual instinct when something gets in the way to prevent desired contact and union with the object. This function of aggression could be seen as equivalent to overcoming a sexual obstacle.

Freud's second phase presents his revised thinking about instincts in *Instincts and their Vicissitudes* (1915), dividing them into self-preservative and *sexual* instincts. The feelings evoked by the transference neurosis convinced him that "at the root of all such affections there is to be found a conflict between the claims of sexuality and those of the ego" (p. 124). Survival and the avoidance of unpleasure are the sole aims of the ego: "The ego hates, abhors and pursues with intent to destroy all objects which are a source of unpleasurable feeling for it, without taking into account whether they mean a frustration of sexual satisfaction or the satisfaction of the self-preservative needs" (p. 138). Furthermore, "Hate, as a relation to objects, is older than love. It derives from the narcissistic ego's primordial repudiation of the external world with its outpouring of stimuli" (p. 139). These formulations suggest the role of aggression as either overcoming obstacles to libidinal satisfaction or threats to self-preservation.

Later on, in *Civilization and Its Discontents* (1930), Freud commented on the relation between the interference of parental authority with the child's satisfaction of instinctual needs and the increment of the child's aggression. He suggested that enforcement of the demand for renunciation of instinctual satisfaction prompts the child's hostility and aggression, which would then be transformed into guilt. The enforcing authority "now turns into the super-ego" (p. 129). In our view, Freud's description of parental figures presents them, simultaneously, as objects of erotic wishes and as obstacles to their satisfaction if self-preservation is to prevail. Aggression, whether directed to the object or the self, is in this sense a reactive response to threats to self-preservation and to pleasure.

The third phase starts in 1920 with *Beyond the Pleasure Principle,* where Freud reclassifies the instincts: ". . . now . . . we describe the opposition as being, not between ego instincts and sexual instincts but between life instincts and death instincts" (p. 53). The death instincts oppose the erotic instincts and tend to "lead what is living back into an inorganic state" (1933a, p. 107). Later elaboration of these concepts (1933b) presented Eros as the instinct tending to preserve and unite, as opposed to "those which seek to destroy and kill and which we group together as the aggressive or destructive instinct" (p. 209). Freud's theorizing had started with clinical observations, but now in this stage moved to considerations of nondemonstrable metapsychological postulates about life and death. Freud's new division of instincts keeps sexual and self-preservative instincts separate, but aggression belongs to neither. However, he still maintained that "[t]he instinct of self-preservation is certainly of an erotic kind but it must nevertheless have aggressiveness at its disposal if it is to fulfill its purpose" (p. 209). Love too needs the instinct of mastery "if it is in any way to obtain possession of that object" (p. 209).

In summary, in Freud's thinking, aggression evolved from being part of the sexual instinct to a nonsexual life instinct (ego instinct), and finally to an aspect of the death instinct. In phase one, the purpose of aggression was to help the sexual instinct overcome obstacles to unsuccessful wooing, thus facilitating contact with the sexual object. This early concept could be seen as a forerunner of our view that aggression serves a need to overcome obstacles to the fulfillment of a variety of wishes, desires, and needs. In the second phase, aggression aimed at preserving the self; it was a reaction to danger or to instinctual frustration. This, again, suggested a need to overcome obstacles and threats posed by the external world or internalized authority figures. In the third phase, Freud's thinking became more difficult to connect with clinical material. Aggression, in the form of destructiveness, now was a manifestation of a postulated death instinct, neither related to making contact with objects nor a reaction to their interference with the satisfaction of instinctual wishes. Aggression thus became primary, not just a reaction to unsuccessful contact with the object, or to unpleasure or to self-preservation. Nonetheless, aggression could also be used to fulfill the aims of sexual and self-preservative instincts. Therefore, in Freud's last formulation, aggression was both a primary instinct and an instinct in the service of overcoming obstacles. We part company altogether from Freud insofar as he understood aggression as a primary instinct in itself with destruction as its aim.

Freud completed his life work leaving psychoanalysts with a confusing drive theory of aggression that has been followed in the last fifty years "by repetitions and reassertions of original opinions" by authors with "clouded vision," as Anna Freud indicated in commenting on the state of the theory in the 1972 International Congress on aggression (p. 163).

Melanie Klein

Klein took Freud's third phase literally. For her the death instinct is not a theory but a concrete reality that he "discovered" in his work (1975a). Klein not only accepted the primary destructive quality of the aggressive drive, but also saw it as dominant in psychic life and development and a critical source of early and life-lasting conflict. Her own clinical observations convinced Klein that the death instinct was a primary instinct and an observable reality that manifested itself as opposing the life instinct, Eros (1975a). She also endowed Freud's original notion of drive with new qualities and functions. Segal (1964) described Klein's views:

> . . . unconscious fantasy is the "mental" expression of instincts and, therefore, like these, exists from the beginning of life. Instincts by definition are "object-seeking." The "experience" of an instinct in

the mental apparatus is connected with the phantasy of an object appropriate to the instinct. Thus, to every instinctual drive there is a corresponding actual phantasy. To the desire to eat, there is a corresponding phantasy of something which would be edible and satisfying of this desire—the breast. What Freud describes as "hallucinatory wish-fulfilment" in Melanie's Klein's view is based on unconscious phantasy accompanying and expressing an instinctual drive. (p. 2)

Segal illustrates graphically the workings of aggressive fantasies:

A hungry, raging infant, screaming and kicking, phantasies that he is actually attacking the breast, tearing and destroying it, and experiences his own screams which tear and hurt him as the torn breast attacking him on his own *inside*. Therefore, not only does he experience a want, but his hunger-pain and his own screams may *be felt* as a persecutory attack on his inside. (ibid., p. 2, italics in original)

For Klein, the connection between the ego and the instincts is mediated by phantasy. Phantasy-forming is a function of the ego:

The view of phantasy as a mental expression of instincts through the medium of the ego assumes a higher degree of ego organization than is usually postulated by Freud. It assumes that the ego from birth is capable of forming, and indeed is *driven* by instincts and anxiety to form primitive object-relations in phantasy and reality. . . . Phantasy is not merely an escape from reality, but a constant and unavoidable accompaniment of real experiences, constantly interacting with them. (ibid., pp. 2–3, emphasis added)

In spite of its rich phantasy world, the kleinian infant is no freer than the freudian. The infant's early ego activity remains "driven" by the power of the instincts: "The immature ego of the infant is exposed from birth to the anxiety stirred up by the inborn polarity of instincts—the immediate conflict between the life instinct and the death instinct" (ibid., p. 12). The aim of aggression is destruction, and hate is its essential affect (1975a). The "subjective experience" of the workings of the aggressive drive appears as hostility, wishes for destruction, and phantasized destructive actions. Greed, jealousy, and envy are also clear clinical expressions of the death instinct (1975a). The aims of these aggressive experiences are (1) possessing all the good an object has (greed), (2) being as good as the object (envy), and (3) removal of the rival in a triangular relation (jealousy). In all three, destruction of the object and/or its qualities or possessions may be necessary to satisfy the wish. If the wish is frustrated, the affect of hate emerges as well as depressive anxiety about losing the object.

Aggression and the death instinct are synonyms for Klein. The death instinct is inborn and active at birth (1975a). Defenses are required to start working at once lest the self be annihilated by its own aggression. The first life-saving defense, projection, places the aggression outside the self, in an external object, and thus relieves the self of its destructiveness (1975b)—this is the paranoid-schizoid position. The difficulty in tolerating the object's and one's own badness brings about further defensive splitting of self and object into good and bad parts and projecting one's own badness onto others. Projection of the death instinct onto an object transforms that object into an external persecutor and arouses destructive hate against it, which further intensifies the need to project and generates persecutory fear of the object. The actual or projected bad object can become persecutory and increase the aggressiveness and hostility of the infant or adult towards it, thus creating a cycle of projection and persecution. This circle of aggression, projection, fear, and hate calls for renewed defensive maneuvers on the part of the ego. The healthy solution is to mitigate aggression with love. If this is not possible, the ego must resort to deflecting aggression outward, or to defensive splitting. The ego may also have to adopt manic defenses to control the threatening object.

The ego must defend against constitutional aggression by whatever defenses it has at hand. The organism is in danger from within, due to the opposition between instincts of death and life. The aggression is constant, always ready to destroy, and cannot be dispelled. It is a reality that can only be mitigated by love or defended against, but it always remains as an inner threat. We might say that Klein's conceptualization of aggression presents it as a built-in obstacle to the capacity of the self to love, that requires constant psychic effort in order to counteract its destructive effects.

Klein's conceptualization of aggression as a primary instinct did not incline her to disregard the consequences of external factors prompting the individual to react with aggressive responses. Frustration of wishes (1975a), experiences of being overwhelmed by confusion, fear, ignorance, particularly before the development of language (1975b), prompt aggressive responses and hateful feelings aimed at eliminating the source of the distress. To the extent that innate aggression poses an internal obstacle to loving, it can only be dealt with by defensive projection and splitting. If there is an external obstacle, Klein believes that the only psychic option is to aggressively destroy it, while hating it. This creates problems because aggression directed toward a human object always returns as persecutory destructive anxiety which in turn may require further defensive activities. Once the cycle of aggression has begun, it becomes self-perpetuating unless the love instinct manages to mitigate the power of the death instinct by fusing with it—as in the depressive position. Klein's view presents a picture of psychic life in which the individual is caught between powerful instincts that rule his life. The psychic subject is, at best, a manager in the struggle between instinctual forces. In any case, the capacity to acknowledge one's own aggression may bring about the possibility of repairing the relation to the now recognized good object. When this happens, the child moves developmentally from the persecutory paranoid position of projected and felt aggression from the object to the depressive position in which object relations become possible.

Klein provided a clinical example that may help to clarify the theoretical points. In her paper "The Oedipus Complex in the Light of Early Anxieties," Klein (1945) presented the aggressive difficulties of Richard, a boy of ten, whose symptoms prevented his attending school. Klein describes some of his problems:

> Richard's anxiety about his aggression, and particularly about his oral-sadistic tendencies, was very great and led to a sharp struggle in him against his aggression . . . he felt in great danger of hurting his mother. He often asked, even after quite harmless remarks to his mother or to myself: "Have I hurt your feelings?" The fear and guilt relating to his destructive phantasies moulded his whole emotional life. In order to retain his love for his mother, he again and again attempted to restrain his jealousy and grievances, deny-ing even obvious causes for them. . . . The repressed anger about frustration in the past and present came out clearly in the transfer-ence situation—for instance, in his response to the frustration imposed on him by the interruption of the analysis. We know that by going to London I had become in his mind an injured object. I was not, however, injured only through being exposed to the danger of bombs, but also because by frustrating him I had aroused his hatred; in consequence he felt unconsciously that he had at-tacked me. . . . I therefore turned into a hostile and revengeful figure.
>
> The early splitting of the mother figure into a good and bad "breast mother" as a way of dealing with ambivalence had been

very marked in Richard. . . . At this stage of the analysis, his actual
mother stood for the "good breast mother," while I had become
the "bad genital mother," and I therefore aroused in him the aggression and fears connected to that figure. (p. 376)

Klein's aggressive drive exercised its compelling force upon Richard's
ego and its fantasies. His ego was "driven" by the instinct and had to
deal with it as best as it could. What the ego cannot do is to be free of
the demand of the aggressive instinct. This demand, however, does
not seek its own discharge. Instead, it forces the ego to form, from the
beginning of life, phantasies of the objects of satisfaction and of the
phantasized and actual actions prompted by the aggressive drive.
Even when the phantasies are ego-created mental conceptions, they
function as if they were actual events capable of causing harm, and,
through projection, bringing about retaliation. That is exactly what
happened between Klein and Richard, making her, in his eyes, "a
hostile and revengeful figure." The great difference in this respect
between Freud's aggressive drive and Klein's is that hers cannot function without human objects providing satisfaction of needs, including
attachment. Another difference is that the aggressive drive obtains
mental representation of its own workings by the mediation of phantasy. Besides, in Klein's view, "discharge" of the drive is not effected
by satisfaction because the construction of bad objects and the phantasy of hostile actions against them keeps the force of the drive continuously active. The construction of bad objects has in it a dim
motivational component in the sense that the object retaliates, as
Richard assumed, because it has been harmed.

In Klein's terms the only way out of the dominance of the aggressive drive is to accept responsibility (an ego function) for the
aggressiveness and to enter the depressive position that moves the
child first to repair the injured object and, then, relate to the good
object. Thus, Klein's aggressive instinct is "experienced subjectively"
through phantasized and actual actions between the child and his
objects. The experience is cognitive and affective. Cognitively, the
child knows his own phantasies and their intentions. Affectively, the
growing person feels the hostility, the hatred, the envy and rage
prompted byphantasies as well as the fear and terror of expected
retaliation.

For Klein, aggression is always affectively hostile and effectively
destructive, intending to harm and hurt. The source of such destruc-

tiveness is the instinct itself, deeply embedded in the child's mind. External frustration may aggravate the intensity of the aggression, but does not create it. The child brings it as part of his or her internal makeup. Thus, the kleinian child, as Richard's example illustrates, is compelled to hate and be hostile and to create bad objects. The child's ego is, at best, manager of a compelling drive forcing him to have bad objects and to try to harm others and then to worry about their "motivated retaliation." Klein's theory of aggression has a subject, but a subject dominated and enslaved by the aggressive drive.

We differ in many ways with Klein's views of aggression, with its integral involvement with the ego, its inevitable association with hostility and destructiveness, and its developmental and defensive vicissitudes. Most important to our present purpose is the clear difference in her insistence that aggression is a biologically given instinctual drive destructive in nature. Our view of aggression as originating in motivations to overcome obstacles clearly separates our view from her drive-driven conception. Further, the motivation to overcome obstacles leaves aggression in our view open to positive and constructive outcomes as well as destructive; it is not inherently and inevitably destructive as in the kleinian view. The determination of aggression as positive or as negative in our view lies in the motivational patterns giving rise to the aggressive action. If these are positive and constructive, the aggression is so too; if negative, so is the aggressive action.

Kleinian views of aggression have enjoyed wide currency, especially in Europe and South America, and have enjoyed greater acceptance more recently in North America. Some of this may be due to a softening of original kleinian insistence on the primacy of the death instinct, greater attention to and more careful therapeutic handling of defensive and adaptive needs, and a greater focusing of aggressive derivatives, following Bion and Racker, in countertransference issues and dynamics (Schafer, 1997a). Betty Joseph, for example, has demonstrated important technical modifications that characterize the modern kleinian approach, focusing more on the here-and-now vicissitudes of transference-countertransference interactions in step-by-step clarifications and interpretations, as opposed to earlier kleinian tendencies to plunge into the instinctual depths regardless of defensive or other needs of the patient. However, in none of these developments is there anything to suggest revision or departure from the basic kleinian model, rooted in the death drive as the biologically embedded and instinctually derived source of destructive aggression. As Schafer (1997b) commented: "Unlike contemporary 'Freudians,' contemporary 'Kleinians' still hew to the idea of the death instinct. In my view, however, they no longer have any well-developed instinct theory, and . . . in practice they are referring essentially to self and other directed destructiveness, not just in the treatment room but as a built-in part of life, and so as a continuing problem for all human beings" (p. 159).

Something similar can be said of Andre Green's (1999) inventive and thoughtful contributions. He adheres closely to the freudian model and tends to write off ego psychological and other developments as treating aggression as reactions to frustration. His adherence to freudian drive theory remains consistent, along with his concentration on affective states which he views as expressions of aggression. He comments: "Affects of an aggressive type demand particular attention: when they are linked to pure, destructive tendencies, they escape anxiety (which affects only the fused erotic and destructive drives). Sometimes the self-destructive tendencies remain the only possible defenses against the expression of the aggressive drives" (p. 96). Also, Green's (2001) reliance on and exploitation of the primary drives, particularly the death drive, are unmistakable and seem closely allied with, if not synonymous with, the kleinian perspective.

CONTEMPORARY DRIVE THEORIES

Among later drive theorists, we can separate proponents of a primary destructive aggressive drive (Hartmann, Kernberg) from those who consider aggression a reaction to unpleasure or frustration or as a function serving a variety of other purposes (Anna Freud, & Mitchell).[2]

Aggression as Primary Destructive Drive

Hartmann

Hartmann (1952) considered aggression as a basic instinctual drive influencing primordial aims and functions of the ego, even before the ego has been established as an organization. However, with development of the ego, it becomes possible to turn aggressive drive derivatives away from unmitigated instinctual discharge into a "neutralized" resource of energy for the use of the ego in pursuing its own aims. "In the course of development, their cathexes will be neutralized, and they will gain a certain degree of autonomy vis-à-vis the instinctual drives" (1955, p. 229). Neutralization, carried out with the ego's autonomous energy, is facilitated by the degree of instinctual cathexes invested in the self (1950). The ego is now able to use the neutralized aggressive energy constructively for its own interests in a noninstinctual mode (1964b). For Hartmann, aggression, once neutralized, is at the service of ego development; it is also available for countercathexis in the service of the ego's defensive operations (1950). Free unneutralized aggression, on the other hand, is destructive and causes conflict.

Hartmann's theorizing (1964a) illustrates the kinds of problems posed when aggression is conceptualized as a destructive drive— problems in devising ways to explain the positive role of aggression in relation to a variety of ego functions, especially self-preservation. Hartmann resorted to more-or-less mechanical explanations involving neutralization and drive fusion and defusion. Stone (1971) wrote to this point as follows: "To ally work for mastery with impulses to destruction as such, or, in the sense of the death instinct, with killing or dying as such, requires the tour de force concept of fusion or a bold view . . . in which the instinct of destruction . . . is placed directly in the service of the life instincts" (p. 225). Other drive theorists, such as Klein and Kernberg, elaborate ideas about defensive projection and splitting, which reduce the aggressively behaving subject to being simply a playground of forces rather than the agent of consciously or unconsciously intended actions, as we propose in our theory. Hartmann's view of postneutralization aggression comes closer to our view, even in terms of motivational perspectives concerned with overcoming obstacles.

Kernberg
The view of aggression espoused by Kernberg (1966, 1967, 1968, 1970b, 1971, 1975, 1984) takes its inspiration from a basically kleinian schema. Focusing primarily on borderline pathology, Kernberg argues for the predominance of pregenital, primarily oral, conflicts and the intensity of pregenital aggressive drive as central to the borderline pathological picture. The condensation of pregenital and genital aims under the dominance of primitive pregenital aggressive impulses causes distortion of the oedipal conflict and consequent developmental impediments. This aggressively determined configuration sets the stage

for oral-aggressive projections onto the mother, resulting in a para-noid-like distortion of parental images and faulty internalizations. Sexual relations are seen as dangerous and destructive. In the effort to deny oral-dependency needs and avoid the rage and fear connected with them, an attempted flight into premature genital strivings frequently miscarries due to the burden of aggressive contaminants. These primi-tive dynamics often find expression in transference paradigms. Closely related to kleinian themes, but also in tune with classical drive theo-ries, aggression is regarded as a primary biologically based drive and is presumed to be destructive. A motivational component in the un-derstanding of aggression seems to be missing.

Aggression as Reaction to Unpleasure or Frustration

In contrast to primary drive theorists, many authors view aggression as much less clearly derived from a primary drive analogous to libido. These contributors write about aggression as a reaction to unpleasure or frustration or as providing means to implement other functions. They fail, however, in our view, to draw any clearly distinguishing features that would define a common factor, among the many types of actions, reactions, motives, aims, and developmental sequences they describe, that can be termed "aggression." It is worth noting that we do not regard our theory as a frustration-aggression theory.[3] There may be no reason to think that encountering certain kinds of ob-stacles may be not attended by feelings of frustration (even anger or irritation), but the distinction of aggression from affects is central to our understanding of aggression. What makes an action aggressive in our view is the effort to overcome an obstacle, and not any affect that might be associated with it—whether frustration or anything else. Overcoming some obstacles might well be attended with pleasure and not frustration.

Stone

Certain aspects of Leo Stone's (1971) view of aggression resemble our own, since he believed that in most cases aggression is a motivated reaction to external stimuli, even though he maintained the tradi-tional view that "certain elements of aggression . . . have an instinc-tual origin or affiliation . . ." (p. 195). Aggression, he wrote, involves an "aggregate of diverse acts, having diverse origin, and bound together, sometimes loosely, by the nature of their impact on objects rather than by a demonstrably common and unitary drive" (p. 195). He expressed concern, similar to our own, about the state of theorizing about aggression: "Where origins, semantic and symbolic contributions, manifestations . . . and motivations are so numerous and complex, it is difficult to feel intellectually secure with a general and intrusive unitary explanation of individual aggression . . ." (p. 239). He added that "the drive toward mastery . . . lies close to the functional center of the aggressive complex in the sense of implementation of any form of a wish, by whatever form or degree of force may be required" (p. 239)—a view that is congruent with our concept of aggression as a capacity of the self put into the service of overcoming obstacles to achieving a goal.

Anna Freud

Anna Freud (1972) drew a comparison between aggression and the libidinal drive, suggesting that "What obscures the analyst's view when he approaches the subject of aggression may be his very experience with the vicissitudes of the sexual drive" (p. 163). She considered such views as "preconceived ideas that handicap an investigation" (p. 163). The confusion comes from a dualistic theory of drives that searches for the source, aim, and object of aggression as parallel with the sexual drive. She believed that the source of aggression must remain an open question. Aggression has no aim of its own; instead "it can associate itself with aims and purposes of extraneous kinds, lending them force" (p. 165). Aggression, therefore, in her view, adds an economic factor to other psychic aims. The object of aggression coincides with the object of love at the beginning of life because "the processes which underlie object attachment do not differ for the two drives" (p. 165). However, "after infancy, the developmental line of sex and of aggression becomes significantly different" (p. 165). The most critical difference is the absence of object constancy in the case of aggression which remains "much longer and more thoroughly, i.e. more closely, tied to pleasure-pain, satisfaction-frustration experiences" (p. 165). She disagrees with Klein's view in that inflicting hurt is not the basic purpose of aggression. "Rather," she says, "we have to conclude that only the aggressive action itself is primary, while its result is accidental initially" (p. 170). She is aware that her answer does not solve the question about the "intrinsic aim of innate, primary aggression" (p. 170).

From our point of view, Miss Freud did not deal explicitly with obstacles to psychic activities. She did, however, indicate that aggression, having no aim of its own, is at the service of other psychic aims, as an economic factor adding enough force to help them overcome obstacles to achieving their goals. This formulation is entirely consistent with the view we have advocated—aggression is an auxiliary capacity called into action when additional force is required to overcome the obstacles to goal achievement. The theories diverge, however, over the issue of agency—for her the agency, as for her father, remains in the drive; for us it belongs more properly to the self.

Mitchell

Drawing from aspects of both drive and nondrive theories of aggression, Mitchell (1993a), acting as the main proponent of the relational perspective in psychoanalysis, presents his view that "[a]ggression is an extremely powerful, universally wired (although individually varied), biological response to the subjective experience of endangerment and being treated cruelly" (p. 368)—a variant of the frustration-aggression theme. He considers the nature of aggression to be inherently hostile and destructive, but not a drive in the sense of classical theory, not "an extrapsychological push deriving from the body" (p. 371). Furthermore, aggression operates not only to protect the "endangered self" (p. 381) in any one instance but also to play "an inevitable and central dynamic role in the generation of experience and the shaping of the self" (p. 373). His views form a bridge to object relational theories of aggression in that "[c]hronic aggression is continually regenerated in the context of ongoing commitments to internal object relations and familiar patterns of integrating interpersonal relations" (p. 373).

Mitchell's view of aggression as a biologically based potential that can be called into action resembles our understanding of aggression as a capacity that can be activated under certain motivational conditions. However, he confines the experience of aggression to affects of hostility and acts of destruction and narrows the conditions for activation of aggression to subjective experiences of endangerment. Our theory of aggression requires only the motivation to overcome obstacles to achievement of aims, whether they be fulfillment of wishes or needs, or the avoidance of distress or threats to psychic equilibrium, including a subjective sense of danger to the self. The affects and actions involved are not confined to forms of hate and destruction; instead they can be highly varied in accord with the particularities of the experiential instance.

Mitchell's place in psychoanalysis is centered on his role as promoter of the relational point of view (Mitchell, 1988). It is not clear to us how his relational perspective connects with his view of aggression, beyond his distancing himself from drive theory. Even so, he proposes aggression as a biological, that is, bodily, potential. Responding to the charge that relational theory leaves the body out of consideration, Mitchell (1995) admitted that "the rhetoric of relational authors (dialectically differentiating themselves from drive theory) sometimes leads them to minimize the importance of the body" (p. 578). But he then went on to explain that the "body" in relational perspective is not the body of classical theory in that the relational body as experienced is constructed in relation to a linguistic, relational, interactional social field, that is, the body as experienced and represented in the mind as derivative from relational processes. In extreme terms, then, whatever of the body that is not constructed representationally does not exist, or does not count (Harris, 1998). A more moderate relational formulation is that the body, outside the scope of relational interaction and meaning, remains unknowable. Thus we would conclude that the relational body has nothing, or little or nothing, to do with the body as conceived in terms of aggressive action, whether bodily or mental. Rather, it seems to relate to the body image, as a component of the self-as-object (Meissner, 1996a, 1997). However, images and representations do not act; they are no more than mental contents. Aggression, however, requires a capacity to act.

Object Relations Views

After Freud and Klein, many analysts have attempted to conceptualize aggression without presenting any essential alternatives to the two basic possibilities: aggression as an innate drive or aggression as a reactive response. Those who consider aggression as reactive usually do not consider destructiveness as its aim, as would Freud, Klein, and other classical theorists. The classical view resorted to Freud's concept of drive fusion, Klein's defensive position, or Hartmann's concept of neutralization, to make self-preservation compatible with a destructive aggressive drive capable of annihilating the self. It remained to other analysts, Fairbairn, Guntrip, and Winnicott among them, to attend to the significance of relations to primary objects for the emergence of aggressive manifestations.

Fairbairn and Guntrip

As one of the primary figures in the object relations approach, Fairbairn (1963) declared his deviation from Klein explicitly: "There is no death instinct; aggression is a reaction to frustration or deprivation" (p. 224), most specifically frustration of libidinal objectives. He still regarded aggression as ultimately subordinated to libido (1952, p. 171). When the aggression is no longer necessary, "it is taken back at the service of the libidinal ego" (Guntrip, 1969, p. 195). In our view these frustrations or deprivations would follow from the interposition of obstacles to specific desires or needs. Guntrip, who closely followed Fairbairn's theorizing, saw aggression as a reaction to fear and human isolation: "Fear of loss of contact with the external world constantly motivates efforts to regain contact with it, but this cannot be done by loving relationships, and therefore can only be done in terms of the other two basic emotional reactions, fear and aggression" (1969, p. 101). Both authors subordinate aggression to the libidinal need to establish object relations: "Libido is the fundamental 'life-energy' and sexual and aggressive energy are specialized aspects of it" (Guntrip, 1969, p. 422). One might also think, as we do, that aggression serves the needs of object relations specifically by helping to overcome obstacles to achieving and maintaining such relations. We would read these formulations of both Fairbairn and Guntrip as addressing a fundamental need to overcome obstacles to libidinal or other fulfillment, and aggression as instrumental in the service of this need.

Winnicott

Winnicott agreed with Klein in many aspects of her theory (Aguayo, 2002). He added, however, his own idiosyncratic conceptions about different aspects of aggression. His ideas are not systematic, but do bring out aspects of aggressive behavior neglected by other theoreticians. Most of his reflections were contained in a posthumously published book, *Deprivation and Delinquency* (1984), where his ideas on the subject are collected. For Winnicott aggression has two meanings: first that it is one of the two main sources of an individual's energy; second that aggression refers to "a reaction to frustration" (1984, p. 92). Winnicott (1958a) affirmed that "the basis for the study of aggression must be a study of the roots of aggressive intention"

(p. 204)—for "intention" read "motivation." The aggression at the beginning of life is "almost synonymous with activity" or motility. It is a self-assertive force directed to being and to obtaining what is needed to be. Aggressive energy prompts behaviors that bring with them pleasure in movement, even in utero, and in the exploration of the world after birth.[4] Aggression is always presented as a developmental force, related to establishing the distinction between self and non-self. Except for reliance on drive considerations, this is not far removed from our own view. To understand aggression one must take into consideration the moment of development and the child's needs.

Winnicott's original use of Freud's and Klein's theories did not question the existence of an aggressive instinctual drive. He believed that it is an energy at the service of creating, in conjunction with love and a good enough environment, the conditions for creation of a real self, a "Me," capable of using objects that exist in their own right, and therefore can be loved and hated without much problem, because they survive. Early destructiveness is accidental and innocent. Later destructiveness appears when the reactive and neglected true self must make new attempts to make itself feel real and to call for the attention of the neglecting environment. All these processes are understood in complex "dynamic" terms referring to the dynamic processes of being oneself in relation to real objects. Winnicott was not concerned with economic factors.

Winnicott (1986) reported the case of a therapist in analysis with him:

> On his way to the analytic session he often stops and gazes at a machine tool in a shop window near my house. This has the most splendid teeth. This is my patient's way of getting at his oral aggression, the primitive love impulse with all its ruthlessness and destructiveness. We could call it eating. The trend in his treatment is towards ruthlessness of primitive loving, and, as can be imagined, the resistance against getting to it is tremendous . . . he needs to get truly in touch with his primitive impulses as a matter not of the mind, but of instinctual experience and bodily feeling. (pp. 83–84)

This was not raw destructiveness. The patient had been talking about some constructive aims with Winnicott in the context of talking about destroying him by eating him. For Winnicott, this patient's destructive aggression is not oral sadism, but aggression at the service of the enhancement of a self that needs to feel real by experiencing the primitive love in the form of eating the object. Destruction is not the aim. It happens but is not malicious.

Winnicott's contribution to the theory of aggression consists in showing that the "dynamic aim" of the aggressive drive can be placed at the service of constructing a true self in the context of real objects in a good enough environment. Reactive aggression responds to environmental impingements and has the effect of either forcing intrapsychic withdrawal with loss of vitality or prompting destructive behavior. This aggressive behavior directed toward the environment reflects a new hope and a dynamic attempt to restore some realness and vitality to a withdrawn individual. Winnicott's aggression is not an instinct as such, in the classical freudian sense. It is a biologically given energy to establish oneself in the world through motility and love by pushing against objects in order to find the crucial developmental moment of differentiating between "Me" and "Not-Me." Winnicott is not interested in the economic aspects of aggression and does not consider it a discharge process. The total person in a personal context is for him the center stage for the dynamic play of aggression. In spite of his original way of considering aggression, Winnicott, not being inclined to theoretical disquisitions, did not challenge the freudian concept of drives.

In summary, aggression is for Winnicott a nonhostile, nondestructive activity that manifests itself in four modes: (1) as a pleasurable source of self-assertion and exploration of the world; (2) as a means to obtain libidinal satisfaction from the object; (3) as a signal behavior to indicate the object's failure to respond to object related or environmental needs; and (4) as a means by which a self (a "Me") can be developmentally established in relation to an environment of objects who are differentiated from the self. Aggression is a constructive energy at the service of development, differentiation, mastery, object relations, and the maintenance of a satisfactory balance between the self and the environment.

Our own theory of aggression shares with Winnicott's view the idea that aggression is not derived from a classically conceived aggressive drive, that it can serve to overcome obstacles to the achievement of certain goals, that it is not inherently destructive, and that it can be associated with a large variety of affects and actions.

Intermediary Theorists—Between Drive and Object Orientations

Brenner

Among the efforts to return to the data of the analytic situation to find a more authentically psychoanalytic basis for our understanding of drives and affects, Brenner (1974, 1975) articulated a theory of affects, focusing particularly on anxiety and depression. His view of aggression would see it antecedently as a reaction to unpleasure and depressive affect, a view that seems to align more with frustration-aggression views. Like other frustration theories, the frustration can serve to motivate the aggressive response, but the aggression is cast in the form of aggressive action. Brenner's view would seem to limit it to a connection with dysphoric affects. We would differ in that in our view the antecedent motivational basis for aggression need not be limited to unpleasure, but might include pleasure as well. Aggression in the service of libidinal aims, for example, may be a matter of increasing levels of pleasurable intensity rather than exclusively a reaction to unpleasure. Or in someone for whom chastity is a meaningful ideal, the lure of sexual pleasure may be opposed by a contrary superego injunction, in which case the obstacles are compounded. If the superego prohibition against such pleasure may pose a dysphoric obstacle to attaining the pleasure, the pleasure itself poses an obstacle to fulfilling the chaste ideal. Focusing only on the dysphoric affect would overly simplify the matter. In fact, in terms of consequent motivation, Brenner (1982) did emphasize that aggression falls under the pleasure principle insofar as satisfaction of the derivatives of aggression is achieved. We should be clear, however, that our differences from Brenner do not hinge on what kind of affect is involved in aggression, since we do not regard affects as part of an aggressive response but as concomitant phenomena (see chapter 6 below). Rather, we view the essential motivation of aggression to be the overcoming of obstacles, whatever the affective quality of the experience may be. Aggression may arise in any context in which the natural attainment of a goal is impeded by an obstacle, of whatever nature, internal or external, fantasized or factual, unpleasant or pleasant, or even pleasant and unpleasant.

Loewald

Loewald (1971) approached instincts from the point of view of personal motivation. He took issue with the mechanistic view of the psychic workings of the drives. For him, "personal motivation is the fundamental assumption of psychoanalysis" (p. 110). Nonetheless, "psychoanalytic psychology postulates instinctual, unconscious, impersonal forces as the motives of our psychic life. Where is the person? Where is the ego or self that would be the source and mainstay of personal motivation?" (p. 110). In Loewald's view, personal motivation is not limited to conscious or preconscious activities, but extends to unconscious processes. Meissner (1993) answers Loewald's challenge by proposing the self, specifically the self-as-agent, as a self-system equivalent to the total person. It is thus the person who acts aggressively, not the drive. He conceives of this self as "a supraordinate and structural construct with the tripatrite entities as component sub-structural systems" (p. 459)—a view that will be further elaborated in this study.

For Loewald (1971), the legitimate use of the instinct concept in psychoanalysis must consider it "only as a psychological concept, and not as a biological or ethological one" (p. 110). Loewald's concept of psychic energy differs significantly from the quantifiable freudian energy. Psychic energy seems to manifest the activities of each of interrelating individuals in the early dyad and the power such intercourse has to bring into being the psychic organization of the neonate:

> Ego and id, conceived as psychic structures, come into being within the psychic unit the neonate is about to become by intricate interaction processes between conflicting, converging, and merging psychic energy currents surrounding and within the emerging psychic system; such interactions result in the organization of psychic structure. It cannot be stressed enough that such organization is most vitally codetermined by the fact of the far higher complexity of an organization of psychic energy obtaining in (for the observer) surrounding environmental psychic systems. It is by the interaction with them that motivational forces of various orders of complexity and integration, and stable motivational structures of any kind, come into being within the newly emerging psychic unit, the child. . . . Structures are understood as more or less systematic and stable organizations of psychic energy; they bring their higher potential to bear on mobile instinctual energy, thus transforming its currents into higher orders of motivational energy. (1971, pp. 111–12)

What, then, in Loewald's conception, is the psychic function of instincts and in particular of the aggressive instinct? What is his psychic energy? He questions whether instincts "are to be understood as elemental component forces of the psyche," or as "forces impinging on the psyche and thus, by definition, themselves non-mental" (p. 115). Freud (1915), Loewald believed, opted at one point for the latter when he defined instinct as "a stimulus applied to the mind," thus using a physiological not a psychical concept. In short, for Freud, instinct is "a factor that operates upon the mind, from within the organism" but "from outside the mind" (1971, p. 116). Freud also called the instinct the "psychical representative" of the somatic stimulation. This second conception was favored by Loewald, who concluded that the specific task of the mind in responding to organismic needs is to represent them psychically in order to deal with them by psychical means. The task of the mind, therefore, is not to "discharge" the effect of stimulation by the instinctual drive, but to generate instinctual activity based on the mental representatives, which include all varieties of representations, including those of affects (pp. 117–18). In this form, as a mental representative of organismic stimuli, the instinct "may be described as the most primitive element or unit of motivation" (p. 119) originating in the stream of mental life itself, the mental life of the human organism. In this respect, instincts are psychic forces, within a psychic system which is itself a "center of endogenous activity" (p. 123).

Finally, Loewald attends to the role of the object in relation to instincts. He asserts: "Instincts, understood as psychic, motivational forces, become organized as such through interactions within a psychic field consisting originally of the mother-child (psychic) unit" (p. 128). The neonate's urges "become coordinated and organized into instincts and assume aims and direction by activities and responses coming from the environment" (p. 130). Contrary to Freud's conception, the experience of satisfaction in Loewald's understanding not only abolishes excitation but also "engenders and organizes excitation processes" (p. 130). The role of the primary object is essential: "In the process of a mother's caring activities, which consist of spontaneous stimulations as well as responses, instincts come into being in the child" (p. 131). Separation from the maternal object brings about the appetitive urges that motivate the child. These are "psychic motives," different from the compelling "causality" of the freudian drive pressuring the psyche to "discharge" the quantity of excitation. For Loewald, it is the memory of interpersonal events with the mother that gives rise to the formation of psychical representatives providing instinctual guidance in the motivational search for or avoidance of the object. Thus the organization of the child's aggressive dispositions is shaped by the type of maternal stimulation and of interpersonal involvement with the child's early urges and needs. The aggressive drive is organized around the particulars of their mutual satisfactions and frustrations.

In summary, Loewald's contribution was to offer an original theory of drives based on the significance of the formation of mental representation of biological urges. These biological urges include the mother-child dyad along with the satisfaction or frustration offered by the mother. Altogether these serve as the foundational elements constituting the appetitively motivated and object-related human instincts. The instinct is not present at birth as such. It is formed as a psychic representative of human interactions and their effects on the structuration of the child's psyche. The mental representative of the instinctual processes encompasses not only the intrapsychic appetitive motivation but also the external response to it. The psychic energy that moves the appetitive motivational search is not the energy of the instinct itself, but that of the psyche. In short, human instincts represent the motivational source of appetitive and relational processes organized structurally in the course of time according to the type of experiences the child has gone through with the mother. In this sense, instincts are not givens, but are ongoing psychic organizations throughout the time of the child's encounter with the environment. An instinct is formed by the convergence in a mental representative of the internal psychic search for something needed and the environmental response to it.

Loewald's theories do not address explicitly metapsychological issues such as psychic energy, the nature of the drive formed in the dyadic encounter, and its economic and dynamic integration in the child's developing personality. They do address some elements such as the memorial representational organization of appetitive needs in relation to the encounter with the environment. This permits formulation of a theory of psychic motivation without resorting to concepts of drives exerting pressure for discharge upon the mind. In this respect Loewald's understanding of the central role of motivations provides a significant background for our thinking about aggression in motivational terms rather than in terms of drive theory.

Kohut and Self Psychology

Other psychoanalysts theorized about aggression from the point of view of narcissism and the development of the self. Rochlin (1973) proposed that aggression arises specifically in defense of the self, responding to humiliation and injured narcissism with hostility and destructiveness, ranging from anger to rage and revengefulness, including violent action. Rochlin's approach appealed to narcissistic motives as instrumental in eliciting aggressive responses. His approach seems congruent with our own insofar as narcissistic injury can be viewed as posing an obstacle to adequate self-esteem or narcissistic equilibrium. However, while fully accepting the impact of narcissistic injury, we would not limit the conditions for aggressive action to narcissistic concerns alone.

Kohut in one dimension moved away from Freud in viewing aggression as an assertive force with potentially constructive objectives—analogous to our view of aggression as potentially positive or negative as a function of motivational factors. This force comes into play in the course of development,[5] and later in life this self-building assertive aggression appears as mature aggression "employed in the service of a securely established self and in the service of cherished values" (1972, p. 647). In mature aggression the people who are its target are seen as objects separate from the self. The opponent is considered an obstacle that "blocks us in reaching our object-libidinal goals" or somebody we hate because "he interferes with the fulfillment of our reality-integrated wishes" (p. 644). This aggression is under ego control. In summary, assertive, nondestructive aggression is for Kohut "one form or quality of the expression of a universal human propensity toward healthy assertiveness that is intrinsic to, and accompanies, any activity of the cohesive self" (Gunther, 1980, p. 191). Destructive aggression appears as a manifestation of disturbances of the self, in particular with persistent failures of the self-object's empathy, that may lead to self fragmentation and primitivization of the expression of aggression, which appears as a "breakdown" product. Kohut (1980) believed that today's historical circumstances present a different prevalence of types of pathology in patients and call for a different type of approach from those encountered by the first analysts. "Freud and his co-workers were more inclined to respond to the conflicts of the cohesive self [endowed with mature aggression] and to assign a place of secondary importance to the disturbed self [liable to destructive aggression and rage], while we are more inclined to see it the other way" (1980, p. 521). However, even in the oedipal neuroses, a self defect may be present and account for the appearance of pathological aggression.

Kohut's (1972) most comprehensive description of the manifestation of aggression is that of a self suffering from narcissistic pathology manifested in narcissistic rage. The vicissitudes of the self in relation to its objects and their changing functions in relation to the needs of the developing self become lasting prototypes for specific forms of security or vulnerability in the narcissistic realm. The raging and destructive aggression of narcissistically vulnerable individuals must be understood as a psychological phenomenon emerging from specific narcissistic pathology in the context of empathic failure by a narcissistically needed object. In this respect Kohut (1972) concludes:

> Human aggression is most dangerous when it is "attached" to the two great absolutarian psychological constellations: the grandiose self and the archaic omnipotent object. And the most gruesome human destructiveness is encountered, not in a form of wild, regressive, and primitive behavior, but in the form of orderly and organized activities in which the perpetrator's destructiveness is alloyed with absolute conviction about their greatness and with their devotion to archaic omnipotent figures. (p. 635)

In any case, his analysis pertained more to the affective state of rage and its determinants in relation to self and self-object connections than to considerations of the nature of aggression. Our emphasis on the distinction between aggression and its accompanying affects, including anger and rage, draws a clear line of separation between our view and the self psychological perspective.

Kohut does not say where this aggression that is "attached" to the grandiose self comes from. He described narcissistic rage as a specific circumscribed phenomenon belonging to "the large psychological field of aggression, anger, and destructiveness" (p. 636). He paid specific attention to the "dynamic" aspects of this form of aggression. Regardless of its varied manifestations, narcissistic rage is characterized by a "need for revenge, for righting a wrong, for undoing a hurt by whatever means, and a deeply anchored, unrelenting compulsion in the pursuit of all these aims" (pp. 637–38). Dynamically, "underlying all these emotional states is the uncompromising insistence on the perfection of the idealized self-object and on the limitlessness of the power and knowledge of a grandiose self" (p. 643). Offenses that injure or shame the grandiose self, or empathic failure on the part of the selfobject, mobilize aggressive rage. The object that is the target of the rage is not perceived as a person on its own right and must be blotted out. "Narcissistic rage arises when self or object fail to live up to the expectations" (p. 644) of how they should function. The deepest offense and shame and the drop in self-esteem experienced by the narcissistically vulnerable person stems from the inability to maintain absolute control over an archaic infantile environment. In its absence, the narcissistically enraged person lacks any empathy for the offending object, experiences unforgiving fury, and feels it must blot out the offense. Dynamically, the failure of the needed object "creates a *psychoeconomic* imbalance" (p. 655, our emphasis), which interferes with ego- and self-regulation.

The only way to modify narcissistic rage is by indirect means, that is, by "the gradual transformation of the matrix of narcissism from which the rage arose" (p. 646). Kohut's interesting description of the dynamic and economic processes involved in the emergence of narcissistic rage as a manifestation of aggression illustrates only the emergence of an *affect* in the context of a particular constellation of dynamic and economic factors. The intentional destructive actions of the enraged individual are not considered separately from the experienced affect. In a certain manner, Kohut seems to attribute "causative" power to the rage affect, its compulsory need to obliterate the offending object and the offense, and makes it equivalent to destructive aggression.

Kohut (1972) presented Mr. P., a "master" of social sadism. Mr. P. specialized in humiliating his acquaintances by maliciously mentioning publicly their minority status in order to embarrass them. Analysis revealed his own fear of exposure and ridicule stemming from violent emotions of shame and rage in childhood. His mother frequently embarrassed him in public. Besides, she humiliated him privately by exposing and checking his genitals to detect whether he had masturbated. "As a child he had formed vengeful fantasies—the precursors of his sadistic enactments—in which he would cruelly expose his mother to his own and to other people's gaze" (pp. 638). This example was intended to illustrate actions motivated by revengeful chronic narcissistic rage. It presents the planned and calculated actions of a person whose intent from childhood has remained to humiliate others as revenge for having been humiliated. This indicates that the motivations involved in the actions include many more aspects of the total person besides the experience of rage. In this respect, Kohut's theory of aggression presents interesting dynamic formulations, but confuses aggressive actions with the affects dominating the person. The actions of the individual require a more complex motivational explanation.

In summary, Kohut's theory of aggression is developmental in the sense that assertive aggression is deemed to be at the service of self-formation. This aggression is neither destructive nor pathological, and remains throughout life available to oppose obstacles[6] that interfere with ego goals and ideals. Pathological narcissistic aggression that finds its severest representative in narcissistic rage is reactive—a disintegration product—to empathic failures during the development of the self and reappears whenever a renewed narcissistic injury or empathic failure reactivates the threat to the pathological survival of the grandiose self and its demands for absolute control and perfect responsiveness. Kohut does not specify whether assertive aggression is a drive in the classical sense, but frequently refers to it using the word "drive."

NEUROSCIENTIFIC RESEARCH ON AGGRESSION

This subject carries us beyond our scope, but it is of such current significance that we feel compelled to at least address the subject even though what we can say about it is rather limited. Neuroscientific research has dealt only indirectly with aggression in the sense we are proposing here. The focus in neurobiological studies tends to fall on affects, including affects that we would presume are frequently associated with aggressive activation, i.e., fear, anger, rage, etc. Our distinction of aggression from secondarily associated affects means that from our perspective neuroscientific studies of aggression are focused for the most part on secondary phenomena rather than on aggression itself.

The experience and expression of affects are areas of central concern with respect to a more complete understanding of aggression insofar as they reflect the complex and simultaneous interweaving of mental and physiological components. Beginning nearly half a century ago, MacLean (1955, 1990) developed the implications of the Papez circuit of emotional integration and defined hierarchical levels of motivational integration.[7] The lowest level, the rhinencephalic system, constituted largely of subcortical brainstem functions, regulated aspects of bodily homeostasis (eating, drinking, sleeping, thermal regulation, etc.). The next level was the limbic system, regulating aspects of social behavior including emotional and attachment behaviors (care-seeking, care-giving, social competition [dominance-submission], mating, cooperation, etc.). The highest system, characteristic of humans, involved the neocortex and served higher mental functions (thinking, curiosity, development of meaning and symbolic capacity, etc.). More recent research, focusing on fear reactions (Armony and LeDoux, 2000; LeDoux, 1989, 1996), suggests that fear is processed through at least two parallel paths, if not more.[8] One elicits an immediate response based on innate reactions (e.g., startle response or unconditioned responses as in fear conditioning) involving a direct path from the thalamus, which processes sensory information and transmits it to other parts of the brain, to the amygdala in which emotional aspects of the stimulus are processed. The second path involves more sophisticated analysis of the meaning of the stimulus: here the thalamus directs sensory information to the cortex, where associative processing appraises meaning, and then transmits it to the amygdala for emotional evaluation. Goleman (1995) explains the process in simplified terms as follows: "Ledoux's work revealed how the architecture of the brain gives the amygdala a privileged position as an emotional sentinel, able to hijack the brain. His research has shown that sensory signals from eye or ear travel first in the brain to the thalamus, and then—across a single synapse—to the amygdala; a second signal from the thalamus is routed to the neocortex—the thinking brain. This branching allows the amygdala to begin to respond *before* the neocortex which mulls information through several levels of brain circuits before it fully perceives and finally initiates its more finely tailored response" (p. 17, italics in original).

The close linkage of brain mechanisms with regard to motives and emotions is illumined by the work of Damasio (1994, 1999), LeDoux (1987, 1996), and others. Psychodynamics are not open to limitless possibility, but are contained by reason of biological endowment and personal history. Damasio, objecting to the separation of higher cognitive and lower affective processes, argues that emotions are the product of combined neocortical and subcortical mechanisms, and that feelings are also cognitive in function. They differ primarily insofar as feelings provide a constant flow of informational feedback

specifically about the body, and are thereby instrumental in influencing our cognitive assessments of ongoing experience. They are particularly influential in our assessments of goodness or badness, pleasure
or pain, and we might add in the assessment of obstacles. He documents the degree to which affectivity contributes to the organization
of cognition, how feelings can disrupt rational thinking and affect
personal and social relatedness, but are also essential contributing
factors to these processes, possibly including mentalization and empathy (Fonagy and Target, 2002; Schore, 2002). In his view, certain
perceptual configurations trigger appropriate affective reactions mediated by the limbic system, amygdala, and cingulate gyrus. These
primary configurations evolve and become more complex in the course
of development and are increasingly mediated by the mediobasal
frontal cortex, which indirectly activates limbic circuits. Limbic influences are then transmitted to the viscera by way of the autonomic
nervous system and to the musculoskeletal connections by the motor
system. These patterns of neural output are accompanied by release
of hormones, regulatory peptides and neurotransmitters in the
brainstem and basal forebrain nuclei, resulting in subjective affective
experiences centered in the insular and parietal cortex of the right
cerebral hemisphere.[9] As LeDoux (1996) and Damasio (1999) caution,
patterns of neural activation may be different for different emotions.
As Davidson (2000) observed: "From the evidence currently available, the right-sided anterior cortical activation appears to be common to both fear and disgust; activation of the amygdala appears to
be more specific to fear; and activation of the insular cortex appears
to be more specific to disgust. These findings are thus consistent with
both discrete and dimensional views of emotion, suggesting that some
circuitry may be unique to specific discrete emotions and other circuitry may code for broader dimensional characteristics" (p. 1152).[10]

For our purposes in the present discussion, we are left with a
degree of uncertainty. What we know with a good deal of certainty,
however, is that the patterns of motivational activation and aggressive
behavior as we propose them are effected by specific brain processes,
but we have only more or less general indications of precisely what
they are. We can be confident that they exist and operate, but we still
do not know what they are, what specific areas of brain they involve,
and in what specific patterns. We would also have to look for further
discrimination between brain processes involved in arousal of aggressive motives and those effecting aggressive action. Insofar as we

distinguish these processes, we would presume that they reflect differentiable patterns of neural activation in the brain. The contribution of any psychoanalytic theory of aggression lies in the phenomenological refinement of aspects of aggressive experience and action, so that researchers working on the brain can have an idea of what to look for. The rapidly advancing pace of neurobiological research offers us the prospect of greater depth and specificity in our knowledge of how brain processes act in expressing aggressive motives and actions and how associated affects are correspondingly induced. In the inevitable dialectic between neuroscience and psychoanalysis, theories that resonate with and facilitate this interdisciplinary interaction will persevere; those that do not will wither and fade.

CONCLUSIONS

All the theoreticians reviewed above, in one manner or another, in one degree or another, consider aggression in terms of drive endowed with an energy that must be discharged, be it at the service of self-formation or destructiveness. It is true that Loewald considered the drive to be organized within the dyadic encounter, but he still considered it a drive. Two questions emerge at this level. The first is about the energy of the drive, an energy exerting pressure on the psyche to achieve discharge. Such a pressure functions as a *cause* capable of exerting its own effects. This causal energy leaves little room for the integration of aggression into the motivational system of the total person carrying out the aggressive actions. There is a need to reconsider the manner in which we conceptualize psychic energy, if we are to propose a motivational theory of aggression that is not based on causality but on human motivation. Revision of the energic concept requires reevaluation of the economic principles regulating psychic functioning, the mind's efforts at balancing external or internal intensity of stimuli, and the finding of outcomes for conflicting motivational situations (Meissner, 1995a, b)

Chapter 4 addresses these metapsychological questions in order to offer a view of energy and of economic principles in psychic functioning that makes room for a motivational theory of aggression. This revised understanding of the economic principle helps to review the role of the regulatory principles of psychic functioning, recasting them as "operational principles determining the stimulus conditions governing activation and integration of receptive and response systems and their adaptive integration in assimilative and accommodative patterns of environmental interaction" (Meissner, 1995b, p. 227).

The oscillation among analytic authors—between those who consider aggression, or at least some aspect of it, as reactive to noxious stimuli or inadequate responses to unpostponable needs, and those who consider it as a constitutive destructive drive present from birth—makes it almost impossible to look at all aggressive phenomena as belonging to the same drive or motivational system. In our view, these theories continually confuse the force and urge of the postulated drive for discharge with the effects of the aggressive actions on others and the environment. When they do not, as in Winnicott, they have to postulate some intentionality, a motivational psychic quality that exceeds the drive itself. Furthermore, most authors, specifically Klein and Kohut, confuse the drive and its effects with the affect that the subject experiences during the aggressive instance. Rage in particular appears frequently as a synonym of destructiveness and other forms of aggression, but it is not synonymous with aggression as such (see chapter 6 below).

What is missing is the dynamic understanding of the motivational process in the emergence of aggressive behavior. The conception of aggression as a drive brings with it a causative urge that leaves little room for dynamic motivational processes that may explain the emergence of aggressive behaviors under specific external or internal stimulus conditions. Kohut made a persuasive case for the significance of injured narcissism in the emergence of narcissistic rage—a position developed concurrently from a different metapsychological standpoint by Rochlin (1973). Nonetheless, he did not see it in motivational terms, but considered the narcissistic injury to have a causative power of its own. This confusion calls for careful conceptual separation of the concepts of causality and motivation and a reformulation of the dynamic principles of psychic functioning. Chapter 5 considers this reformulation in relation to our revised theory of aggression from the motivational point of view. Chapter 6 offers a clarification of the necessary differentiation of the affects frequently present in the aggressive situation and their relation to aggression itself.

Kohut explicitly pointed to the great significance of the self in psychic life and in aggressive experiences. Kohut's self, however, is not any freer of the causal pressure of the aggressive drive than Freud's psychic apparatus. For Freud, the apparatus had to discharge the urging demands of the drives, libidinal or aggressive. For Kohut, narcissistic failure or neglect has a causative power in bringing about aggression and narcissistic rage. Similarly, the cure is effected by the reparation, under analytic regression, of the original narcissistic failure. The individual is the locus where these injuries and repairs take place. What is missing is the complexity of dynamic options, not as the field of events but as regulated by the agency of the self. Thus, a motivational theory of aggression also necessitates reformulation of the notion of the self-as-agent.

This revision of "the field's most elementary theoretical generalizations" (Kuhn, 1970, p. 85) permits us to offer a coherent theoretical foundation for our revised theory of aggression. We see aggression not as a drive exerting its pressure for destructive discharge on the mind, but as a capacity of the mind—that is, as a capacity of the self-as-agent—activated under appropriate stimulus conditions of encountering an obstacle interfering with an intended internal or external action. This concept is broad and comprehensive enough to be able to encompass in its explanatory power all examples of aggressive behaviors presented by the different authors mentioned in this overview. We believe that our manner of understanding aggression and its supporting metapsychological modifications of psychoanalytic theory offers an alternate paradigm to understand aggression as an economically and dynamically conditioned manifestation of the self as agent of its own unconscious and conscious actions.

Chapter 3

A Case of Aggression in Analysis

"I ALWAYS HURT THE ONE I LOVE— AND LIKE IT"

The concepts and theoretical revision we have introduced above and will be considering in greater detail below remain suspended in conceptual midair if they are not tied to and rooted in the concrete soil of clinical application. We need to focus our argument on specific clinical material, not only to facilitate communication and understanding of our perspective, but also to keep the development of our argument attuned to clinical realities. Any case presentation can neither demonstrate a metapsychological point, as in our concept of aggression as a biologically rooted psychic capacity aimed at helping the attainment of the goal of intended actions, nor prove the clinical accuracy of the formulation of the analytic process. We offer this case, nevertheless, as an illustration aimed at helping the reader understand in clinical terms the way in which we conceive theoretically the dynamics of one form of aggressive pathology and the organizing fantasy accompanying it.

THE CASE

Mr. T, a forty-three-year-old professional man, came to analysis requesting help to improve his relationships with women. It was immediately obvious that he was extremely bright and had an unusual
capacity to articulate his inner states. He was divorced and had minimal
contact with his ex-wife and children. He prided himself in being able
to seduce women, but lamented that he could never find the right
woman. Most women were stupid and enraged him. He was aware
that he was getting old and wished to marry again. He had tried to
live with some of his girlfriends, but the relationship had always ended
in sadistic fights. He had acquaintances but no true friends. No one
could satisfy him. Mr. T was a man alone and isolated, despite his
active social life and constant dating. He lived in a state of chronic
rage, feeling acutely the "stupidity" of others and their inability to
recognize his value and superiority over them. He was always ready
to humiliate people or pick a fight, if he felt the slightest offense.

His work situation was solidly established but colored by constant strife. His father too had been a steady worker and excellent
provider. Mr. T described his father as a good man of few words, who
was physically very strong but somewhat absent from home due to
his long working days. Mr. T's mother had died during his late teens.
He had failed to recognize that she was dying, even though she had
been ill and hospitalized on and off since his grammar school days.
He did not know for sure what illness had afflicted her and caused
her death. He described her as intrusive, meddling with his schoolwork, and dragging him from teacher to teacher. They fought constantly, particularly during his adolescence. He was a poor student
and did not graduate from high school. It was only after moving away
from his home state that he finally got a high school diploma, went to
college, and then graduate school. Mr. T was accepted to Ivy League
colleges and graduate programs, but he could not accept them. He
finally settled for what he called a "second-class" professional degree.

During the first analytic hour, Mr. T presented two dreams. He
described the second: "I am in the Army with others. I am wearing a
captain's uniform but it has no insignia. I am marginal, always marginal. I am never in the main stream of things. I never make a full
commitment." The dream anticipated the next six years of analysis.
He experienced endless rage with people's inability to appreciate him
and used elaborate and persistent machinations to control, cajole,

overpower, outsmart, and win over others, regardless of the humiliation he inflicted on them. This was his way of forcing them to recognize him. The analyst did not escape from his manipulations. He made every effort to force the analyst to give him what he wanted. If he thought he had tricked the analyst into acquiescing, he laughed with self-sufficient satisfaction, mocking the analyst.

Early in the analysis, Mr. T talked about his wish to have power over all things and people so that he could force them to respond to him. He was overtly grandiose in his wishes for power. This grandiosity, conscious, explicit, and intensely satisfying, alternated with fits of rage and fury. The slightest contradiction or event that did not fit his wishes provoked him into dangerous actions and constant entanglements in actual life as well as in the analytic situation. On the street, if he found the driver ahead of him driving too slowly, he would pull ahead, cut in front of the other vehicle, get out of the car, and insult and physically threaten the driver. Hour after hour of the analysis was spent listening to his disparaging comments about women and his wishes to "fuck their brains out" for their offenses, such as wearing mini-skirts or having breasts that enticed him.

The atmosphere in the analysis was always tense. Every word or tone of voice of the analyst that displeased him, or suggested to him some limitation in the analyst's understanding, prompted him to ridicule and devalue her. He demanded her absolute attention to his words and perfect remembering of each one of them. Frequently, in moments of intense rage for feeling disregarded, he would threaten the analyst with the most graphic descriptions of how he would rape her, trying to convince her that he could make her a plaything for his sadistic and murderous wishes to penetrate and destroy her. He was extremely vigilant, certain that the analyst was going to cheat him or "fuck him over." He constantly monitored the minutes and seconds of his hour to prevent being cheated out of his time. Mr. T's entire life was dedicated to showing himself superior to others, seducing women, demanding special attention, going into rages when he felt it was not forthcoming, and being incensed at the stupidity of people who "didn't get it."

In the midst of this chronic narcissistic state of enraged and entitled excitement, the history of his relationship with his mother began to emerge. Mr. T had spent many hours of every day with his sickly mother. He became her little helper, providing her with company and physical care. He massaged her, rubbed medicines on her back, attended to her sore feet, and brought her medications for her. He felt very alone during the times she was hospitalized. Their emotional involvement was intense and deeply ambivalent. Each Friday afternoon, when classes were over, he would use some of his allowance money to buy her flowers. He loved the good meals she cooked, and was very taken with her attractive looks and the good care she took of her appearance. He desperately wanted to gain her attention and approval, hoping she would in some way show she loved him. The mother, in turn, was focused on the great dreams she had for her son's professional future (a barely disguised substitute for her own unfulfilled intellectual ambitions) and became persistently enraged with his poor academic performance in grammar and high school. His father remained aloof and uninvolved in his studies, but his mother made every effort, from paying for tutors to changing him from school to school, to help him succeed, but to no avail. It was not so much that he wanted to rebel against her, but that he could not concentrate because his psychic life was taken over by sexual fantasies about his mother and fantasies of compensatory narcissistic triumphs which found expression in constant masturbation. The enticing bodily presence of his mother, the smell and feeling of her skin, her perfume, her genitals under her clothes, continuously excited him to try to obtain her loving response, to overcome her rejection of him. The uncontrollable masturbation expressed his inability to master the excitement and the narcissistic satisfaction of his fantasized, if ephemeral, success.

The post–World War II events deeply affected the household. The father's side of the family had left their Eastern European country of origin much before the arrival of Hitler. The mother, on the other hand, had left on her own in the early 1930s, leaving her family behind. Her entire family was sent to concentration camps. She desperately hoped that one of her relatives might have survived. Her life centered on the special radio broadcasts listing the names of the people who were still alive. Her tragedy became entangled in the endless fights with her son, when she repeatedly accused him of being like Hitler. In some of their intense fights, she would deeply humiliate Mr. T with words and actions. Her most humiliating action was to spit on him to show her utter contempt for his failures.

The patient felt torn between his extreme attachment to his mother and a great hatred of her. He felt that she was not there for him, that she was like an impenetrable wall. There was no way he could either have a decent conversation with her or get her to be really interested in him. His father, on the other hand, was gentle and patient with him, took him places, particularly sharing some physical activities together, like swimming or fishing. He was a tall and physically very strong man, whose athletic competence evoked admiration, envy, and fear in his son. Mr. T enjoyed his father's company, but lamented that the father was a laconic man of action and not inclined to talk more openly with his son. He wanted his father to protect him from his mother, but the father insisted that she was his mother and he had to respect her. The father was attentive to the mother's wishes and demonstrated his affection by buying her expensive jewels.

The analysis became a constant invitation for the analyst to be involved in a sadistic fight, centered around Mr. T's persistent efforts to seduce her, and his continuous berating of the analyst for her incompetence and stupidity. The countertransference required acute and ever-alert self-monitoring to contain temptations to respond to his provocations. The analyst made a conscious and continuous effort to use words, expressions, clarifications, and questions that conveyed to Mr. T that, no matter how many threats he made or how much he tried to devalue her, his words would not be met with retaliation, but with a sustained effort to understand them and him in them. The analyst decided, in view of Mr. T's compelling need to be superior, to use few and carefully selected interpretations, and these only after having helped him with questions and clarifications to do his own search of his thoughts, feelings, and wishes.[1] He seemed to accept this manner of working, constantly bragging about his capacity to work in analysis always—in his opinion—one step ahead of the analyst. Slowly, however, Mr. T began to concede that in fact the analyst was trying to help him, that she did remember most of what he had said, and that some of her remarks were not as stupid as they seemed.

The recognition of the analyst's efforts to help him and the slow discovery that he was coming to know aspects of himself that he had not been previously aware of prompted Mr. T to explore in greater detail his life and behavior. He described his relationships with his girlfriends and his wish to "force" them to be for him what he wanted them to be. His "forcing" involved sadistic behaviors, like pinching their breasts or "fucking" them with such force and destructive desire that the women would beg him to stop. Progressively, he came to recognize that deep down he wanted to kill the woman. In a couple of situations, he was not far from strangling the woman. The motive for the wish to kill was always the same: the woman's inability to respond to him exactly as he wanted. Frequently, he would explode with insults and deeply hurtful remarks. If the woman cried, he felt satisfaction for reducing her to nothing, and contempt for her weakness. Pain would force her to deal with him. It was during the discussion of one of those intensely sadistic moments that Mr. T acknowledged and put into words what has become the title of this chapter: "I always hurt the one I love—and like it." What he liked was the feeling of power, of overwhelming the woman and "forcing" her to recognize him and his superior knowledge and wisdom.[2] If the woman was hurting, she had no choice but to take notice of him and to beg him to stop. That response would put him in the superior position of controlling the relationship. This manner of relating also obtained in his relationships with his coworkers and all the people he came in contact with in everyday life.

The progressive analysis of these repeated events and Mr. T's acknowledgment that the analyst did not have to be "forced" to listen to him, even when he had seen her all along as a prostitute he paid to hear him, gradually produced a transferential change. Previously, Mr. T had continuously demanded to have his way and insisted on receiving sexual favors from the analyst. The analytic regression brought to the fore childhood longings for maternal love and memories of his desolation when he experienced his mother as an unresponsive wall. He acknowledged that all his provocations had not succeeded in distracting the analyst from listening to him as himself.[3] He confessed that at some moments he did feel understood and attended to. He had tears of painful recognition in his eyes when he began to feel that something he had tried to express all his life had finally been understood. It was through repeated experiences of this type that he began to feel "fond" of the analyst. After some time, Mr. T began to believe he was in love with her. The feeling of being in love with the analyst made him realize that he had never really loved anybody in his life. Love was a new feeling he had not known before. Enticed by these new feelings, he wished to understand what had happened to him that made him unable to love, and to have such compelling needs to be superior, to humiliate others, and to be hurtful to the people he wanted and needed the most. He wished now for a relationship in which he would not have the need to fight all the time.

The last two years of Mr. T's six-year analysis were devoted to reconstruction of the external and internal conditions that contributed to his rages, grandiosity, destructive wishes, and sadistic behaviors. He acknowledged that his failure to seduce the analyst and engage her in a sadomasochistic relationship had helped him see that there were other ways of relating to people. The picture emerging from the reconstruction unveiled his profound sensual and sexual entanglement with his mother. He recalled the afternoons they spent in bed together, the smell of her body, the great stimulation he felt being near her genitals, and the enacted fantasies, carried out with his pillow, of having sex with her. These fantasies had continued throughout his adolescence and adult life. Hours were spent in analysis listening to his desire and demand to have perfect sex with his mother and with the analyst. The sexual overstimulation and fantasizing were, as soon as he was old enough, incorporated into his constant masturbation. From that moment on, he had increasing difficulties concentrating on his studies and his grades consequently went down. His failure enraged his mother, who could not understand why he was failing. Intense fighting between mother and son began and escalated to a high pitch in adolescence. On one occasion the fighting actually became physical. He stopped, in terror, when he realized that if he kept hitting his mother against the wall he was going to kill her.

The dynamic components determining this mother-child sadomasochistic relationship included both Mr. T's intense preoedipal and oedipal frustration with her. Preoedipally, he wanted "fusion" with her. He wanted her to attend to him exclusively, to really hear and see him. The mother seemed to have involved him deeply in her own needs, both physical and emotional, and to have been unable to respond to his wishes for closeness with her, particularly after he began to fail. Her illness and hospitalizations, and, most specifically, her depression about the loss of her family in the Holocaust, combined to make her personally remote and unable to attend and respond to her son. Earlier, she seemed to have been able to show him some tender, even if limited, affection.

These wishes and feelings for his mother appeared in the transference, in Mr. T's desire for fusion with the analyst and the concomitant terror of losing himself forever. He came to see that rage served him as a protection against such dangerous wishes. Progressively, he relaxed the rageful defense and began to express more overtly his wishes for tenderness, "softness," and mirroring. He tearfully described how his mother was not tender and did not want to see him as he really was. She could not respect him. He recognized that the analyst did respect him. This acknowledgment permitted him to become aware that his way of relating with himself was actually a continuation of his way of relating with his mother. He said: "I insulted myself. I don't hear me . . . It is *me* that is missing. I feel love and affection for you but a 'me' is missing." He reflected: "In analysis I am getting back something that is really mine. I have to have a sense of security about myself. There is goodness in you. Myself, my 'I,' I have to find what is behind the 'I,' behind 'me.' . . . If I trust you I can trust myself."

He felt intensely the regressive pull: "It is *amazing*! The longing for Mama. I feel this pre-arousal, the wish to penetrate, to merge. I say to myself, 'I am in love with her' [the analyst]." He hurried to say: "I hate you: you can't have me. I am in love with myself." At this moment, Mr. T became acutely aware of his intense ambivalence and asked himself: "How do I remain friendly but not fused? Do I have to sell my soul to be a member of the beloved?"

The countertransference at this point became that of the mother of a young child. The analyst needed to attend carefully to the developmental level of his wishes to maintain the analytic stance mentioned earlier of giving the patient the lead in his progressive discovery of himself. Tender feelings were present on both sides of the couch. A subtle, soft shared sense of humor developed between them, and was used by the patient each time he found himself trying to avoid an issue or returning to his old narcissistic trick of rejecting the analyst out of fear of being rejected. During this period, his prevailing fantasy was that of returning to his mother-analyst's virginal womb, a womb never occupied before by anybody else. That would make him truly special.

The oedipal components were equally strong in this second part of the analysis. Fantasies about perfect sex with his mother returned in full force, together with tremendous sadistic and revengeful wishes because of his not having obtained it. When the analyst interpreted that his persistent masturbation showed that his penis was his mother between his legs, he agreed that it was 110% correct. He commented: "Anger supports my penis." The anger was not only against the rejection, but also his own protection against the dangerous vagina dentata (he had several dreams and conscious fantasies about this fear), and the fears of closeness and of his own murderous wishes. He felt the pain of his empty struggle: "When I am revenging myself on a woman I feel like a piece of meat, completely humiliated." He realized that sex alone could not satisfy him and that he had spent his life between "fighting and fucking." He concluded: "It is the soul that I want to touch."

The sequence of events just described illustrates the progressive evolution of Mr. T's psychic change. First, he found his "I," one that he could call "really mine," emerging from the trusting relationship with the analyst. In the context of regression to early and later libidinal wishes for a maternal analyst, he was able to separate his penis from his mother and from the desire for her and to claim it for himself. The separation from the fixating maternal object, the mourning of the compelling sexual desire for her, and the sense of ownership of his own self facilitated the emergence of a wish for meaningful object relations, a wish to "touch" the soul.

After much discussion and persistent clarifications and interpretations, he reconstructed his oedipal struggle: "My mother did not belong to me. She betrayed me sexually. She betrayed me as a child because I couldn't go to her with a problem. We had no language between us. . . . I had no right to speak. . . . Mother's rejection was compounded by my and her disrespect. I feel the full impact of the rejection. . . . My capacity to kill the people I love scares me. I did wish to murder her. . . . We were like ships in the night." The discovery followed his explicit acknowledgment that he had been persistently disrespectful of the analyst, while the analyst had kept her stance of personal and analytic respect, even in an instance in which she caught him doing something mildly dishonest.

He confessed stealing his mother from his father, and lamented how hard it was to be a male when his father was so strong and a real "stud." He concluded: "My relationship with my mother was a lie. I was not able to be the perfect child. I chose to put myself between my parents. I lied. I was inferior. I felt superior. I want to cry for ages." In this respect and at this moment of the analysis, Mr. T experienced the guilt of being so close to actualizing the oedipal experience that Rothstein (1979) described in several patients with narcissistic personality disorders. He recalled the shock and rage of a moment during his teens when he returned home at a time his parents were not expecting him, and found them on the back porch holding hands and staring into each other's eyes. He felt that they both had betrayed him, particularly his mother. In a sober mood he concluded that he had to grow up and put his parents together as a couple in his mind.

Mr. T connected his relationship to his mother to all relations with women. He could not talk to women without feeling humiliated.

The humiliation awakened in him intense wishes for revenge, manifested in his sadistic behavior with them. Finally, he uncovered the key unconscious conviction that prompted him to "force" women to respond to him. He said: "If I couldn't conquer my mother, how could I conquer anybody else?" His phrase was close to Freud's point regarding aggression in the service of libido:[4] he had attempted to sadistically overcome in all women his mother's "resistance" to his wooing.

Mr. T recognized that he had to accept his losses. He said: "If I accept that I lost my mother and she lost me, I can be free. Then, I can love a woman." He reviewed his past behaviors:

> I am understanding my narcissism. I'll never be the same after I leave this office. We men soothe ourselves with our penises. I feel shame. I spent a life sexualizing rejection to undo a rejection [by his mother]. . . . Why didn't Father or Mother ever say, "I love you? . . . I kept myself safe by not having relationships. I conned people to get love without getting burned. I don't like my dependency. . . . I am realizing how bad and corrupt I am. I feel ashamed. [He laughed in a slightly embarrassed and soft manner.] I can tolerate the shame. I have tears in my eyes. The problem was that we had dishonest communication, corrupt messages with my parents.

These discoveries brought him to a reappraisal of his mother. He did not change the story of rejection and humiliation of him on her part, but was able to recognize her goodwill. He said: "I apologized to Mother. She did her best. She tried. I was involved in self-debasement. She tried to help me with my home work. I never realized how arrogant I was. I needed your help."

Apologies were now also extended to fellow workers and acquaintances when he found himself trying to put them down. He changed his dating style and allowed himself time for the development of a relationship with the woman he was seeing in order to curb his inclinations to "force" her to love him. The transference also evolved in new directions. He was able to experience renewed tender feelings for the analyst and wished to touch her face affectionately. He noticed at once the emergence of rageful feelings, but was able to see their defensive function. He commented that he wanted to play with the analyst and added: "How wonderful it is to feel connected [to you], to have psychic space. . . . In growing up, the more I showed respect for my mother [he bought her flowers every Friday] the angrier she got with me."

The transference became intensely positive. He declared: "My love for you is in a very special place. If I trust you, then, I can trust myself. . . . I am changing my perception of women. There is respect here. I have respect for you. You love me as a child, as a son. I love you as a teacher." He declared solemnly: "I am opening the door for affection in me." The statement indicated the termination of the analysis. It signaled the transformation of revengeful sadism, as repayment for the humiliation of being unlovable, into the recognition that he had been understood and that he did not need to "force" anyone to love him. He could see now, after having experienced it in the analysis, that he was able to love. That capacity alone was the main contributor to his feeling lovable. His core conviction had been reversed.

DISCUSSION AND CONCLUSIONS

As our understanding of aggression makes clear,[5] analysis of the dynamics of sadomasochistic relations often reveals a series of obstacles to be overcome. The first obstacle encountered in development is the inability or resistance of the parental objects to provide something that is needed psychically and developmentally. In Mr. T's case, his mother and father found it difficult to give him personal recognition and indications of their love. From his early latency to the end of her life, his mother showed overt contempt for him, comparing him to Hitler, confirming his already present sense of being unlovable. He felt his mother had failed him both as a small child and as a sexually excited boy. Preoedipally, she seemed to have responded only in limited ways to Mr. T's craving for closeness and tender affection. As a result of his frustrated cravings and the emergence of vivid sexual fantasies, he developed a fear of the phallic mother as intense as his wish to be the sole inhabitant of her womb.

Oedipally, Mr. T felt the excitement of offering her the ministrations she required for her enticing body and of behaving like a little husband in fulfilling his responsibilities (buying her medicines, bringing them to her, running her errands, being her companion in her outings). He wished to become her sexual partner during the long afternoons they spent together in bed. He felt enraged for her ignoring the intensity of their sensual and sexual involvement, for he wanted exclusive possession of her. But instead she wanted Mr. T's father. His more sublimated efforts, the weekly gift of flowers, did not find in her the sought-for affection and closeness. She did not seem to have been aware of the powerful sexual excitement he felt for her body. On the contrary, both parents gave unmistakable signals that the father was the sole possessor of the mother, and that she favored her husband over her son. This otherwise normal oedipal configuration was distorted by the fact that it was the child, not her husband, who ministered to her bodily needs and spent most of his after-school hours caring for her, while his father worked until quite late at night and did not get involved with the family affairs of the day when he came home.

The paradox was that Mr. T, in fact, had his mother to himself all day long, but he could not have her emotionally or sexually. Added to this failure was his contemplation of his father's impressive physique, which increased Mr. T's feelings of inferiority and impotent competition. There was nothing he could do to overcome his mother's resistance to being involved with him in a personal way, whether preoedipally or oedipally. His oedipal defeat was complete. Mr. T became convinced that if his mother couldn't love him, nobody could, least of all a woman. This narcissistic injury led him to elaborate compensatory masturbatory and nonmasturbatory grandiose and sadistic fantasies in which he made himself the victor, thus overcoming the internal obstacle posed by his defeat. The affects of anger and rage fueling the fantasies could become transformed into exhilarating grandiose fantasies, which isolated him socially and interfered with his studies, and in the end, made him even more withdrawn and depressed.

But now, as an adult, when he was in the presence of a woman, the anticipated feeling of repeating his past humiliation and rejection elicited in him defensive and compensatory rageful affects, which enabled him to justify to himself his humiliation of the woman. In his impotence, in order to feel he could be accepted, he flaunted his compensatory superiority, while simultaneously feeling that he could not impress her because she was too stupid to "get it." The only way he could obtain something from her was by resorting to the last effort he could make to obtain her response: to sadistically force the woman with his overpowering sexual penetration, his hostile words, and his physical infliction of pain, to make her recognize and love him. This desperate added effort to achieve the response from the object represents a clear illustration of what we are calling aggression, which in his case resulted in sadistic fantasies and actions. The external aggressive actions, however, did not help him to overcome his internal obstacles because, regardless of what happened with the woman, he could not feel loved or lovable. He only felt "like a piece of meat." The internal conviction of worthlessness interfered with his being able to accept whatever recognition, affection, or respect the women or his fellow workers might offer him. His narcissistic rages, his intense murderous wishes, his wishes to humiliate people, his abuse of women, were simultaneously an effort to prevent people from discovering how worthless he was and a way of averting the expected repetition of his failure to have his mother notice and love him. This was the insurmountable internal obstacle motivating his sadistic behaviors. He had to resort aggressively to any available psychic maneuver to avoid feeling this terribly painful inner sense of being worthless and unlovable.

The intensity of Mr. T's rage and his determination to demonstrate himself superior to others by making them face their stupidity was dynamically a compensatory maneuver to displace onto others his unbearable feeling of being unlovable and inferior. The hateful feelings and behavior, as Gabbard (1991) suggested with respect to borderline patients, served to contain his envy of those who could love and be loved. There was also an identification with his mother spitting on him in contempt and humiliating him with harsh words. Unlike Gabbard's patients, Mr. T did not experience himself as hateful or revengeful. He felt that his effort to correct others and force them to behave the way he wanted was a kind of special mission he had to carry out for their own good, to help them see themselves as they really were. His continuous mocking efforts to catch the analyst in not remembering, or contradicting herself, or showing her inability to attend to him adequately, were directed to proving that she could not possibly care for him and could not be an honest working analyst. As far as he understood it, it was his task to show human beings what they really were: people who only under duress and when absolutely forced to do so would respond to him. What he had against them was not that he hated them: he hated the fact that they would not spontaneously want to show appreciation for him and make room for him in their lives. It was to no avail that his second wife tried very hard to respond to him. He couldn't believe it and attributed ulterior motives to her caring. Only in the fourth year of analysis, after he was able to understand his rejection of others, did he came to understand that his now ex-wife had actually loved him.

How did the analysis help Mr. T to change from a sadistic individual to a man capable of tender feelings, from a sarcastic interlocutor to a humorous speaker? The technical handling of the analysis was based on the analyst's early dynamic diagnosis considering Mr. T's narcissistic stance as a defense against his wish for love and affection. During the third evaluation hour, however, when the analyst was worried about taking him into analysis, given the severity of his pathology, a brief and vivid countertransferential "vision" the analyst experienced help her decide to accept him as a patient. The analyst "saw" a boy of five or six looking longingly while standing forlorn in the corner of a room. Continuous recollection of that vision subsequently sustained her in her being able to tolerate—not without great effort and constant vigilance—all his attacks without retaliation. That attitude represented the containment function several authors (Boyer, 1986, 1989; Buie and Adler, 1982–83; Carpy, 1989; Chessick, 1977; Epstein, 1979; Gabbard, 1989, 1991; Giovacchini, 1975; Grotstein, 1982; Little, 1966; Meissner, 1988, 1996b; Searles, 1986; Sherby, 1989) have suggested as a condition for treating borderline patients. Mr. T was not a borderline patient. In his case the containment was intended—as Freud recommended (1914, p. 154)—to allow him to display his entire pathology in "almost complete freedom," without interfering with it or responding with either sadistic attack or masochistic surrender to what he said or did.

Questions, invitations to explore his feelings, observations, clarifications without any interpretation that would have challenged his need to be superior, were the prevailing technical approach. For a long time, interpretations were almost nothing but enlargements and rephrasings of his discoveries. Only after he developed some affection for the analyst and acknowledged that she wanted to help him did the interpretive work proper begin. Mr. T experienced this behavior on the analyst's part as profoundly respectful of him, and later verbalized his feelings about it, indicating that such respect had been critical for his changing his stance from sadistic rejection to acceptance of the analyst's interventions. If he was respected, he could respect in turn. Dynamically, this technique contributed to creation of the psychic space that permitted progressive interpretation of his injured narcissism and its compensatory grandiosity. It also gave him time to experience the complexity of his feelings without having them interpreted beyond their here-and-now meaning.

The repeated emergence of similar patterns of feelings led him to see that all he was doing was nothing but manipulating people, through his rages, his displays, his overpowering attitudes, without achieving any relief of his own psychic pain. Finally, he came to see that in his narcissistic rage it was he who had been blinding himself and could not see others as they really were—in other words, that he was doing to others what he claimed his mother and father had done to him. He acknowledged that it was he who had refused to accept the analyst and her efforts to help him. He recognized that to assuage his pain he had covered it up with rage and revenge, his prevailing affects, while continuously machinating ways and means to make people do what he wanted. These machinations manifested what we are calling the aggressive extra effort directed to overcoming an obstacle. In his case, it was an internally persisting obstacle that could only be changed through analytic work. In the end, he was able to change significant aspects of his self-structure and representation, and to revive through regression early affectionate feelings for his mother that had been completely sequestered from his conscious experience, and to integrate them by means of extensive working through.

It is our view that the sadism in Mr. T's fantasies and actions was not elicited by an aggressive drive. It resulted from motivational activation, through complex psychic processes in Mr. T's mind, directed to overcoming a seemingly insurmountable internal obstacle.His all-encompassing sadistic behavior only revealed the persistence of his ineffective efforts to overcome this obstacle and finally achieve his goal of feeling loved. When that obstacle was removed and he began to believe himself lovable and acceptable, the sadistic behaviors lost their function. We hope to have shown that Mr. T's sadistic and aggressive behaviors, fantasies, and wishes were motivated by clearly identifiable dynamic processes at the service of helping him maintain a modicum of narcissistic equilibrium in facing the near-insurmountable internal obstacle of feeling and believing himself to be inferior and unlovable. Every human relationship, particularly with women, threatened to repeat the stimulus conditions of his developmental years, when he could not obtain the maternal response he longed for. Under such stimulus conditions, he felt internally compelled to overcome the internal obstacle. Unable, as he was, to achieve such a result, he resorted consciously and unconsciously to every displacement, projection, and behavior that could "force" the object at hand to respond to and notice him.

SUMMARY

Psychoanalytic theory considers sadism a manifestation of the aggressive drive, but we are proposing a revised theory of aggression suggesting that aggression is not a drive but a biologically rooted psychic capacity that can be called into action by appropriate stimulus conditions and motivational contexts. The activity of this aggressive psychic capacity is aimed at overcoming obstacles, whether external or internal, that interfere with the achievement of the goal of an intended physical or psychical action.

This chapter presented the case of a sadistic man to illustrate the application of this theoretical approach in an effort to show that it is not necessary to postulate an aggressive drive to understand sadism. The dynamics of sadistic behaviors and wishes originate in complex and multidetermined motivational sources, as we will demonstrate further in chapter 8. We are also suggesting that at the center of these motivations in sadism there is an internal obstacle: the conviction or profound self-doubt about being lovable and acceptable as an object. Most sadistic behaviors and wishes represent efforts to overcome this insurmountable internal obstacle. The intrapsychic situation created by this internal obstacle calls to action, in moments of intrapsychic or interpersonal stimulation, the intervention of the biologically rooted aggressive capability to carry out any external or internal action deemed capable of overcoming such an obstacle. The repetition of sadistic actions and fantasies is only a measure of continuous but ineffective efforts to overcome the internal obstacle.

Section II

Theoretical Perspectives

Chapter 4

The Agent of Aggressive Action

INTRODUCTION

The case of Mr. T, presented in chapter 3, opens the way to further considerations of the theoretical substructure supporting the analytic process, with particular emphasis on the role of aggression conceived as a motivation directed to overcoming obstacles rather than a drive-based theory. We can make the following observations about the case material regarding Mr. T:

(1) Nowhere in the case presentation or discussion is there any mention of aggression as a drive, or of any other drives.
(2) The constant focus in the clinical material is on the meaning, contexts, conditions, genetic determinants, and motives providing the reasons why the patient acts and reacts in the manner he does.
(3) The emphasis in the analytic process falls on the interaction between analyst and patient, first in relation to transference and countertransference, and second in relation to alliance factors finally enabling analyst and patient to engage with each other in a process of self-inquiry and self-exploration that increasingly draws the patient away from intensely sadomasochist transference involvements to more productive engagements in the analytic process and with the analyst as analyst.

(4) At each step in this process, obstacles had to be overcome—on the part of the patient, obstacles posed on one level by his sado-masochistic defenses displayed in the transference, and on another level his powerful narcissistic needs. We would argue that overcoming these obstacles in the course of the analytic process required mobilization of the patient's aggression and its direction to increasingly therapeutic purposes. The gradual shift in the patient's position entailed a differential mobilization of aggressive action from the defensive needs and motives enacted in the transference involvement to a redirection of action into more therapeutically productive channels. At each step, it was the same aggressive capacity that was called into play, but the motivational contexts were distinctly different and served distinctly different needs and desires of the patient.

(5) *Pari passu* with the shifts in aggressive orientation on the part of the patient, the analyst's aggression had to be mobilized, at first in the service of circumventing the countertransferential traps being set by the patient—either to become the masochistic victim of his sadistic attacks or to counter his onslaught with a domineering and sadistic retaliation of her own. Her aggression had to be brought to bear on sustaining her analytic stance and reinforcing her alliance position in the face of his attempts to undermine the analytic relation. Much of her aggression was directed against intrapsychic obstacles—e.g., the "temptations" to succumb to his transferential pressures—in order to establish some semblance of alliance. But an even further measure of aggression had to be brought to bear in sustaining the alliance, in circumventing the patient's efforts to draw the analytic interaction onto more real ground, and to increasingly facilitate the patient's ability to enter into the analytic work and become the active investigator of his own pathology and its meanings and reasons.

(6) The interpretive dynamic in this case at no point makes reference to drives or drive derivatives as explanatory of the patient's orientation, attitudes, or behaviors. Rather, the direction of inquiry and interpretive focus is toward the motivational basis for the patient's behavior and life pattern—toward the meaning, motives, and reasons behind his actions. An important aspect of this case that played a special role in the process was that any implication of mechanisms driving his behavior that he could not control or

anticipate would have been so traumatizing and injurious to his fragile grandiosity that they would have been totally rejected and might well have completely disrupted the analytic process. The analyst had to play her cards with careful consideration of his narcissistic vulnerability, and find a way to engage his capacity for self-exploration and self-understanding that would yield therapeutic benefit while circumventing the pitfalls of possible submission to the authority of the analyst and the analysis and corresponding narcissistic injury.

Our purpose in this study is to develop a principle of aggression that is motivational rather than energic. Cases like the above challenge us to rethink how we understand the mental processes in both analyst and patient to guide us in working with our patients in terms that are more closely aligned with the actual practice of analysis rather than with a preconceived model of the mind that leaves a gap between theory and actual clinical application. In approaching this problem, our purpose is not to refute or debate the merits or demerits of the drive model; we regard that enterprise as more or less a closed book, that has been effectively accomplished by others. While many, particularly in the postkohutian and more recent postmodern developments in psychoanalysis, have declared the drive theory as dead and buried, the fact remains that it is still a majority view whose remnants can be found, either directly or indirectly expressed, on nearly every page of much of the current analytic literature. Thus, reports of its demise may have been somewhat premature. Part of our task is to persuade the body of readers who still maintain some variant of the drive theory, along with others who have abandoned the drive concept but have yet to find an adequate replacement, that a view of aggression as motive has both theoretical and clinical advantages. Given this context for our discussion and our presumption that drive theory has been sufficiently critiqued by others, we still find it advantageous for the purposes of exposition to contrast our view of aggression with the traditional drive theory—as way of asserting and clarifying our own approach. Thus, we are not the first to challenge the drive theory, but we feel confident that we are making the effort to move beyond drive considerations to fashion a different theory specifically of aggression as motive and as functioning within a modified metapsychological framework—elements that we do not find elsewhere in the analytic literature.

In replacing the drive theory with a theory of motivation, we encounter the problem of agency, that is, to the extent that aggression is conceived as motive and not as cause, how do we account for aggressive action? We are not the first to pose this problem or to attempt to answer it. Some years ago, Roy Schafer (1976) advanced his view of an action language to replace what he saw as an outmoded metapsychology. Schafer's criticism was directed against the methodology and the form of psychoanalytic thinking based on a natural science modality of theorizing that had become second nature to most of us. The inevitable direction of such natural science thinking was toward reification and anthropomorphisms, essentially substantializing mental processes—as though the mind were divided up into a series of lesser minds, to each of which we attribute intentions, goals, characteristics, and qualities. While on the clinical level we deal with our patients as symbol-making and meaning-oriented personal agents, on the level of theoretical discourse, he charged, we deal with them as aggregates of psychic machinery. To this extent, the personal agent has been a constant embarrassment to metapsychology and has never found a satisfactory place in the theory. Instead of a psychology of the personal agent who performs many actions, we have a psychology of many minor subagencies acting upon and interacting with each other to bring about complex psychic resultants.

Many have laid a critical axe to the inherent difficulties in metapsychology,[1] but few have taken the further step of delineating an effective and useful alternative. Schafer did take a further step, arguing that, in fact, there are no such entities in the mind, no such minor agencies; there is only the human being who is a personal agent performing actions for specifiable reasons, with specific purposes, and directed to the attainment of specific goals. His replacement took the form of his action language, which, if it had the advantage of focusing on personal agency and responsibility, resulted in a somewhat stilted clinical language that seemed to imply a kind of word-magic, namely that verbal reformulation would somehow effect structural modification. Moreover, insistence on the action language seemed clinically to employ a frontal assault on the patient's defenses that many found less than helpful. One difficulty his theory encountered was that, in doing away with notions of force, energy, and drive on the grounds that they are substantive terms which are implicitly personified by having aims and intensity imputed to them, such propulsive entities were thereby eliminated as initiators and sustainers of action. To take a single example, translation of a drive impulse as conditional action—that is, action that one refrains from doing, or action that one would do were it not for certain inhibiting circumstances—seems to provide a pallid reflection of what is implicit in the original notion. It would be accurate to say that if I have an impulse to expose myself, but do not do so because of the presence of other people, the action in question, namely exposing myself, is a conditional action insofar as I might have done it had not that immediate set of circumstances prevented me from doing so. But to leave the matter at that seems to leave out what is relevant to the impulse itself and to focus rather on the related action to which the impulse is directed. What is not included is precisely the impulse, or perhaps more accurately the impulsivity, that is, the quality of forcefulness, peremptoriness, and pressure for discharge that the notion of impulse connotes. We would argue, in contrast, that impulsivity and its related characteristics are qualities of motivational import, and are a function of quantitative factors related to internal need states, and the contexts and characteristics of stimulus contingencies. Thus Schafer's approach points in the direction of our theory insofar as it brings into focus the personal agent acting for reasons and directed to goals. But a motivational theory entails more. Reasons are statements of motivational purpose, but the theory must also account for the mechanisms of motivation thrust and activation.

The action language asserted that it was adequate for purposes of understanding to describe actions accurately. The modes of actions and the need for understanding are adequately satisfied, so Schafer contended, by relating those actions to the reasons the personal agent has to perform them. Explanation is cast in terms of reasons, intentions, and meanings with the consequence that the causes of action, precisely because they reflect the natural science approach, are ruled out of court. In our view, explanations in terms of reasons, reasons that are often hidden from the subject himself, and of discovering what in fact are the real reasons rather than the given reasons, provide only a partial explanation. If one limits the scope of inquiry to answering why questions, then the demand of the question is satisfied by asserting reasons for the action. But science cannot simply rely on why-questions and reason-answers as the basis for explanation and understanding. We must ask questions about how the behavior is performed, its possible underlying causal sequences, what mechanisms and processes contribute to its being performed in that manner and not any other, etc. In other words, there are whole areas of questioning that have to do with our understanding of the structure, composition, nature, organization, and functioning of the agency in question which relate to a whole realm of factors that are not touched on by why-questions and their corresponding reasons. It is the business of science to ask about and to try to understand not only the why-questions that address reasons, but also the how-questions that address the causes of behavior. If the personal agent acts for reasons—and we concur that it does—the reasons must be further stipulated in motivational terms, and the capacity of the agent to act must be explained as well.

However, as we are arguing, motives motivate; they are not causal, that is they do not act as sources of action. As long as and to the extent that a motive is effective, it offers of itself no basis for action. Action is possible only when, in response to motivational appeal, a source of activity is called into operation. Motives are ineffectual without a source of agency capable of responding to their motivational attraction. Analogously the rules of chess do not move the pieces—they state the rules by which the pieces can be moved; the pieces are moved by the motor power provided by the players. Or, more to the point, the player's desire to move the pieces in order to gain an advantage over his opponent (a valid reason) does not move the pieces; the player himself must do so by a physical action, motivated by his desire and directed by the rules of the game. This was not a problem for traditional drive theory since the drives were regarded as causal and sources of action. The present chapter attempts to address the fundamental problem of the nature of the agency responsible for aggressive action in a motivational theory of aggression. The following chapter will take up the dynamic nature of aggression itself specifically as motive.

It should be immediately clear that locating the source of agency in the self runs counter to current postmodernist trends in analytic theorizing. The relational and intersubjective approaches have thrown the whole question of agency and subjectivity into a limbo of uncertainty and doubt that we do not share. These schools have equivalently diluted and dissolved personal agency and subjectivity into an amorphous co-construction of an intersubjective dyadic entity in which issues of motivation, causality, and responsibility belong to neither partner in the analytic dialogue, but must be ascribed to a putative third which is neither analyst nor analysand. One such formulation suggests that "a well-synchronized and well-attuned dyad be viewed as *an integrated system wherein space and time is shared, as a single organism-like system.* A system is thus produced in which it is no longer possible to say who activates whom and who begins an interaction. Each partner influences and modulates the emotions and movements of the other" (Arnetoli, 2002, p. 750, emphasis in original). In terms of our own theory, we would have no difficulty in accepting the final sentence, since such interactions are transparently the stuff of analytic interaction. But for us both analyst and analysand are independent agents and enjoy independent and private subjectivities which de facto cannot be shared (Meissner, 1999d, e). Yet the partners in the analytic dialogue continually interact and modify each other's responses in complex patterns of ongoing mutual influence. But they do so as individuals, acting, reacting, and interacting with each other in the interpersonal matrix of the analytic relation. We see no need and no basis for dispensing with individual and personal subjectivity and agency, in that the personal self is not only capable of profoundly meaningful and involving relationships with others, but cannot develop psychologically or live successfully without them (Meissner, 2000d, e).

THE CONCEPT OF AGGRESSION

The essential elements of our understanding of aggression can be summarized in the following points:

1. Aggression is *not* simply a biologically based drive in a constant state of activity or discharge. It is rather a biologically grounded capacity requiring appropriate stimulus conditions to elicit activation or response.

This view of aggression clearly diverges from the classical drive notion. Aggression here differs from the theory of instincts in that it does not regard aggression as a form of biologically determined instinctual drive constantly seeking discharge and exerting pressure on the mental apparatus. Instead we see it as representing a basic capacity called into action only under stimulus conditions in which overcoming of an obstacle is required. The difference is clear in the developmental context: drive theory would see development of aggression as a process in which the mental apparatus strives to integrate the aggressive drive derivatives impinging on it from below, i.e., from an innate biologically given drive; in contrast, the present motivational theory would see development in aggression as reflecting the organism's experience of dealing with and overcoming obstacles in the course of which action potentialities or capacities are activated and integrated. Aggression is thus a given capacity that comes into play only under appropriate stimulus or motivational conditions. Rather than a biological force, aggression becomes a psychological construct related to and reactive to specifiable stimulus conditions including relationships with objects. The emphasis shifts from biological determinants to the motivational context of aggressive action.

2. The motivational (as opposed to drive-discharge) aspect of this model of aggression arises from the conditions of activation, namely the need for activating stimuli, the goal-oriented or purposeful character of the response, and its inherent connection with wishes, desires, meanings, and intentions.

Motivation in a general sense refers to a disposition to purposive or intentional action, whether conscious or unconscious. Motivation in this sense is distinct from sheer energic discharge, although it may secondarily involve energic components as an aspect of the causal efficacy involved, not in the motive, but in the action. Motives may express themselves in varying degrees of complexity, intensity, modes of displacement, and levels of psychic integration (G. Klein, 1967). Wishes, in this hierarchy of motivational terms, rather than expressions of drive impulse or discharge, involve a cognitive dimension which lends direction and intention to the action expression, usually through linkage with a mnemic image. In Freud's view, fulfillment of a wish is a psychic act aimed at reproducing "the perception, which had become the sign of satisfaction" (Laplanche and Pontalis, 1973, p. 482). Motivation intends achievement of a particular aim. The aim may be satisfaction of a need, fulfillment of a wish, attainment of psychic equilibrium, or avoidance of distressful affect. Any interference with accomplishment of the aim of a motivation becomes an obstacle. The obstacle may be extrinsic to the individual or intrapsychic.

Once a mental representation of a motivational aim has been formed, an action can be elicited to obtain it. If an obstacle interferes, the self may call any available psychic process into play to overcome it. Aggression utilizes any resource of the organism, from physical force to defense mechanisms, in its persistence toward reaching and attaining the motivational goal. In this sense, aggression requires participation of several psychic agencies and a rearrangement of the defensive system. Certain aggressive behaviors involve a minimal number of psychic processes, while others may require participation of all three psychic structural components of the self. In this view aggression is not a force, but an action capacity for integrating psychic functions in the service of attaining a motivational aim.

3. The common element in aggressive behaviors is the striving or exertion for the purpose of overcoming an obstacle. In the clinical setting such obstacles are exclusively nonphysical, insofar as they can be cast meaningfully in either psychological or moral terms. Aggression only comes into play at that point at which an action, otherwise naturally, easily, or comfortably effected, becomes inhibited, impeded, or otherwise counteracted by an obstacle to that action. By implication, therefore, it is not the action that determines the aggressive nature of the activity, but rather its motivation, i.e., overcoming the obstacle. Consequently, even destructive actions would not be specifically aggressive because of their destructiveness, but rather because of the effortful component called forth in the overcoming of an obstacle. One could presume that destructive activity is usually aggressive, but only by reason of the fact that other forces would naturally or inevitably be called into play, opposing the action and setting an obstacle to its accomplishment. Some aggressive actions may be destructive, but conversely destructive action need not be aggressive. The same point is reinforced by Parens's (1979) use of the category of nonaggressive destructiveness.[2]

4. Such a motivationally based view of aggression requires certain key distinctions. First, there is the distinction between aggression and its accompanying affects (see chapter 6). Aggressive acts may be accompanied by a variety of affective states, whether fear, anxiety, lust, love, joy, or even anger and rage. However, an essential note of the present view is that aggression is not defined by its accompanying affects. The intrinsic motivation or purposive dimension of the aggression itself, namely, overcoming of an obstacle, whether psychological or physical, is not linked with any specific affective response, but may be connected with a variety of affective components derived from peripheral or secondary sources and reflecting the motivational conditions of the aggressive response. In this sense, rage might be a response to narcissistic injury rather than an expression of aggression.

The affective quality of the response has more to do with the stimulus context and conditions than with the eliciting of an aggressive response as such.

5. A second distinction we propose is that between aggression and its associated actions. Freud's failure to make this distinction plagued his early thinking about instincts. He regarded instincts as inherently active, that is, as exercising a degree of force on the psychic apparatus. In *Instincts and Their Vicissitudes* (1915) Freud wrote: "By the pressure of an instinct we understand its motor factor, the amount of force or the measure of the demand for work which it represents. The characteristic of exercising pressure is common to all instincts; it is in fact their very essence. Every instinct is a piece of activity; if we speak loosely of passive instincts, we can only mean instincts whose *aim* is passive" (p. 122, emphasis in original). In contrast, we insist on the distinction between cause and motive; in our view of aggression, the causal or power component is attributed to the self-as-agent (Meissner, 1993), the source of all of the organism's activity, physical and psychic, and the motivational component is attributed to the agent's aggressive capacity.

In discussing the theoretical underpinnings of this concept of aggression, we regard economics as encompassing firstly statements relevant to the causal principles of action and their regulation, and secondly to issues relevant to quantitative variation. Dynamic principles, in turn, are related to the status of aggression as a motivational principle. Thus our theoretical revision retains both economic and dynamic principles as essential to the understanding of aggression, while specifically divorcing it from any dependence on drives or drive derivatives. We are proposing a metapsychological shift from appealing to drives as sources of both motive and causality to an understanding of the locus of causality as inherent in the self, specifically the self-as-agent, and recasting aggression as a form of motivation prompting and directing the self to action.

The Economic Principle and the Question of Agency

The economic principle in psychoanalysis has fallen into disrepute, largely because of connection with Freud's energic model, giving rise to questions as to whether it has outlived its usefulness and now actually hampers our advancing understanding of the mind's functioning. Can the concept of psychic energy, of which aggression was accounted one of the primary forms, have any validity or reality at all? Might not psychoanalysis find firmer theoretical footing in other more contemporary explanatory models?

In the contemporary setting, there is an emerging consensus that Freud's energic hypotheses are not only scientifically outdated, but are no longer adequate for the theoretical demands of psychoanalysis. Certain writers have unequivocally endorsed abandonment of an energic base for psychoanalysis, regarding Freud's concept of psychic energy as little more than metaphoric. While there may be reasons for abandoning the energic hypothesis, we can find a way to jettison the bathwater and retain the baby. One danger in abandoning the energic hypothesis is that we find ourselves without a theoretical foundation for any capacity for causal action or agency. Our position in the present study is that psychoanalysis cannot abandon its claim to scientific status or maintain the validity of its position as an understanding of human psychic functioning without a metapsychology, but not necessarily metapsychology as narrowly conceived by traditional theorists (Meissner, 1981b). We would further contend that the economic principle does not depend on the energic model Freud originally proposed, yet psychoanalysis cannot do without an economic principle—that any meaningful theoretical account must embrace economic issues in some form, and that any hope of integration of psychoanalytic propositions with contemporary scientific understandings of the human mind and its biological substrate becomes meaningless without an operative economic principle.[3]

Our purpose is to propose a motivational theory of aggression. While the classical theory of drive activation regarded drives as sources of both motive and action, we stipulate that the motives and causes of action are distinct, and that while aggression continues to serve certain motivational functions leading to action, it is not part of the causal sequence producing the action. As was the case for Mr. T, the analytic interest was not focused on the causality of his aggressive actions, but on the motivation. All of his actions, aggressive or not, express the causal efficacy and potential of his inherent agency, i.e., of the potential for action of his self-as-agent (Meissner, 1993). The recurrent question in the analysis, then, had to be: What obstacles were inherent in the situation or the analytic interaction that would have stimulated him to the effort of overcoming them? What were the obstacles in him that provoked his modus operandi, and what obstacles did he create or find in the world around him that provoked aggressive responses?

The drive-discharge model interprets aim in terms of discharge, thus blurring any distinction between drive and motive. For Mr. T this would have meant that the reasons for his behavior would have been interior and indistinguishable from the causality of his action. But in clinical and life contexts, for example, libido and sexuality do assume significant connotations of meaning and motive (G. Klein, 1976). Even if meaning and motive do not exclude quantitative dimensions, the quantitative cannot substitute for the qualitative. But even so, we can question whether the range of behaviors and motives is exhausted by appeal to sexual and aggressive drives.

Beyond economic issues involved in quantitative variation, it seems clear that any concept of efficient causality effecting transformation and real change requires an energic basis—there is no causality without a potential for action or work. In this sense, psychic change occurs as the result of psychic work, so that in some sense energy, as the principle of work, is required to explain the maintenance of psychic integrity, and by defect disturbances and disruptions of psychic equilibrium (Badalamenti, 1985). But the locus of psychic action in our view is not to be found in drives or even in disparate psychic structures, but in the self conceived as synonymous with the human person. In whatever context aggressive motives arise for overcoming an obstacle, they stimulate and direct the activity of the self-as-agent, utilizing whatever capacities of the self are appropriate for the obstacle and context in question. The capacities required for thinking through a difficult problem in solid geometry are different from the capacities called into play in wrestling a formidable opponent.

At the same time the notion of energy is itself problematical and elusive, not unlike the concept of gravity: we know it's there and has effects, but we don't know what it is. As in nature, energy is nonspecific—it differs according to the instrumentality in which it functions, e.g., fire is one form of energy, electricity another, chemical energy another, and so on. In physics, the concept of energy is multipurpose and difficult to specify. In its various forms it is measurable—degrees of heat, decibels of sound, intensity of illumination, electrical charge, and so on—all by its effects and not directly. But in each case, the energy involved in the production of the corresponding effects or work reflects a common denominator. The general meaning of energy in its modified forms is determined by the medium of expression. In other words, there is no pure energy. To push the argument to its limits, we might ask what is the energy contained in a weight, for example an iron ball, raised to a given height? We call it "potential energy" and attribute to it a quantitative measure. When the body falls the potential energy is transformed into kinetic energy—and if the mass and acceleration are large enough, it can do plenty of damage. But the body itself does not change physically until it impacts the ground, if at all. If we haul it back up to its original perch, it has the same potential energy as before. What then is the energy so measured? Conclusion: not only does the concept of energy have multiple meanings and implications, but in their most elementary sense these meanings are merely quantitative, do not extend beyond the capacity to exert causal effects, and remain essentially unexplained. Certainly the concept of energy in the iron ball is a far cry from Freud's elaborate energy model.

To take another analogy, the nervous system uses forms of neurophysiological energy to generate action potentials as well as subthreshold electrotonic charges. But as knowledge of the functioning of neural networks advances, energic considerations fade in importance and signal functions and information transfers related to such shifts in energy distribution take precedence. The discharge of action potentials in a given neural system requires energy, but the rate of firing has more important informational functions. Just as conduction of signals from the retinal neurons to cortical visual centers cannot take place without energy, more complex mental processes cannot take place without energy. Speaking metaphorically, psychic energy is the gas that runs the psychic motor—whether the motor belongs to an automobile, a speedboat, or an electrical generator, the gas is the same. But without it the motor does not run. A psychic system without psychic energy would be like a powerful computer that is not plugged in.[4]

THE SELF AND AGENCY

To summarize this part of our reflections, we can draw the following conclusions regarding the causality of aggressive action, keeping in mind that our interest is in aggression as motivational aspect of psychic functioning.

(1) Psychoanalytic theory requires an economic principle as an integral part of its theoretical account of the human mind and its
functioning, particularly with respect to the origins and regulation of psychic causality.

(2) Psychic energy is regarded as a principle of work, that is, as the
capacity for psychic structures to perform specific functions. Energy in this sense is no more than the capacity of psychic functions and/or systems to operate and to perform their respective
functions. Thus energy is merely the capacity to do work, in
whatever form or expression such psychic work manifests itself.[5]
Running is work, thinking is work, feeling is work, imagining is
work, even unconscious fantasy is work.[6] But whatever energy is in
question, it is not substantial, it is not any kind of entity, it is not
hydraulic, nor does it involve any form of recognizable charge or
force. It is the inherent capacity of the psychic apparatus and its
component parts to function—no more, no less. Psychic energy
is, then, a potential for action. The economic principle, in contrast, is thus a quantitative expression of the intensity, level, duration, and regulatory conditions for implementing motivational
determination and/or causal power of the organism as the source
of psychic agency. This conclusion equivalently specifies causality as a capacity of the self-as-agent and dispenses with the drive
theory as causal, including the concept of aggression as drive.

(3) Interpretations of economic principles in psychoanalysis specify
the conditions of causal activity in the self with reference to psychic activities and their causal determination and regulation. The
regulatory principles are statements of the necessary and sufficient conditions as to how the system works and produces effects.

(4) Energic concepts still have a limited role in psychoanalytic theory
in accounting for causality and work effects. They do not represent driving forces impelling psychic activity, but are *a priori*
conditions necessary to complete the understanding of causal
efficacy. The libidinal and aggressive aspects of behavior, classically attributed to the respective drives, are refocused as motivational states eliciting behavior responses as motives and not as
causes. My desire to eat the apple sets the causal sequence involved in my eating in action, but my desire is not part of the
causal sequence, but rather motivates it; the desiring, along with
the subsequent decision to eat and the eating, are actions of the
self-as-agent. Adam's desire to eat the apple was overdetermined—

by his wish to taste a new fruit, by his need to please his wife Eve, and by his narcissistic wish to have the knowledge of good and evil like God—but all these motives, while prompting him to make his fatal choice, were not any part of the causal sequence that began with his self-determination and decision leading to his actual eating.

(5) The separation of issues related to causality or agency from questions related to motivation is central to our understanding of aggression. How, then, in our theory of aggression, do we understand psychic functioning and action? If we abandon the appeal to biologically generated drive forces as principles of psychic action, where do we locate the principle of action and agency? The approach we are taking responds to this issue in terms of the role of the self-as-agent (Meissner, 1993), whereby agency belongs to the self as the theoretical construct standing for the real person. In this sense, agency belongs to the person, not to the drives.[7]

With respect to aggression, the term "aggression" connotes no more than the motive eliciting that capacity required for effective functioning or for performance of work against a given resistance or obstacle, thus shifting the explanatory focus from causality or agency to the eliciting conditions and their motivational import. It is our sense that this shift in emphasis is more faithful to the actual modality of analytic thinking as it actually develops clinically in the analytic process—as seems evident in discussing the case of Mr. T above. As clinicians, our interest does not lie in the putative drive as such, or for that matter in any causal process or agency, but in the circumstances, contexts, events, and relationships that provide the context of whatever aggressive expression is in question. However we understand the patient's capacity to act, even to act aggressively in overcoming obstacles, that knowledge does not help us to understand what motivated his behavior, what contextual conditions and factors, whether intraspychic or interpersonal or other, lie behind and illumine the reasons for that behavior. We also recognize that such motivational contexts involve the patient's history, developmental and experiential, the derivatives of which contribute to setting the analytic stage on which aggressive action is played out, as well as the complex network of relationships that play a significant role in his ongoing life experience. We recognize this dimension of the analytic experience most poignantly, but not exclusively, in the transference.

Economic considerations represent the capacity or potential of the organism to respond to the stimulation of the schema with greater or lesser degrees of force and activity. The activating and eliciting capacity of the motivational schema would be without effect if the energic capacity to respond were missing, but the capacity for action lies in the self-as-agent. The integration of power and information concepts provides a more satisfying theoretical foundation for psychoanalytic thinking about action. If we grant that no psychic action takes place without involving psychic energy, does that imply drive involvement in any sense? In the theory we are proposing, our attempt to rethink the concept of aggression, performance of an action does not require activation of aggression to explain the activity— psychic structures are capable of functioning in themselves without need for any drive to explain action, i.e., they have an inherent capacity for activity that involves their own specific energic potential as part of the inherent causal efficacy of the self. Aggression enters the picture when motivating circumstances for activation of the aggressive capacity are present—denominated in our reformulation as "overcoming an obstacle." Aggression is a capacity activated under stimulus conditions calling for overcoming an obstacle, whether external or internal (intrapsychic). The classic drive, then, is replaced by a capacity or potential of the self that can be called into operation when required under certain motivational conditions. The same argument applies to the libidinal drive—not every appetitive desire or tendency need be driven by a libidinal drive, but libidinal desires and actions can be elicited by specifically libidinal stimulus conditions.

These dimensions of the analytic experience are displayed in detail in the case of Mr. T. First, the therapeutic effort was directed to unearthing, exploring, understanding, and putting into perspective the multiple factors in his early life experience. These included his difficult relationship with his mother, the connection between that level of his experience and his adult narcissistic need and vulnerability, and the defensively motivated sadistic attacks against the women in his experience, including the particularly intense provocations with his female analyst. Second, the interpretive focus that gradually emerged from the conjoined efforts of Mr. T and his analyst were focused on the meaning of these events and relationships and the motivational impact they had on his attitudes, orientation to life, and his behavior generally. This shift brings the motivational structure into the foreground and appeals to an entirely different metapsychological perspective than the classical derivation from drives. In other words, the understanding of Mr. T's embattled narcissism and his need to attack and demean the significant women in his life appealed to the meaning, contexts, and motives of his behavior rather than to the effect of an impersonal drive-force and its vicissitudes. It may well have been this dimension that George Klein (1969, 1970, 1975) had in mind in distinguishing between the metapsychological and the clinical theory in psychoanalysis. It is our persuasion that this shift in theoretical perspective regarding the understanding of aggression, for example, serves to diminish, if not close, the gap between theoretical formulation and clinical praxis.

How, then, are we to understand psychic agency? Our preferred response moves in the direction of developing a more comprehensive theory of the self in psychoanalysis (Meissner, 1986a, 1993, 2000c). The principle of agency in this frame of reference does not lie in a set of biologically determined drives, but in the self as an autonomous, self-initiating, self-generating, and self-directing source of psychic action.[8] But our concern in regard to the dynamic principle is not with the source or cause of action in economic terms,[9] but with the nature, quality, form, purpose, intention, direction, and meaning of any such action. Any form of action attributed to ego, superego, or id is in effect an action of the self acting in specifiable ways characteristic of these component subagencies (Meissner, 2000f, g, h). Thus, the self may act in ways characteristic of a predominantly id-orientation so that action becomes impulsive, imperative, expressed more in a modality of peremptory discharge and primary process organization rather than of purpose and control. Or the self may act in ways characteristic of the ego in which the capacity for delay, direction, defense, regulation, secondary process organization, purpose, and reality-orientation predominates. And similarly regarding the superego, whose characteristic expression is evaluative and ethically oriented.

Chapter 5

Aggression as Motivation

THE DYNAMIC PRINCIPLE

This above reformulation of the economic principle as pertaining to aggression by implication involves retrenchment from the theory of drives. The argument leads inexorably to the question of what explanatory alternatives are available for interpreting phenomenally identifiable behaviors previously thought of as drive-related or drive-derivative, if we no longer appeal to drives as sources of action and motivation. This is singularly relevant to the understanding of aggression as intimately involved in action and the production of effects. And we are particularly interested in focusing our conclusions on the analytic process where dynamic issues take precedence.

Our purpose in this chapter is to explore the ramifications of this theory of motivation and to try to bring into focus the differences in emphasis and direction of thinking called for in a revised understanding of dynamic principles when an appeal to the drives as the sources of motive force have been abandoned. The economic principle discussed in the previous chapter accounts for the conditions for psychic functioning so that under appropriate stimulus conditions psychic functions are activated or deactivated, intensified or modulated, and their respective potentials for action are called into operation or the reverse, whether amplified or modulated. Additional questions, however, remain regarding the relationship of these processes to motivational conditions that give rise to and modify patterns of behavior and action.

MOTIVATIONAL PRINCIPLES

Motivational issues have particular relevance to the role of aggression, but there are significant issues pertaining to the connection between motivational systems and principles of action and causality that deserve separate attention (Meissner, 1995c). It was one thing to understand the expression of Mr. T's aggressive onslaughts against his analyst and another to grasp the immediate intentionality of that behavior, namely the overcoming of the obstacle posed by her therapeutic stance and her unwillingness to comply with his transference demand—to become the masochistic object for his sadistic attacks—and still another to fathom the motivating reasons in his dynamic unconscious and its roots in early life history that gave rise to them and sustained their ongoing intensity. These require a clear formulation of the determining influences as more specifically informational and meaning-related. The aspects of motivation calling for clarification would include the basic definition of motivation, appetition, the relation of wish and motivation, the distinction of cause and motive, the relation of reasons and motives, the relation of motives to needs, the question of nondrive motivation, the expression of drive-like characteristics, and finally the status of motives as determining behavior. We can address these issues in terms of the differentiation of the classic theory (Rapaport, 1960a, b) from alternative nondrive motivational systems, and an exploration of aspects of other than drive-determined bases of aggressive action and motivation.

(1) Primary definition. In the classic theory motivations were defined in terms of internal forces of the mind, distinct from external stimulation and/or any form of physiological process providing internal stimulation. These forces may be variously experienced—as passive, peremptory, compulsive, feeling beyond control (ego-dystonic); or at times actively, as willed (thus ego-syntonic). By implication, the direction and magnitude of any affect force was determined by conditions of drive force and discharge, rather than by any consideration of external goals or purposes. In these terms, the motivational principle lay in the disposition of drive forces and motivation was to be understood in these drive-determined terms. Further, motivation and causality were conjoined in the drive concept—the drives not only motivated but were sources of psychic action.

Against this, we would argue that motivation pertains to the stimulus conditions (both internal and external) and contexts of meaning that elicit a response from the organism, providing the circumstances stimulating the organism to respond. These responses are actions of the self as the source of agency, not of drives. The difference here lies between execution on one hand and intention or motivation on the other: execution is causal, intention appetitive.[1] Motivation lies in the aim of the behavior, not in the source. The classic view of motive seeks to account for both action (energy) and direction (force), whereas a non-drive theory of motivation would seek to account only for the "direction" and intentionality (purpose) of the behavior. This impinges on the issue of the distinction between cause and motive (see below).

(2) Motives as appetitive. The classic view included the note of motives as "*appetitive internal forces*" (Rapaport, 1960a, p. 865, italics in original).[2] Appetites were defined by: (a) peremptoriness, which may be subject to degrees of delay or control, but is not voluntary; (b) cyclic character, subject to rise and fall on the basis of accumulation or discharge of energic tension, also subject to variation and attenuation; (c) selectiveness, implying that direction of the motive force is determined by the object and the circumstances in which the object may be obtainable; and (d) displaceability, in terms of which objects leading to or substituting for the primary object may trigger the consummatory action.

But none of these characteristics require an instinctual drive theory. These qualities of action can just as well be determined by stimulus conditions, including the conditions determining response readiness in the organism. For example, if the lion, snoozing in the midday sun, is well fed and satiated, the dancing gazelle prancing across his visual field will elicit no response. The lion snoozes on. But lions get hungry. The hungry lion does not snooze, but goes into his predatory mode and begins to prowl in search of game. If the same gazelle dances across the field at this juncture, he will be a goner. Is this a "hunger drive"? Or does the internal state of hunger set the conditions in which the dancing gazelle becomes a motivating stimulus eliciting the aggressive predatory response?

We should note that selectivity becomes salient insofar as it affects the stimulus conditions eliciting the response. The predatory behavior of the lion is motivated by an intentionality to catch and devour the prey. The gazelle only assumes its character as prey when the lion is in the predatory mode, otherwise not. The hunger acts only as an internal state setting the conditions of need for stimulus response. There is no internal force impelling the lion to aggressive behavior. In fact, it can be reasonably argued that the lion's hunting and killing may not even be aggressive, even though it is destructive (Parens, 1979; Rizzuto et al., 1993). Motivation in this sense is not meant to explain the causality of the action, but merely to account for the conditions in which the agent is aroused to action. Or, putting it another way, motivation is meant to explain appetition or the eliciting conditions for action, not action. Regarding appetitiveness in clinical terms, George Klein (1976) suggested:

> The clinical theory is not obliged to assume that the appetite is itself the consequence of a peripheral condition (a "drive") independent of itself. Its focus of inquiry is the motivational context. In the clinical theory, sexuality is viewed as appetitive activity within a reticulum of motivational meanings rather than the manifestation of a linear force impelling itself against a barrier. In the clinical theory, the structural nature of sensual craving is not that of a flow of something but an activated schema—a cognitive structure in action. (p. 41)

Behavior is appetitive in that it seeks to gain an objective, reach a goal, perform an action—but this intentionality is determined in relation to the eliciting conditions, not by the causal apparatus of motion or effectance. Exploratory behaviors or forms of curious behavior, for example, even if not consummatory, that is, not directed to or attaining a specific object, are still aroused by a set of stimulus conditions in which the unknown or the uncertain intersects with the desire to know, to find out, to clarify or explain, inherent in the human capacity to know and understand.[3] The need or desire to know is satisfied by knowledge, just as the hunger need is satisfied by food. It was precisely the failure to account for exploratory behavior and forms of curiosity that prompted White (1959, 1963) to propose his view of effectance and competence.

(3) *Wishes*. On Freud's terms wishes involved a model of internal motivational forces extending beyond his early reflex arc model. Despite his reliance on simple energic models, wishes held a central position in Freud's clinical thinking, providing the basic motivational term in the *Studies* (Breuer and Freud, 1893–95), the Dora case (Freud, 1905a), and particularly in *The Interpretation of Dreams* (1900)—as Holt (1976) commented, "[Wish] is a cognitive-affective concept, framed in terms of meanings and potentially pleasant or unpleasant outcomes

of possible courses of action" (p. 179). Wishes are forms of mental expression of motivational states, whether conscious or unconscious.[4]

In the classic theory, the memory trace of pleasurable satisfaction, associated with the lessening of tension from instinctual demands, was required for formation of a wish. The wish requires activation, not only of the memory of satisfaction, but of the stimulus conditions of the situation of satisfaction.[5] The mental image associated with satisfaction referred back to a previous excitation of a need that had earlier found satisfaction, so that when the need arose again it sought association with the memory image left by that earlier satisfaction and thus evoked the experience of satisfaction. Satisfaction of the wish in dreams, symptoms, and fantasies all carry this impression of compromise in realizing fulfillment by recovery of the memory of satisfaction, but for wishes whose adequate fulfillment requires some accomplishment in reality, these processes are half-measures. It is one thing to dream about getting the top grade in a final examination, another to actually do so. Wishful thinking may carry some of the burden of wish-fulfillment, but it is fulfillment falling short of accomplishment. The notion of wish-fulfillment emphasizes the dynamics of the wish and its fantasized satisfaction, whether conscious or unconscious; reality is kept aside, as in dreams (Laplanche and Pontalis, 1973). This reasoning was implicit in Freud's insistence on the complementarity of the pleasure and reality principles.[6] The wish of itself is, then, by definition, always incomplete, unsatisfied, frustrated—an emptiness yearning to be filled; if and when it achieves satisfaction, it is no longer a wish.[7]

The transition from need to wish as a motivational state was stated succinctly by Schur (1966): "The emergence of the 'wish' marks the beginning of the functioning of what we call psychic structure. I have also stressed the difference between the physiological concept 'need' and the psychological concept 'wish'" (p. 68). The psychological shift implied in the notion of wish carries with it the implication of purpose and direction to a goal. Holt (1976) stated cogently: "With the concept of wish, we can assert, in answer to the behaviorists and other mechanistically inclined theorists, that behavior *is* purposive, that fears, longings, plans, fantasies, and other mental processes are not epiphenomena, but must be central to any adequate psychology of human behavior, and that the person is often not conscious of what his purposes are" (p. 180). From the beginning, Freud's notions of defense, repression, and conflict were impregnated with meaning and purpose. Purposes remained clinical and related to dynamic considerations of conflicting motives and aims.

The Sandlers (1994) have extended the implications of the distinction between drive and wish. In their view, "not all unconscious wishes can be regarded as being motivated by instinctual drives seeking discharge" (p. 1004). Humans experience wishes for safety, assurance, affirmation, even narcissistic gratification, which do not qualify as drive derivatives, but are motives nonetheless. They continue: "It is, we believe, a fundamental error to consider every unconscious wish as being an instinctual wish or even as being a drive derivative. So, for example, the urge to cling to a maternal object, or simply to what is familiar as a response to anxiety, should not be regarded as always being motivated by a partial oral drive or be regarded as some form of drive derivative. The motivating force is much more likely to be anxiety" (p. 1005).

E contra, in terms of the preceding argument, this view, if not detracting from the classic view of drives, puts it in a very different context vis-à-vis motivational functions. We would push the argument a step further to suggest that not only is psychoanalytic motivation much more complex than the instinctual theory might allow, but that the instinctual patterns themselves are subject to motivational conditions such that seemingly drive-like conditions are called into action only as a result of eliciting conditions interacting with internal dispositional states; they do not exist antecedently in a state of constant activation and seeking for discharge.

By the same token, we have become increasingly aware that the range of nonconscious mental activity is much wider and more diversified than previously imagined. Much nonconscious activity can be categorized neither as preconscious nor as repressed and unconscious, as, for example, schematic and scripted patterns of functioning, nonconscious influence of goals and behavioral plans, and a variety of procedural rules guiding behavior, particularly in sociocultural contexts, none of which may find representation at a conscious level, and none of which can be attributed to unconscious id-related dynamics (Emde, 1993). Illustrations might include grammatical rules that govern the use of language but are not consciously declared, or complex rules governing social interactions, even including aspects of moral behavior—the rules may determine the patterning of behavior without any explicit representation or reference (Kihlstrom, 1987). Yet such behavioral components are motivated not by drive-derivative components, but by stimulus conditions and contexts calling the appropriate procedural codes and normative references into play.

Thinking in these terms tends to drive a wedge between the concepts of drive and wish, so that we no longer need to think of drives as the only source of wishes, conscious or unconscious. Wishes may operate on other grounds—undoing or avoiding narcissistic injury, or wishful fantasies driven by anxiety, shame, or guilt, as was evidently part of Mr. T's problems. This also opens the door to wishes based on other than instinctual motivations—curiosity, incentive motivation, effectance, competence (White, 1963). Part of the remarkable turn-around in the trajectory of Mr. T's clinical course was the emergence of an entirely different set of wishes and therapeutically oriented intentions to engage more productively in the analytic work so that he began to entertain the possibility of finding self-understanding, meaning, and hope for himself and his life. These wishes were wishes of a very different order than the perverted wishes behind his transference struggles.

(4) Causes versus motives. By equating motivations with forces the classic theory attributed causal efficacy to them. Motives, in this sense, "move" the organism to action as causes of execution. On these terms, when I reach for a piece of bread, the motive is to be found in the series of muscular and neural mechanisms controlling my movement as well as the prompting impulse thrown into gear by hunger stimuli arising in the body and transmitted through hypothalamic centers regulating hunger and satiation. We would submit that the distinction between causes and motives is essential, but the view of internal drive forces acting as causes makes them instrumental in providing the source of spontaneity and the causal agency behind action, particularly consummatory action, i.e., action directed to a goal. This is the *vis a tergo* concept of drive activation. In this sense, past experiences, including the infantile and archaic, were regarded as determining and causal.

In a revised theory, however, motivation lies elsewhere. To take a crude example, if I jump out of a skyscraper window, gravity is a cause of my earthbound trajectory, not a motive. My jumping is also both caused by the sequence of motoric causes, and motivated. My motives inducing me to follow such a course of behavior can only be cast in terms of reasons for the behavior. A confusion arises between a broader and narrower connotation of the term "cause"—the broader usage refers to anything contributing to an outcome; the narrower usage is specific in referring to the action or motoric sequence or process that produces effects in the order of execution or efficiency as distinct from the order of intention. In this sense, to call such motives causal only confuses matters, since motives are "causal" only in the broader analogous or metaphoric sense that they contribute to eliciting certain behavior, not in the sense that they belong to the motoric, executive, causal sequence producing the actual behavior. Causes in the modern sense are efficient causes, i.e., causes that produce effects. In the above example, my motives for jumping are different than my act of jumping. That action sequence is not altogether physical since the entire sequence is preceded just by psychological processes involved in deciding to jump, and the action sequence must be initiated by an act of will setting the physical sequence in motion. The situation would be quite different if I were skydiving and my chute failed to open. The causes would be similar, but the motivation quite different. One might suspect hidden unconscious suicidal motives in such a case, but it might also happen that a chute that should have opened didn't. In the latter case, the initiating motive was to enjoy the thrill of the skydiving experience. But that motive is purposive, looking to the future rather than the past for its explanatory potential. Further, my behavior can be motivated by external circumstances—if I drive under the speed limit, my behavior may be motivated by civic virtues or by not wanting to get a speeding ticket. These would be motives, not causes.

Another example. The pitcher's intention (purpose) as he releases the pitch is distinct from his act of throwing, even though one leads to the other. The intention is mental, the throw physical; the intention is motive, the pitching motion causal. By the same token, the batter's intention to park the ball in the bleacher seats is distinct from his actual swing, which may or may not accomplish his intent. Causality enters the picture with his self-actualizing decision to swing, setting the physical sequence resulting in the swing and possible hit in motion. But, on these terms, the decision is not externally caused, but is motivated and thus determined. And, of course, it is not his intention that parks the ball in the eighteenth row. Thus the act of volition setting an action sequence in motion is causal, but is different from the intentions and motives that lie behind the volition, whether it involves choice or not.

This revised schema would shift the accent from causal sources and processes to stimulus qualities and contexts requiring cognitive evaluation and assessment, and on the inherent meaning of the stimulus complex—all of which are basically cognitive and informational (G. Klein, 1967)—rather than on causal factors producing the response pattern. There would be no drives acting as causal forces driving the psychic apparatus from below, but rather capacities that can be elicited and triggered into action and direction by appropriate stimulating conditions providing the necessary conditions for motivation and effective functioning. Libido and aggression would, then, take the form of specific motivational capacities or potentials capable of being activated by specific stimulus conditions. Libidinal capacities would operate only in contexts of libidinal arousal and interest; aggression would only come into play in circumstances calling for overcoming of an obstacle (see chapter 1).[8] The crucial component, then, would be the qualitative meaning of the stimulus rather than merely the quantity of energy release or tension reduction (G. Klein, 1967). These formulations are entirely consistent with Arnold's (1960) emphasis on "appraisal" or Tomkins's (1962, 1970) view of motivational feedback.

As a theory of motivation, then, ours is not a theory to explain the motoric or causal aspects of agency (which lie elsewhere), but a theory aiming at understanding the conditions prompting the agent to move from inaction to action and determining the course and direction of his activity. The mechanisms of action, in contradistinction, are causal and not motivating. The classic theory emphasized action, and appealed to drives as originating principles of both action and motivation. Our revised theory locates the principle of agency in the self-system (Meissner, 1993) as the originating source of causal activity, whereas motivation pertains to the stimulating and eliciting conditions giving rise to and directing behavior. Thus motivation provides the guidance system, not the motor power behind the action.

(5) Motives and reasons. Motives also involve and can be expressed in terms of reasons and purposes. Reasons are statements of factors motivating an action or series of actions, answering to the question "why?" Purpose, on the other hand, addresses the objective, the goal, the achievement that is intended to satisfy the desire or wish, the "what" to which the desire or wish is directed. Reasons, in this sense, would connote the action as determined; purpose carries the connotation of the action as determining and open to future

possibilities and comes close to the implications of Freud's appeal to "aim" in his discussion of instincts. My purpose may be to climb Mount Everest; this primary goal may be accompanied by secondary purposes, some conscious, some not—to gain fame and recognition, to please my mother, to fulfill ambitions related to my ego ideal, to satisfy my wish for narcissistic self-enhancement, to counteract my sense of worthlessness and unimportance, to escape the coils of my depression, and so on. These secondary purposes are also reasons for my undertaking the ascent of the mountain, but they qualify as reasons only insofar as they explain the purpose. Reasons serve to explain purpose. Stating the purpose—here, to climb Everest—does not address the why-question. Reasons offer some understanding of the "why" of the purpose. Thus, motives are purposive, reasons, as reasons, are not, although they can also serve as statements of subsidiary purpose. Thus reasons are explanatory rather than purposive. In the example, my wish-purpose of gaining fame and fortune also expresses one of the reasons for the climb.

(6) Motives and needs. Motivations are by and large linked to need states—both in regard to physical needs as well as to emotional, intellectual, or other higher order needs. Need can be regarded as any state of thwarted or frustrated satisfaction, expression, or attainment. Needs occur at many levels and in many contexts according to the aspects of the self-system called into play. Hunger is a need arising from lack of nutritional intake. Thirst is a need determined by lack of water. There are corresponding needs related to the entire hierarchy of functions and capacities inherent in the organism. There is a need for exercise lest muscles atrophy. There are needs for intellectual and emotional satisfaction. There are needs for achievement and accomplishment, for recognition, acceptance, and meaningful human relationships. These dispositions become needs when their expression or fulfillment is blocked or frustrated. We can think of the needs involved in Mr. T's sadistic and domineering behavior—needs for narcissistic compensation, frustrated needs for love and the sense of himself as lovable, and so on. This need-condition or conditions can then set in motion the internal dispositions calling motivational systems and their expression into action. But clearly, needs and wishes are not synonymous. When Schur (1966) argued that the transition from need to wish marked the emergence of psychic structure, he was likely thinking of physical needs, but we would contend that the distinction is operative with regard to nonphysical needs as well.

(7) Nondrive motivation. Freud centered the theory of motivation on the drives, which he presumed to be necessary to explain certain pathological phenomena, other irrational but not necessarily pathological behaviors, experiences and behaviors seemingly beyond conscious control, and other seemingly spontaneous behaviors not attributable to other causes (Rapaport, 1960b). But difficulties arose from using the drive theory to explain too much, as Rapaport (1960a) complained, and neglecting other determiners of behavior, as though no other form of motivation was open to psychoanalytic understanding. Thus the role of other factors, both internal (ego factors other than defenses) and external (physical or social stimuli), as codeterminers of behavior was short-changed. Understanding behavior as overdetermined would tend to open the way for nondrive determinants. Despite his insistence on the role of the drives, Freud never intended his drive theory as exclusive (Rapaport, 1960b). In fact, Freud's 1926 ego theory led to the development of a theory of ego autonomy and a corresponding hierarchy of instinctual drive derivatives of varying degrees of neutralization (Hartmann, 1939, 1964a) and to theories of psychosocial adaptation and development (Erikson, 1950, 1959).

While the classic theory left room for nondrive motivations, our theory leaves no room for drive-related motivations. Motivations are divorced from any consideration of drives; in effect there are no drives. Drive motivation is replaced by patterns of motivation setting the conditions for and eliciting responses from the self-as-agent. Stimulus conditions and contexts of meaning can elicit patterns of behavior reflecting instinctual levels of motivation that would previously have been attributed to instinctual drives. Abandoning the drive theory does not do away with instinctual motives, but rather attributes them to motivational conditions rather than drives.

In any case, one function of the drive theory was to protect the relative autonomy of the psychic apparatus from stimulus dependence and explain the origin of nonvolitional behaviors that were characteristically irrational, peremptory, primary process in organization, and beyond conscious regulation. However, the drive theory is not necessary for the first objective, as long as the agency of the self is recognized as in itself autonomous or relatively so. In this sense, the agency of the self is never either totally autonomous or stimulus dependent. Rapaport's effort to bolster the autonomy of the self from external stimuli by appealing to dependence on the drives can be seen as a matter of misplaced autonomy. A revised theory would locate the root of autonomy in the self-system; the so-called autonomy of the drives would then merely reflect the capacity of the self to act in descriptively drive-like fashion under given eliciting conditions. The patterning of self-generated action is, however, responsive to eliciting stimulus conditions and contexts within limits—not caused by such determinants, but motivated by them. Experiments on stimulus deprivation have shown the degree to which self-regulation and patterns of self-orientation and adaptation can be modified in regressive terms, but the contribution of "stimulus nutriment" is never completely determinative; the degree of structural integrity and capacity to maintain self-organization is a reflection of developmental and even constitutional differences that vary from one individual to the next.[9]

Nor is the drive hypothesis necessary to account for the second objective of explaining nonvolitional behavior. One of the profound discoveries of psychoanalysis is that the self, however conceived, is not unitary or simple, but multiple and compounded not only of different, but even contradictory, substructures and functions. This means that certain aspects of the functioning of the self-as-agent are unconscious, out of the regulatory and self-aware capacity of the conscious subjective self (Meissner, 1999d, e), but nonetheless remain functions of the same self-system operating under the direction of other variant configurations of purpose, desire, and intentionality than are immediately available to subjective awareness. These latter intentionalities can be opposed and contradictory to conscious objectives and purposes of the self. This is the essence of Freud's discovery of intrapsychic conflict and his theory of the unconscious. The theoretical question is whether appeal to a drive hypothesis is at all necessary to encompass these clinical phenomena. We would argue that it is not, that the essentials of the understanding of the unconscious and the phenomenon of intrapsychic conflict can be preserved without creating separate sources of agency within the mental apparatus. The problem of unity in diversity can be dealt with well enough by recognizing that the psychoanalytic self is heterogeneous, composed of often contradictory levels of functioning , and capable of multiple, complex, and often oppositional motivational states simultaneously.

(8) Drive-like characteristics. The primary characteristic of drive expression is the primary process manifestations, which are characteristically peremptory and beyond the capacity of will and conscious effort to control. In this regard, it seems particularly difficult for ana-

lysts to conceive of peremptory behavior without attributing it to intrinsic drive activation, even though attribution to motivational terms is perfectly logical and consistent. Peremptoriness can reflect motivational stimulus conditions that elicit a response that has the qualities of urgency, demand, imperativeness, seeking immediate satisfaction, and so on. Secondary process behaviors are, in contrast, subject to some degree of control, but this can vary across a spectrum of degrees of more or less voluntary control. Rapaport, following Freud, looked to drives as guarantors of internal spontaneity and autonomy, but in so doing left the mind open to being driven by internal forces over which it had no more than questionable control. However, there does not seem to be any a priori exigency to attribute the capacity for autonomous expression to drives rather than to the person himself. If drive activation is not seen as constant and creating an unremitting pressure on the mental apparatus for discharge, the situation changes. The self then enjoys an inherent degree of autonomy by reason of the coherence and stability of its internal structural organization. The source of the capacity for action resides in the self-as-agent (Meissner, 1993) and the nature of the action patterns is influenced by stimulus and contextual conditions including both external contextual and internal dispositional factors.[10]

The self, then, preserves its autonomy from external determinants by reason of its interactive relation to environmental determinants, which may be adaptive or maladaptive, but these outcomes are not determined solely by external factors. Autonomy from internal determinants is guaranteed by the role these factors play in the overall economy of action and adaptation—the range of behaviors available to the self are influenced by internal dispositions in conjunction with stimulus conditions and contexts operating as motives and not as causes. The causality lies in the self-system, specifically in the resources of the self-as-agent. There are, then, no drives as such, but rather capacities of the agent that may operate in drive-like fashion when such a pattern of behavior is elicited by appropriate conditions. This would apply equally to unconscious behaviors of whatever sort, since these behaviors are also proper to the self-as-agent.

(9) Motives and determinism. The principle of determinism means that all behaviors that are actions of a psychic agent are motivated and that the motives can be expressed as reasons, conscious or unconscious, for the behavior. At the same time, not all behaviors are motivated—knee-jerks and eye-blinks are caused but not motivated—

but all are caused.[11] In the freudian scheme, drives can be regarded as contributing to such reasons, functioning as motives; otherwise they serve as causes. But in a theory without drives, the causality lies elsewhere, i.e., in a source of agency not contained within motivational parameters. What psychoanalysis customarily regards as drive-dependent or drive-derivative behavior refers to the activity of the agent in question (self-as-agent) operating in a mode of peremptoriness, spontaneity, cyclicity, selectivity, and appetitiveness as described above. These are not drives as in the classic theory, but capacities for action elicited under determinative stimulating and dispositional conditions. In this schema, all actions are caused, that is, they are actions of the self acting as causal agent—some conscious, some unconscious, some deliberate, some indeliberate, some voluntary, some involuntary, but all actions of the self-as-agent (Meissner, 1993).

DESIRE

The concept of desire requires some comment, since it has acquired broader connotation as a motivational term, and has attained a more central place in analytic thinking through the contributions of Lacan, for whom it served as the primary motivational term. As such it is distinct from need and demand, and occupies a place intermediate between them. Need aims at a specific object in which it finds satisfaction, while demand addresses itself to others from whom satisfaction is sought (Laplanche and Pontalis, 1973). Like other motivational terms, such as wish or purpose, desires cannot be confined within the scope of the pleasure principle without admitting the role of the reality principle and the associated relevance of the real as the object of intentionality (McIntosh, 1993).

The operative freudian term to express the dynamics of desire is "wish" as discussed above, but is usually applied in reference to single acts or specific objectives. The French translate the German term *Wünsch* as *désir*, setting the stage for Lacan's usage, making desire a more general and largely subjective dimension of the human agent. For Lacan, desire is not restricted to the seeking of satisfaction of a wish or need. In the gap between need and demand, there is a "wanting-to-be" transcending satisfaction of particular needs and demands. Any demand is addressed to another, but, whatever the specific object of the demand, what is really sought from the other is his love, the deepest and most persistent desire of the subject. "Desire, then, is a want-to-be in the subject that is unsatisfiable either through gratification of his needs or acquiescence to his demands" (Muller and Richardson, 1982, p. 281). The transition from this approach to desire to the lapidary lacanian formula, "Desire is the desire of the Other," is ready enough, but carries with it some weighty assumptions. Between desire as insatiable and desire as desire of the Other lies the supposition that desire as well as demand are transmitted in the symbolic order and that the other in question is not only the Other whom I can address in speech but the other within the self, i.e., desire is the desire of the unconscious.

But in searching for the derivation of this fundamental desire, Lacan (1992) extends the argument to its most infantile sources. At the root of desire, then, the place of the thing which serves as the ultimate object of desire is occupied by the mother of infantile experience, embedded in the complex psychology of mother-child interaction and developmental experience expressed in less than satisfactory fashion by categories of dependence, satisfaction, and frustration. Thus, "Freud designates the prohibition of incest as the underlying principle of the primordial law, the law of which all other cultural developments are no more than the consequences and ramifications. And at the same time he identifies incest as the fundamental desire" (p. 67). In short, for analysis there is no other sovereign good, only the mother, the object of incest, a forbidden good, but there is no other.

Without venturing further into the opacities of the lacanian metaphysics of language, this view of rudimentary motivational dispositions posits desire more as a constant state of need that is inherently unfulfillable. Whatever the implication and meaningfulness of this concept of desire, it seems to depart substantially from the original freudian notion, and brings into focus more profoundly existential concerns that have greater relevance to the philosophical understanding of man's nature than a more restrictively psychoanalytic account. The extent to which identifiable psychoanalytically relevant desires remain linked to such primitive and fundamental desire remains an open question. The lacanian view of the infantile root of desire provides almost a mirror image to the kleinian view of the primal destructiveness inherent in the paranoid-schizoid position. It would seem to us just as questionable whether the root of all desire can be located in the primal desire for the unreachable incestuous object as whether the root of all aggression and sadism can be derived from the primal destructiveness of the death instinct. There can be little doubt that his desire for the mother and the frustrations it entailed played a fundamental and decisive role in Mr. T's psychic life, but would it be fair to him or theoretically accurate to derive the total complexity of his motivational life from that single root?

Turning back to clinical experience, it seems more satisfying to view the desires pertinent to analytic concerns as assuming various forms and functions within differentiating contexts. If desire is to serve as a motivating principle, it must be highly diversified and heterogeneous. We must decide whether it is a single, unitary, originating principle, or whether it consists of multiple, multifaceted, and highly diversified forms that may effectively stand on their own. In the former instance, the argument would require demonstration of the connecting links between the primal desire, however conceived, and particular specific contextual desires. Within a lacanian framework, we would have to demonstrate the connection between, for example, the desire to pass an examination or to consume a plump red apple and the primal incestuous desire to possess the mother. If the symbolic connection between apples and breasts might facilitate this task, we would still have to substantiate the claim that such a meaningful connection was in fact operative. The theoretical symbolic equation does not demonstrate the fact. The desire (wish) of the student to pass the examination may be more meaningfully related to complex ambitions and wishes to master certain material, accomplish certain goals, gain some form of recognition, achieve a level of accomplishment and earning capacity, and so on. The motivational concerns, in other words, may be more relevant to particular goals and purposes related to the exercise of cognitive capacities than to a primordial state of infantile desire. Even eating the apple may have more to do with the wish to satiate hunger pangs or even to enjoy the taste and flavor of a delicious fruit. As an explanatory account of this piece of behavior no more is required; the effort to extend the analysis to infantile derivatives may accomplish little more than strain credibility.

Our theory would argue instead that every constituent subsystem, capacity, functional process, and structural component of the psychological apparatus can be connected to goals and purposes specific to its nature and capacity. Setting goals and directing effort to the achievement of such objectives is accomplished through the organization of motivational states. The intellectual capacity of the human mind, for example, has goals and purposes that are suited to its nature, the attainment of which is sustained by the pleasure principle in conjunction with the reality principle. Learning, the development of communicative skills, mastery of complex tasks, development of linguistic competence, development of economically valuable and work-related skills, development and expression of talents, and so on, constitute goals and purposes that suit the intellectual aspect of the human mind. The list could be expanded, but the point is that these relatively specific objectives have validity and motivational impact on their own recognizance without appeal to any infantile or primal motivational state. The potential linkages to other levels and contexts of motivation remain open to exploration: it may turn out that some part of the student's motivation to study intensively in order to do well on the examination is related to wishes to please his mother and gain an added degree of recognition and acceptance from her. This additional component would point our attention to other dimensions of the complex motivational state as an aspect of the overdetermination of the behavior—readily recognizable in terms of oedipal dynamics—but the added dimension does not replace or invalidate the former intentionality. The analytic perspective thrives on the potential for the analytic process to unearth hidden, usually unconscious, components of motivation, but we should not lose sight of the fact that such unconscious motives are codeterminants of the behavior and, however useful or important they may be for clinical understanding, they are not the sole motivational components, and often are not the most important. The range of variation in such cases is wide and complex.

Desire versus drive. This perspective puts the meaning of "desire" and its congener "wish" in a somewhat different light. Instead of arising from a source that provides a push *a tergo* as in the classic drive theory, motivational states arise from setting goals, implementing purposes, translating hopes and ambitions into effective action, and so on. The motivational determinants lie in the contexts and circumstances within which the organism operates, some external, some internal. The athlete gifted with certain locomotor and coordinative talents may ambition becoming a star in the NBA and earning millions of dollars in the process. This goal and purpose motivates him to train, practice, and develop his skills to their maximum potential. Fundamental to his motivational state is his desire to achieve and accomplish not only immediate objectives (shooting a jump shot) but long-term goals. The desire for wealth and status may carry its own validity; it may also be overdetermined by other related wishes—to prove he can achieve a greater status and earning power than his father, for example. Both motivational components can be understood and explained on their own terms without appeal to infantile or instinctual motivations—even competition with the father. The circumstances and contexts for both contributing motivations may be sufficient to understand their effects on their own terms. The appeal of power and wealth in a consumer society in which affluence is highly valued, especially for a poor boy whose family could barely eke out a minimal existence, has a high valence. But competition with the father may, and probably will, involve oedipal dynamics. Just as other channels of motivation do not depend on or derive from infantile motives, they do not preclude them either.

Even the obviously oedipal competition with the father can be recast in terms of developmental needs for self-assertion, self-validation, and parental recognition and acceptance. The circumstances of parent relationship and involvement can stimulate fundamental desires for love and acceptance without appealing to a libidinal drive—libidinal needs, yes; libidinal drive, no.[12] By the same token, issues of competence, independence, and competition can be rendered intelligible without appeal to an aggressive drive. Needs for love, acceptance, and recognition are endemic to the human condition, but the eliciting of such needs and their engagement in a motivational state need not be determined by a drive pushing from the rear, but can be activated and elicited just as meaningfully by the conditions and context of relationships and mutual involvement with significant others. In other words, the same dynamic issues and concerns addressed by the classic theory in terms of drive derivatives can be addressed in motivational terms related to goals and purposes without any linkage to drive considerations. Action directed toward the achievement of such goals and purposes does not require any drive force for their accomplishment, but only activation of the capacities of the self-as-agent.

We might even conclude that the appetitive desires operative in the infantile mother-child interaction can be adequately conceived in similar terms. Given the primitive state of infantile dependence, the conjunction of survival needs of the infantile organism with the nurturant and ministering functions of the maternal object can give rise to the forms of attachment, anaclitic dependence, and mutual cuing and responsiveness that characterize the infantile mother-child symbiosis. The stimulus conditions for this complex interaction are not only hunger or elimination needs, but more fundamental needs for response, mutuality, empathic resonance, and attunement, qualities that transcend the merely physiological and have a prepotent impact on the course of psychological development. Here again, the pleasure-unpleasure principle holds sway, but not necessarily as the expression of a libidinal drive (Meissner, 1995a, b). Along the same line, Basch (1979) commented:

> Affective reaction provides inherent basic controls for adaptation by placing a qualitative value on percepts thereby providing the motivation for goal seeking behavior. The interaction and union of ever more complex sensorimotor schemata guided by the affective tone of past experience, results in a network of error correcting feedback cycles which are perfectly adequate for the infant's needs and, most important from the psychoanalytic point of view, explain how it is possible to permanently embody a record of an infant's affective/behavioral transactions before recall or reflection is a possibility. (p. 16)

MOTIVATION IN ANALYSIS

The complexity of desire, along with its multiplicity of levels both embracing and transcending levels of instinctual motivation, then, opens the door to clinical implementation by directing analytic attention to the multiplicity and complexity of motivational components that come into play in the analytic situation. In the classical framework, the explanatory potential of drive forces does not reach much beyond the dynamics of the transference. But the analytic context involves much more: transference is only one piece of the analytic interaction. A broader conceptualization of the analytic relation would have to include the real relation and the alliance as differential and contributing components of the analytic context along with transference.[13] By implication, these nontransferential components open the way for more diversified, non-drive-derivative motivations to enter the analytic process and action. If I read him correctly, Friedman (1995) seems to espouse a similar position:

> To the extent that they believe that patients can work at treatment in other than a transference enactment, analysts are assuming the presence of non-libidinal motives. Those motives are usually buried

in the definition of the ego. . . . Lichtenberg's exploratory-assertive motive is just the sort of thing that would make it reasonable for an analyst to expect a patient to undertake analytic work that is not transferentially gratifying, such as allowing himself to separate from the analyst and to undercut his transference wishes by honest reporting. It is of the greatest important to analytic theories of many different shades to have some reason to suppose that patients may be driven by other-than-attachment motives. (p. 457)

We would want to emphasize that the dynamic principle cast in terms of meanings and motives comes closer to the demands and interests of the clinical context, particularly as it comes to life in the analytic process, as is evident in the discussion of Mr. T's analysis. Analytic exploration leads in the direction of exploring the contexts and conditions, historical and present, conscious and unconscious, that serve as the motivating factors involved in the patient's behavior throughout the course of his past life, in his present life engagements, and particularly in the analytic process and in relation to the analyst. These narratives involve much more than can be adequately encompassed by an appeal to reductive drive forces. If aggressive or libidinal capacities are called into play, they are the result of motivating circumstances and conditions that elicit such patterns of response. To call into question the role of drives as motives does not mean that the patient does not act libidinally or aggressively, but that motives or reasons for such behavior lie elsewhere than in impersonal and constantly pressuring forces, and that the source of action also lies elsewhere—in the person himself operating as the relatively autonomous or relatively nonautonomous source of action in the self-system.

Chapter 6

Affects and Aggression

INTRODUCTION

The common assumption in analytic discussions of aggression is that the affective states commonly associated with aggressive action—anger, rage, hatred, irritation, etc.—are synonymous with aggression and are counted as expressions or manifestations of the aggressive drive. In this chapter we focus on these affects and draw a clear distinction between aggression as motive and these affective resonances. We recognize that analytic thinking about affects is currently in a state of considerable flux and diversity, and consequently do not intend to present a theory about the nature of affects. Affects are one of the most difficult and confusing subjects in psychoanalysis. No past or present-day psychoanalytic theory is comprehensive enough to provide full understanding of subjectively experienced affects. In fact, psychoanalysis cannot of itself produce an all-encompassing theory of affect. The neurological, chemical (neurotransmitters), and hormonal conditioners and determinants of affects lie beyond or outside of the scope of analytic theory. Much has been learned about the psychology and neurobiology of emotions (Damasio, 1994, 1999) and significant challenges lie ahead for integrating such rapidly advancing neuroscientific findings with psychoanalytic phenomenology and theoretical understanding. The unique and exclusive contribution of psychoanalysis to the understanding affect consists in its ability to trace the intrapsychic conscious and unconscious processes (perceptions, memories, memory traces, wishes, desires, and defenses) that contribute to the establishment of unconscious affects and the experience of conscious feelings. Many psychoanalytic theories about affect have emerged in recent decades, but, in the end, when it comes to the technical analysis of the emergence of affect in the clinical situation, we still find ourselves relying on Freud's understanding of the dynamic organization structuring affective experience (Green, 1999).

THE MEANING OF AFFECT

The term "affect" requires clarification. Affect is used in psychoanalysis either as a metapsychological concept or as the clinical description of a perceived emotion or feeling such as rage, sadness, or envy. As a theoretical term, it refers to Freud's and others' efforts to understand affects as psychic functions in terms of economic, structural, and dynamic organizational principles. As a clinical term, affect refers to a complex expression of subjective feelings, behaviorally observable emotional expressions, correlated physiological changes, and moods which are for the most part describable in the everyday language. The analyst's task in the clinical situation consists in helping the patient understand the dynamic motivational sources of concrete affective experiences. As a dynamic process, affect belongs exclusively to the psychology of the person. It denotes on one level an unconscious dynamic process accompanying certain unconscious motivational states, and on another level a subjective feeling experience that can be partially expressed to another while its intrapsychic and interpersonal meaning can only be determined by the detailed analysis of its component elements, i.e., personal motivations and desires, intrapsychic and interpersonal circumstances, and the facilitators or impediments for achieving intended psychic goals, much of which transpires on an unconscious level. In this respect, a subjective feeling is always narrower than the affective dynamic (conscious and unconscious) structure conditioning its emergence.

Freud established that the constant aim of the mind's dynamic processes is to avoid unpleasurable affect. This aim, however, may be pursued at a high psychic price, and yet it does not fully succeed in suppressing the experience of painful feelings. Dynamically understood, painful affect may bring about a lesser suffering than one caused by the awareness of even more intolerable internal or external situations. Freud's model of affect emergence describes the great complexity of affective processes and the continuous efforts of the psyche to seek satisfaction through dynamic reorganization of mental representations. The Freudian model has two pillars. The first is that psychic economic processes activating and stimulating the person to carry out certain actions must find proportionate fulfillment in terms of the pleasure principle (Meissner, 1995b). The second is the persistence of memory traces of past experiences that are easily and continuously linked to past moments of pleasure or unpleasure. The dynamic organization of character structure in each individual is, in psychoanalytic terms, the structural recording of psychic responses to past moments of motivational excitation and of having obtained or failed to obtain satisfaction of its goals in adequate objects. Infant research and object relations theorists have focused on the great significance of the human object for the experiential and dynamic motivational organization of affects for the child's early and later relationship with himself and others. However, this necessary focusing on early objects of satisfaction does not change the clinical requirement for tracing in the present the intrapsychic dynamic motivational components of the experience of particular affects in the adult.

INTERRELATIONS BETWEEN AFFECT AND AGGRESSION

Early in his work, in *The Interpretation of Dreams* (1900), Freud had observed the tendency of affects to persist in influencing the psyche in spite of defensive efforts to stop their emergence into conscious awareness. He said in referring to the complex formed by ideas (*Vorstellungen*, representations) and affects: "In the case of a psychical complex which has come under the influence of the censorship imposed by the resistance, the *affects* are the constituent which is least influenced (*der resistente Anteil*, the resistant part) and which alone can give us a pointer as to how we should fill in the missing thoughts" (p. 461).[1] Freud also observed the persistence of the same affect regardless of how long ago it had been experienced for the first time: "A humiliation that was experienced thirty years ago acts exactly like a fresh one throughout the thirty years, as soon as it has obtained access to the unconscious sources of emotion. As soon as the memory of it is touched, it springs into life again" (1900, p. 578).

This observation about the great perdurance of affect does not seem to apply equally to all affects. Some are transient affects that cannot be retrieved unchanged, in contrast to others such as humiliation with the rage and indignation it evokes, for which ready retrieval is not only possible but a familiar experience in analysis. In fact, it seems possible to assert that the most perduring affects, those that can be made "to spring to life" by conscious recollection of a related event, are, more frequently than not, negative affects such as anger, rage, envy, humiliation, fear, and others. Positive affects are frequently more subdued in their experience, expression, and retrieval, even when they may arise as sudden experiences such as falling in love instantly or becoming very fond of a newly met person. The perdurance and easy reawakening of negative emotions under particular circumstances may account for the persistent tendency in psychoanalytic theorizing to equate negative affects such as anger, rage, and envy with aggression conceived as a drive.

Our understanding of aggression, as a biologically rooted capacity activated by appropriate stimulus conditions involving the presence of an obstacle interfering with achievement or complete of an intended aim, requires a clear distinction between affect and aggression. We insist on a clear distinction between motives and affects: they are not the same although they may be and often are associated. The motivation for the aggressive activity to overcome the obstacle can and must be distinguished from the intrapsychic sources that under particular internal or external circumstances result in the emergence of a particular affect. The motivation for aggression is always the overcoming of an obstacle, be it internal to the psyche or present in external reality. The affect experienced just before or at the time of the carrying out of an aggressive activity may find its sources in a multitude of past or present experiences always linked to the emotional history of the individual and the concrete stimulus conditions that appear as an obstacle to the intended action.

A brief example from everyday life may illustrate the point. Two persons on a sidewalk are suddenly confronted by a car out of control and threatening to kill them. The car is obviously an obstacle or threat to their self-preservative wish to continue living. Both react in the same way by jumping aside to avoid the car. When the car stops, one person collapses and trembles with fear. The other, however, becomes enraged, grabs the driver, and beats him, shouting, "You murderer, you want to kill me!" The first impulsive aggressive action, avoiding the car as a destructive obstacle, is the same for both. The reaction is prompted by fear and results in avoidance, mediated by the nearly instantaneous transmission of neural impulses through direct thalamo-amygdalar connections and resulting in a reflex fear-flight response (LeDoux, 1987, 1989, 1996, 2002). Such a response is not subject to any reflection or extensive processing but takes place rapidly and, as we would say, "instinctively."

In contrast, the affect in each of the two persons is drastically different: one individual is overcome by fear of death and injury, while the other is enraged. This second level response follows a separate but parallel neural path involving complex interconnections of cortical associative and decisional processes, thus calling into play memory and associative connections reflecting patterns of reaction to life-threatening stimuli based on the individual's life history and previous experience. In both cases, the affects of fear in one and rage in the other are not in themselves connected with the aggressive activities, but find their sources in the two individuals' respective personal histories and dynamic experience of the moment. The fearful person may be reexperiencing occasions in which his life was threatened or he feared or imagined it was. The second person may have linked the threatening car and driver to childhood and adolescent experiences of narcissistic humiliation and danger, when he was physically overpowered by peers, the deeper injury being not physical but the impotent humiliation. Now, the reawakened feeling of impotence itself that sustains the rage has also become, in turn, an internal obstacle to his narcissistic equilibrium. The secondary aggressive action on the part of the second person, to start beating the driver, may not motivationally be directed against the driver as much as to overcoming the obstacle posed by the internal feeling of impotent humiliation reawakened by the situation, by transforming himself into the powerful person who seizes and can retaliate against the driver. The fearful person responds by traumatized collapse and retreat; the aggressive person mobilizes his capacities to overcome the obstacle posed by the threat and acts aggressively to overcome it. The motivation of the first is driven by fear, that of the second by aggression.

Human life is continuously colored by affect. In ordinary circumstances the affect may be quietly present as a background, not-well-defined feeling that we do not need to explain. We take it for granted as our mode of being at the moment. Nonetheless, discrete affects such as sadness, anger, rage, or affection imposing themselves on our conscious attention require motivational understanding. If the sources of the feeling are not self-evident, such as sadness because we have lost someone we love, we search for the motivation of our feelings.

We ask, "Why am I sad, angry, furious?", "What makes me so jealous, envious?" We know that our feelings have a motivational explanation that can be answered by searching within ourselves until we find the type of internal or external event or events that we can recognize as having prompted us to feel a particular feeling.

Psychic life consists of an endless sequence of internally initiated motivations and of motivated responses to external and internal events requiring our reaction, a reaction which in turn, is motivated by our manner of perceiving and interpreting the events confronting us. In each instance, be it an internally initiated motivation or an external circumstance that invites a response, the motivation is inevitably linked with affects. In either case, be it an internal motivation or a motivated response to events, the course of the intended action or actions, intended to achieve specific motivational aims, may encounter an obstacle that interferes with its completion. At this point, aggression, as we understand it, enters the picture, enhancing the motivation to complete the action, particularly in relation to overcoming the obstacle. Whether aggression facilitates overcoming the obstacle or fails to do so, the individual responds with affects of different types according to the outcome. This description permits us to present a sequence of psychic and actual events taking place in any aggressive activity:

(a) Motivation to carry out a psychic activity colored by a particular affect(s).

(b) Initiation of the psychic action and/or external activity aimed at completing the intention of the motivation. The activity itself has its own emotional tone.

(c) An intrapsychic or external obstacle is encountered that directly interferes with completion of the motivational aim. Awareness of the obstacle and of its interruption of the action evokes different affects according to the emotional dynamic taking place within the subject and the manner in which he interprets the meaning and significance of the obstacle.

(d) The individual may give up the effort to achieve the intended aim, in which case the affect he would experience depends on his interpretation of the meaning of being left with an incomplete or frustrated activity. The person may also continue to feel the need to complete the action. This need is related to its own affect, conditioned by the dynamic motivation of the need to complete the action and the self-valuation involved in being one who will do what is needed to complete the action.

(e) To complete the action, the person calls upon aggression as a biologically rooted capacity activated by the stimulus conditions presented by this particular obstacle to completion of the intended aim of the motivation. The aggressive actions available to the individual for overcoming the obstacle are as varied as the obstacles encountered. If the obstacle is physical, physical force may be required. If the obstacle is psychical, such as an interfering thought, or a superego demand, the action may take the form of a psychic defense, such as suppression or repression.

(f) Once the aggressive action has been carried out effectively, the obstacle has been removed, and the activity completed, the subject may experience various other affects. They can be as varied as the meaning this particular success may have for the individual at that specific moment of his life. In turn, the psychic or external effects of the aggressive action, once perceived, may evoke other types of affect such as regret or satisfied revenge, if the aggressive action has been harmful or destructive. It may also prompt joyful feelings of satisfaction, triumph, self-assurance, etc. regardless of whether or not some destruction has occurred. If the aggressive action has failed to remove the obstacle, the cycle may be repeated. Either the person gives up or further aggressive actions are summoned up to try again to overcome the obstacle. This new action in turn comes with its own affects. A negative feeling may be the fear of being too "aggressive," while a positive feeling maybe a self-valuation as "persistent" or "determined."

The preceding sequential description makes it clear that a complex array of affects are present in any aggressive act aimed at removing an obstacle in order to complete an intended action. The affects experienced by the individual depend on the emotional dynamic context of the person at the moment and on the meaning he attributes to his internal and external circumstances. The motivation for aggression depends exclusively on the need to overcome the obstacle. In other words, the motivation for the affects comes from the most diverse psychic sources, while, in contrast, the aggressive activity itself is motivated solely by the need to overcome the obstacle.

This schematic description of the psychic sequence encountered in the carrying out of an aggressive action raises many questions about the relation between affects and aggressive action. Can an experienced affect contribute to activation of aggression? What is the role played by the awareness of the obstacle? Or can the obstacle be perceived preconsciously, without conscious awareness? Can affect itself become an obstacle? Could the expression of affect itself be equivalently an aggressive action, a manner of overcoming an obstacle? What role do anger and rage, the affects customarily linked to aggressive actions, play in summoning aggression to overcome an obstacle? Is there a *causal* connection between the experienced affect of anger and the aggressive activity? How does narcissistic injury relate to so-called narcissistic rage? These are complex and difficult questions that cannot be answered immediately until the detailed examination of clinical events allows us to analyze the psychic components of affective experiences related to the expression of aggression. In any event, such questions underline the differentiation of affects and aggression and offer the prospect of bringing us another step closer to understanding their relationship.

ANALYTIC VIEWS

But before we examine clinical examples it would help to locate this discussion about the relation between aggression and affects in the context of prevalent psychoanalytic thinking. Moore and Fine (1990) define the aggressive drive as "[t]he manifest strivings, either physical or verbal, to subjugate or to prevail over others. . . . Manifestations of the aggressive drive range in intensity from non-hostile, self-assertive, and self-preservative mastery, through irritation, anger, and resentment, to the extremes of fury and murderous violent rage" (pp. 10–11). This definition explicitly asserts that the negative affects of anger, resentment, fury, and murderous rage are "caused" by the aggressive drive. This is a position held most emphatically by Melanie Klein and her followers. Heimann and Isaacs (1970) assert: "Anxiety itself, however, arises from *aggression*. It is evoked by the aggressive components in the pre-genital stages of development. It is the destructive impulses of the child in the oral and anal phases . . . which are, through the anxiety they stir up, the prime causes of the fixation of the libido" (p. 175, emphasis in original). Klein herself (1970) insists on the connection between aggression and anxiety:

> I still believe that aggressive impulses are at their height during the stage in which persecutory anxiety predominates; or, in other words, that persecutory anxiety is stirred up by the destructive instinct and is constantly fed by the projection of destructive impulses onto objects. For it is inherent in the nature of persecutory anxiety that it increases hatred and attacks against the object who is felt to be persecutory, and this in turn reinforces the feeling of persecution. (p. 235)

The kleinian view, therefore, seeks to establish a *causal* relation between the aggressive drive and the affects experienced by the subject.

Affects such as rage, fury, resentment, or anxiety either "manifest" the aggressive drive or are "stirred" by it. Such a conception narrows the dynamic understanding of complex motivations of affects to the effects of the activation of the aggressive drive. A similar line of thinking pervades Green's (1999) efforts to probe and struggle with the complexities of the original freudian drive-representational model of affects. In his view, aggression and the destructive instincts give rise to and find expression in anxiety and related hostile affects. The theme is echoed in Kernberg's (1982) modification of the dual instinct theory:

> The term "instinctive components" for inborn perceptive, behavioral, communicative, psychophysiological, and subjective experiential patterns, that is affects, seems appropriate, in contrast to the use of the term "drives" for the motivational systems, libido and aggression. . . . Having explained how I see the relation between drives and affects, I hasten to add that drives are manifest not simply by affects, but by the activation of a specific object relation, which includes an affect and wherein the drive is represented by a specific desire or wish. (p. 909)

Even with his more encompassing manner of defining the "instinctive components," Kernberg maintains the idea that affects are "manifestations" of a drive that also has the capacity to establish wishes and object relations. This conceptualization still sees the "instinctive components" as causative of and manifested in affects, and consequently narrows the source of affective experience to instinctual sources, thus neglecting the complexity of simultaneous intrasystemic psychodynamic motivational processes present in all psychic processes.

In our view, the dynamic sources for concrete affective experience stem from a variety of compatible and incompatible motivations that converge on the point at which the individual intends (preconsciously or consciously) to achieve a particular aim. At the point of the formation of the intention, there is no aggression. Instead, aggression is summoned up as a resource available to the individual when external or internal obstacles begin to interfere with the achievement of this aim.

CLINICAL RELEVANCE

A clinical example may illustrate this point. Ms. H, a young woman, in the middle phase of her analysis, developed a wish that her analyst call her by her first name. The analyst invited her to explore her wish. The patient insisted that it was only a wish and that there was no reason for the analyst not to call her "Sally," instead of just saying "you" or "Ms. H." She felt neglected, standardized by the analyst's formal address. Besides, she had noticed that the analyst had a pleasant and affectionate tone of voice in talking to her. She liked that voice. She wanted to hear her name in that voice. She became insistent. Why didn't the analyst "break the rules" with her? She needed the analyst to say her name. She threatened, mildly, to leave the analysis if the analyst did not respond to her need. The analyst must have known that she "needed" it. This last point provided the analytic opportunity to explore the "need." After much careful analysis during several hours, a conviction, which was also a wish, came to light. Ms. H described with deep sadness how her father had no affection in his voice when he addressed her. His voice was harsh, cutting, and he conveyed with it that he had neither affection nor appreciation of her. In hearing her analyst's voice, especially when addressing her as "you," she began to feel the indignation of having been mistreated by her father. Such indignation was very frightening to her because she was terrified that it could easily be transformed into dangerous murderous rage, an omnipotent rage capable of killing its target.

In the analysis she had hoped for a double result: that by "forcing" the analyst to say her name with a nice and affectionate voice, she would be able to overcome on the one hand her rage at her father, which was threatening to erupt in the analysis, and on the other hand, to undo the deep narcissistic injury of his manner of addressing her by demonstrating (to him and herself) that she could be addressed in a different manner. The motivating affects from the past were humiliation, indignation, and fear of impending dangerous rage, all reactions to her frustrated desire for love. She had felt these painful feelings as a child and in the analysis, and they had to be contained at all costs. The affects in the present were about transferential wishes for the analyst-father's love to undo the injury and repair the past hurt, together with feelings of entitlement stemming from her success in seducing men in her adult life to make them do what she wanted. She encountered two obstacles, one intrapsychic, namely fear of her own rage at the deep narcissistic injury inflicted on her by her father, the other external, the unwillingness of the analyst to submit to her wish. The obstacles converged into one in the analysis, because she was afraid of becoming ragefully murderous, with an analyst she very much needed, and whose voice she cherished. Her conviction was that, if she could get the analyst to say her first name the way she wanted, she could overcome the obstacle of her emerging rage at recalling the humiliation her father had imposed on her. After the analysis of her experience, the patient no longer felt the need to have the analyst address her by her first name. She "confessed" that she knew the analyst cared about her.

The episode has a succession of moments: (1) At the beginning of this analytic moment, Ms. H experiences the wish to have the analyst call her by her first name, and feels strongly about having her wish fulfilled. She carries out verbal actions to induce the analyst to do want she wants. When the analyst opposes completion of her wish, becoming an obstacle, aggression to overcome this obstacle is expressed in the form of threats to leave the treatment, reinforced by her further effort to overcome the analyst's resistance by insisting that he break the rules.

(2) When the analyst invites her to explore the nature of her wish, Ms. H returns to the exploration of her prior experience. A preconscious memory of the way her father addressed her becomes a consciously retrieved memory. The memory elicits intense conscious sadness, while she realizes that preconsciously she was aware all along that letting herself fully feel the frustration experienced with her father would bring about intense and, in her opinion, dangerous, if not murderous, rage. This rage had been all along and, particularly at this point, was still a most frightening obstacle for her, because she feared its intensity and the analyst's rejection of her if she expressed it. Therefore, the rage as an affect had become an internal obstacle she had to avoid at any price. At the time of this reconstruction, it became clear that her wish to have the analyst address her with a soft and affectionate voice was her fantasized manner of overcoming not

only the narcissistic rage of her humiliation but also of undoing her past impotence with her father. Making the analyst "break the rules" was not only a present aggressive action to overcome the analyst's refusal to do so, but also a retroactive and displaced manner of undoing the humiliating impotence of her father's rules.

(3) The analysis of Ms. H's motivation to "force" the analyst to say her name, her reexperiencing in the analysis of deep and very old affects of love and hatred present in her wish, together with the actual experience of the joint exploration with the analyst of her wishes, feelings, and fears, constitutes an extended form of analytic aggressive action, helping the patient overcome her obstacles in the analytic situation as well as the intrapsychic obstacle posed by the reawakening of her intense rage.

We hope this example answers some of the questions posed earlier. The first question, whether experienced affect contributes to the activation of the aggression, can be answered positively. But it is not the affect alone that leads to aggression, but the affect in conjunction with a motive, namely the wish for a loving response from the analyst which then encounters an obstacle. The loving feelings Ms. H experiences in relation to the analyst's voice reawaken past and present wishes for love, but also threaten to bring forth the always ready feeling of intense rage. Both feelings and the motivational processes they reflect converge to prompt her to act aggressively, to force the analyst to express love for her by saying her name and, in so doing, to become able to contain internally the emergence of conscious rage. But the affect does not *cause* the aggressive action. The consciously or preconsciously perceived affect, reflecting what at that moment was still an unconscious motive, prompted Ms. H as a total person, a self-as-agent, to attempt to overcome both obstacles by carrying out the aggressive action of trying to force the analyst to call her by her first name. In short, the motivationally derived and subjectively experienced affects facilitate the person's recognition of intrapsychic and external obstacles to intended psychic actions. The example also indicates that very frequently in psychic life affect becomes a significant internal obstacle that must be overcome by a variety of internal and external actions, as is evident in different ways in each of the cases we will present further on.[2] In this respect, Anna Freud (1936) observed:

> The ego is in conflict not only with those id-derivatives which try to make their way into its territory in order to gain access to

consciousness and to obtain gratification. It defends itself no less energetically and actively against the affects associated with these instinctual impulses. . . . Love, longing, jealousy, mortification, pain and mourning accompany sexual wishes, hatred, anger and rage the impulses of aggression; if the instinctual demands with which they are associated are to be warded off, these affects must submit to all the various measures to which the ego resorts in its effort to master them, i.e. they must undergo metamorphosis. . . . Obviously, however, one and the same ego can have at its disposal only a limited number of possible means of defense. (pp. 33–34)

Even though Anna Freud understands aggression as a drive linked to the affects of hatred, anger, and rage, she does see in those affects one form of obstacle the ego must overcome with active defensive measures. We agree with that aspect of her understanding, i.e., an affect can be an internal obstacle. This being the case, we can then assert that the activation of an ego defense in order to suppress an affect permits us to conceive of such an ego's defensive activity as an intrapsychic aggressive action motivated by the desire or need to overcome an internal obstacle.

Another clinical example may help understand the connection between hostility as an affect expressed in action and the aggression necessary to overcome the impeding emergence of an affect experienced as an inner threat, i.e., an obstacle. Mrs. Y, a woman in her late forties, had come to analysis because she felt compelled to be involved in extramarital affairs. She did not want to leave her husband, but could not get herself to fully appreciate him. The affairs she had followed a similar destiny. At first, the men seemed ideal, intelligent, affectionate, and admiring of her. After a time, she experienced them as inferior to her and boring. The fate of her woman analyst was different. From the beginning the patient found many faults with her. She frequently called the analyst stupid and incompetent, and criticized her looks, her clothes, and the decoration of her office. As the analysis proceeded, her childhood history began to emerge. She was the child of a depressed, incompetent, and possibly psychotic mother. Her sister was much like her mother, with whom the mother had established a symbiotic bond. The father, a very prominent man, lorded over the house from his distant study. Mrs. Y was a gifted and enthusiastic child, but continuously curbed by her timorous mother. The young girl felt very much alone and tried to side with her father.

Recalling her childhood suffering brought many tears to Mrs. Y's eyes. The analyst believed that now they could attend more carefully to Mrs. Y's difficulties, in particular her need to devalue the people she needed most.

At one point, while working in this manner, the patient developed a pattern of response deeply disturbing to the analyst. When the analyst believed that she and the patient had reached an emotional moment of closeness, she tried to offer her some carefully formulated interpretations of what Mrs. Y was talking about. The patient listened attentively, and then, when the analyst was emotionally fully involved in what she was saying, Mrs. Y would shout with a shrill and sarcastic voice: "You mispronounced that word. You're stupid. Your English is horrible. Couldn't you improve it?" The analyst was so startled that for a few seconds she could not remember what the words were. After some time, patient and analyst traced her behavior to very painful interactions with her father during latency and early adolescence. She desperately wanted to get his attention and be appreciated by him. To achieve this, she would study advanced subjects he proposed to her to further her education. Then he would test her. She prepared herself to an excessive degree for these examinations. Her knowledge was impeccable, and yet inevitably, her father would interrupt her to say contemptuously, "You missed . . ." He would be referring to something completely irrelevant. What he could not do was to recognize her effort and be appreciative of her abilities. Mrs. Y was devastated each time the situation repeated itself. She could not satisfy her father.

The vignette illustrates her identification with the aggressor-father and her reversal of passive into active. That understanding is in fact correct, but does not explain why at that particular moment of her analysis Mrs. Y had to repeat with the analyst her father's behavior with her. The analysis revealed that the greatest danger for her was the reawakening of frustrated childhood longings for closeness, affection, and recognition. When the analyst was interpreting so attentively to her, she reexperienced the preconscious longing for closeness and the danger of being devastated by its frustration. The affect that had become intolerable, in life and in analysis, was her hunger for closeness. She had to stop its development at any price. That was the obstacle she tried to overcome by berating the analyst in midsentence. Although to all appearances, her behavior was truly hostile to the analyst, the motivation for her action was not to hurt the analyst, but to overcome the internal obstacle posed by her increasing desire for closeness with her. She had to overcome the temptation to let herself wish for that closeness. Thus, even when her action was visibly hostile and destructive to the analyst, it was so only accidentally. Her intention of the aggressive action was not directed at hurting the analyst, but at suppressing the emergence of a severely dysphoric affect in consciousness.

AFFECT AND AGGRESSIVE ACTION

The question of whether the expression of affect could be an aggressive action, a manner of overcoming an obstacle, needs some further consideration. Valenstein (1962) coined the term "affectualization" to refer to a particular type of defense in the analytic situation:

> A superfluity of affects is unconsciously utilized for defensive purposes, often in association with instinctual derivatives and their discharge; and this overdoing of affects is habitual enough in certain patients, and possibly specific enough to justify its designation as a mechanism of defense. This would be consistent theoretically with an approach to tension management and modes of drive discharge, with defenses which evolve from them, as follows: thinking, and its unconsciously determined excessive use for defensive purposes, i.e., intellectualization; action, and its unconscious use in fantasy-organized "doing" for defensive purposes, i.e., acting out; affect, and its intensification and excessiveness, with unconscious use or exploitation for defensive purposes to avoid the cognitive appreciation of emotionally charged issues and the rational recognition of explanatory connections, i.e., affectualization. (p. 318)

He went on to illustrate his concept with the following case:

> A young woman with a hysterical character neurosis undertook psycho-analysis because of depressive periods, and difficulties in her ties to people due to injudicious acting out of Oedipal and pre-oedipal conflicts. From early childhood she had been an emotionally volatile and stormy person. She would over-optimistically develop intense attachments and interests in which euphorically she would enthusiastically invest all her energies. Then when disillusioned or disappointed, she would respond with despondency alternating with outbursts of angry recrimination.
> For some time she predominantly reacted to the frustration

of the psycho-analytic situation and to interpretive interventions with argumentation and negativeness which often regressed quickly into crying, shouting, scolding temper tantrum storms. Towards the end of such emotional episodes she would become more accessible. She had always been taxed by intense feelings of inadequacy and incapacity, and she was very much afraid that psycho-analysis would bring out not only very undesirable traits and depraved interests, but also an essential worthlessness. Furthermore she was afraid that psycho-analysis would limit her freedom of action and reduce her to a state of well-adjusted mediocrity.

It appeared that her emotionalism, and in particular her tantrums, was not only an infantile reaction to frustration and a consequence of her narcissistic vulnerability, but also served, like a smoke screen, to obscure the psycho-analytic field; to interfere with the spreading out of her associations, and the availability of that degree of introspection and intellectual self-awareness which could have made both her behaviour and associations meaningful and subject to appropriate interpretations and the development of a deepening insight. And gradually she became aware that she often fostered excesses of emotion to avoid or blur knowledge of which she was afraid.

Towards the end of this phase, as she became less threatened by the analysis and the insights gained through it, she settled down a great deal. . . . At this point she reported the following: "Often during the analytic hour I wonder what I am doing in analysis; why have I put myself to such a task. There is a strong pull in opposite directions—desire to know the mysteries within me and being frightened to discover the unknown about myself. One of the greatest threats of discovery is what to do with the new knowledge." (pp. 318–19)

In terms of our understanding, "affectualization" was used aggressively as an external but also more specifically as an intrapsychic defense to overcome the obstacle posed by dangerous associations threatening to bring out frightening aspects of herself or forcing her to become mediocre. Obviously, she must have had many frightening fantasies about who she was deep down. Her fantasies and convictions—as Valenstein understood it—blur such awareness, the obstacle for her wish not to become mediocre and discover forbidden aspects of herself.

Another patient, Mr. R, illustrates the motivation for using affect—in the form of "affectualization"—as a defense to overcome dangerous awareness of his libidinal clinging to his erotized mother. Each time his associations would bring him dangerously close to recognizing his sexual desires for his mother, he would enter an agitated state of religious despair. He cried and bitterly lamented that he had been cursed by God from the beginning of his life. He was the cursed scapegoat, there was no hope for him, he had been sent forever to be alone in the desert (Girard, 1986). The emotional storm subsided as soon as he managed to change the direction of his associations. As Valenstein's (1962) view suggested, his loud tears were a defense to overcome the obstacle posed by preconscious awareness of his sexual attachment to his mother. God's purported aggressive action against him conveniently transformed his own desire to get rid of his father, who was the main obstacle to his desired access to his mother. His hostile wishes against his father were manifested in his constant pre-occupation with his father's health and the fear that he would die. Mr. R could only accept that he was the victim of unjust rejection in order to maintain his ego-syntonic self-image of a good nonsexual boy who loves his parents. As it happens with many obsessive neurotics, Mr. R continuously tried to suppress the preconscious awareness of his sexual and hostile wishes toward his parents. The need to maintain a good-boy self-image was the continuous obstacle requiring aggressive sup-pression and affectualization to ward off unacceptable desires.

Mr. R documents the intrapsychic use of aggression in the form of psychic defenses (affectualization, displacement onto God) to over-come the internal obstacle posed by incestuous and murderous pre-conscious desires to realizing a favored self-perception as an innocent victim. In our view, anger and rage are not in themselves expressions of aggression. As shown in the preceding examples, motivations for angry and rageful feelings have their own dynamic sources that may be independent of the aggressive intrapsychic or external activity. That was the case with Mr. T,[3] whose physically hurtful behavior with women was not motivated by his anger with them but by the convic-tion that they could not acknowledge him unless he forced them to do so. That belief motivated his aggressively forcing them to recog-nize him. His anger and rage were motivated by the impotence and despair he felt when he became aware that no amount of forcing could give him what he wanted.

Similar considerations apply for narcissistic injury and the evoked narcissistic rage. The affect of narcissistic rage is elicited by a pro-found threat to the integrity of the self (Kohut, 1972; Rochlin, 1973). The aggressive action to overcome the obstacle posed by the threat may take many different intrapsychic and extrapsychic pathways. Among several intrapsychic options, the person may simply block out the injury from conscious awareness, may undergo an hysterical conversion, or may somatize its effects. Similarly, external behavior also has many pathways to overcome the obstacle, ranging from making the other person eat his words to actual murder.

SUMMARY AND CONCLUSIONS

Affects as experienced in the clinical situation and in ordinary life have complex motivational sources stemming from the dynamic context of the moment when they are felt and are qualitatively conditioned by the personal dynamic history of the person who experiences them. Affects in themselves have no causative power to produce aggressive intrapsychic activities or external behaviors. Aggressive responses, if elicited at all, are prompted by a motive that draws the agent into action but does not itself cause the action. The aggressive activities, be they intrapsychic defenses or external actions, find their sole motivation in the psyche's disposition to overcome or remove an obstacle that interferes with intended actions, and these actions are effected, i.e., caused, by the agency inherent in the self-as-agent.

Our manner of conceptualizing aggression and affect has definite consequences for clinical work. Anger, rage, and a variety of negative affects directed against the self, or against the analyst, or against others, need to be analyzed in order to understand their dynamic motivational sources in the present and the dynamic past of the patient. They cannot and must not be explained away as expressions of an "aggressive drive" that causes the patient to feel or to act in a particular manner—as if the person were not the responsible agent for both affects and actions.

Similar considerations apply to wished for or performed activities that bring about the forceful completion of an intended psychic or physical action. The forcefulness of the action is not an indicator of the existence of an aggressive drive compelling the person to act. Instead, each individual forceful activity must be analyzed separately in order to ascertain the nature of the obstacle the patient is confronting, the dynamic meaning of such an obstacle in the patient's personal history and present moment, as well as the psychic motivations in selecting a type of action and degree of intensity of activity to overcome that particular obstacle. All these aspects of the patient's emotional experience and personal actions are, as is all psychic life, deeply rooted in the dynamic organization of his past experiences with significant objects. In conclusion, our approach suggests a careful *independent* examination of the motives for affects and actions and the obstacles they encounter, which, in contrast to the formulations of some other theories, are postulated as causally linked to each other as components of a postulated aggressive drive.

Chapter 7

Developmental Perspectives on Aggression

The aggressive capacity we have been describing is an inborn resource of the organism, present from birth if not before. From the very beginning of life, that capacity enters into and plays its role in the complex interaction and integration of action and reaction that serve as the basis for development. As that process unfolds, the defensive and adaptive aspects of the aggressive capacity are called into play in negotiating the challenges and achievements of the growing organism and the developing psyche. The various theories of the nature of aggression we have discussed[1] envision that process in quite different terms, and it is incumbent on us to set forth our view of the developmental process as it impinges on and involves aggression. We will argue in this chapter that our view of aggression as motivational capacity directed to the overcoming of obstacles has valid application throughout the developmental sequence and that the various categories and description of aggressive behavior from infancy, through childhood, and on into adolescence and adulthood have the same motivational direction and involve the same dynamic processes. Obviously child developmental theorists argue their case on the basis of their own theories of aggression, not on ours. They may and often do take anger as an expression of aggression, whereas we would not unless it were associated with overcoming an obstacle in some form. In most cases of behavioral observation, such is in fact the case. The infant expresses hostile affect in a context of confronting an obstacle or striving to overcome it. For the most part, the following material, based as it is primarily on infant observation, involves such externally expressed aggressive actions.

For the sake of exposition and clarity, we will take advantage of the detailed work of Henry Parens (1979) on the development of aggression. Parens's categories of aggressive behavior provide a useful starting point for a discussion of the developmental aspects of aggression and allow us to focus our thinking and our view of aggression in relation to the psychic development of the child. In the course of that discussion, we will make clear the aspects and extent to which we find our view congruent with his as well as the points at which we differ. The issues are complex and controversial; other theorists have developed independent appraisals of the development of aggression, some in reaction to Parens's work, some quite separately. We will pay particular attention to the positions of Winnicott and Kohut, whose contributions to the understanding of the development of aggression have been especially controversial and noteworthy. Throughout, our objective is to extend and clarify our thinking about aggression and to specify how our understanding of aggression is exemplified in the developmental process.

PARENS ON AGGRESSION

The views of aggression in developmental theories hinge on the distinction between aggression simply as destructiveness as opposed to a more general view of aggression, including nondestructive and assertive modalities. The most substantial and elaborate consideration of the nature of aggression is in the study of the early development of aggression by Parens (1979), based on systematic and analytically informed observation of children during the first three years of life. The children were observed along with their mothers, but not with their fathers. Parens primarily holds to a drive theory of aggression, regarding various types of aggression as forms of drive discharge, concluding that "aggression is an instinctual drive and not an ego function" (p. 124), coexisting with the libidinal drive.

In contrast to the view we are developing, he regards documented manifestations of aggression as "discharge" phenomena. But then he adds that functionally, "aggression inherently serves and *motivates* the ego's task to master and to adapt" (p. 124, emphasis added). He regards destructive behaviors and intentions, however, not as drive-related but as reactive responses: "Hostile destructiveness, rather than being a constitutionally determined drive which obligatorily presses for discharge, is activated by specific experiences which have a common denominator, excessively-felt unpleasure" (p. 122). Parens concludes: "The reformulation of aggression advanced in this work proposes that experiences of excessive unpleasure, when too numerous, too frequent and too harsh, lead to *increases* in the mobilization of destructive impulses in the human child" (p. 122, emphasis in original). This manner of conceiving the aggressive drive brings Parens close to Freud's early conceptualization of aggression as a self-preservative drive, and away from the later concept of the death instinct.

Parens also develops a typology of variant forms of aggressive behavior which extend along a continuum reaching from the destructive to the nondestructive poles, including both destructive and nondestructive aims and both affective and nonaffective forms of expression. He describes four types: unpleasure-related discharge of destructiveness, nonaffective discharge of destructiveness, pleasure-related discharge of destructiveness, and finally nondestructive aggression.

Unpleasure-related discharge of destructiveness. This form of aggression reflects an innate primary destructive drive, present in the infant at birth in the form of rage and elicited by antecedent conditions of cumulative and sufficient unpleasure; it does not result from a "biologic vegetative cyclical activity" (p. 5). When the threshold of unpleasure or frustration is reached, it leads to a reaction of rage or hostile destructiveness. This reaction does not occur spontaneously, but only in reaction to frustration or provocation, and it aims to inflict pain or harm on the offending object or to destroy that object. It has two significant features. Excessive unpleasure is the condition for its emergence. It can be prevented by "the mother's arresting the unpleasure which caused the infant's rage" (p. 5). Parens concludes: "From the *dynamics* of this discharge of destructiveness, we inferred that the *affective* state created by excessively felt unpleasure *causes* an all-important modification in the aggressive impulse, the aim of which becomes to inflict pain, to harm and destroy the object in order to rid oneself of the psychic pain incurred" (p. 5, emphasis added).

Parens illustrates how this category is present from birth by presenting the moment when twelve-week-old Rosa, gripped with mounting exploratory motor excitation, cannot reach the block that attracts her. At that point, "unpleasurable affect appears on her face, and she begins to cry. She is, in our judgment, frustrated and angry. After two or three minutes, the intensity of her valiant effort to reach the block peaks and is followed by evidence of frustration. Unpleasure and destructiveness are manifested" (p. 19). Parens relates this observation to Freud's (1915) conclusion about unpleasure: "The ego hates, abhors and pursues with intent to destroy all objects which are the source of unpleasurable feeling for it" (p. 138). Parens concludes that the capacity for this type of destructiveness is a potential of the aggressive drive. He does not believe, however, that such a potential emerges spontaneously or "accumulates" (as energy might in the model of spontaneous discharge). It emerges only as a response to unpleasure.

This form of aggression would be somewhat at variance with traditional psychoanalytic drive theory, which tends to see the aggressive drive as constantly seeking discharge, rather than as elicited in reaction to frustration (Shane and Shane, 1982). Parens (1982) himself is not slow to endorse this conclusion when he writes: "What I do *not* believe to be primary is the large negatively-valenced trend *hostile destructiveness*; that is, I do not believe that anger, hostility, and rage are inborn; they are reactive, experientially produced phenomena, and therefore to a degree can be prevented and mitigated" (p. 315, emphasis in original). Thus far we would agree, but our emphasis would fall rather on the motivational conditions that elicited the destructive wish or intention. Again the action in our view is aggressive not because it is destructive, but because its function is the overcoming of obstacles.

If Parens is exercised to dissociate himself from the traditional drive-based view of aggression, he has also been criticized for maintaining a drive theory of aggression at all. Lichtenberg (1982), for example, would prefer to speak of "perceptual-affective-action patterns" in preference to drives. He would then translate Parens's "unpleasure-related discharges of destructiveness" into "the rage reactions of infants in distress." Parens (1982) is of course unhappy with this translation. He regards the rage reaction of infants as paradigmatic for the entire class or range of destructive behaviors. He regards it as a more convenient paradigm than anger, hate, or revenge, which would also be included in this behavioral-dynamic category, precisely because it is found in earliest infancy, whereas the others may be found in later stages of development but not in the earliest stage. Consequently Lichtenberg's reduction of the paradigm with its more extensive range of meaning to simply one of its manifestations would be to dismiss the spectrum of destructive behaviors it embraces.

Kohut

In contrast, Kohut attempted a new formulation of psychoanalysis centered on his conception of the self. Conceptually, Kohut's self is "a supraordinate configuration (supraordinate to the mental apparatus and the agencies) [that] must be assumed to be present, albeit in a rudimentary form, the moment we speak of a 'psychology' in the human infant. This rudimentary self, then, is the earliest, smallest, primal unit of complex psychological experience" (P. Ornstein, 1978, p. 102). Early in development a "nuclear self" is established. "This structure is the basis of our sense of being an independent center of initiative and perception, integrated with our most central ambitions and ideals—and with our experience that our body and mind form a unit in space and a continuum in time" (Kohut, 1977, p. 177). The nuclear self is a cohesive and enduring configuration. Each definition of the self covers a different territory. Ornstein addresses Kohut's metapsychological conception of the self as a supraordinate structure, while Kohut's second definition responds to the subjectively perceived self as the unifying center of initiative in time and space. The subjective definition describes the situation of the optimal self when development has gone reasonably well.

Where do drives, in particular the aggressive drive, fit in Kohut's self? He affirms:

> It will bear repeating that the tenets I propose with regard to the experiences of aggression and rage also apply to the libidinal drives. The infantile sexual drive in isolation is not the primary psychological configuration. . . . The primary psychological configuration (of which the drive is only a constituent) is the experience of the relation between the self and the empathic self-object. Drive manifestations in isolation establish themselves only after traumatic and/or prolonged failures in empathy from the side of self-object environment. Healthy drive-experiences, on the other hand, always include the self and the self-object. . . . If the self is seriously damaged, however, or destroyed,[2] then the drives become powerful constellations in their own right. (1977, p. 122)

This quotation reveals Kohut's rejection of the freudian notion of drive at one level while he retains and modifies it at another. The freudian drive exerts pressure on the psyche demanding discharge. The kohutian drive does not drive anything. It is present as a reactive component of the experience between the self and the self-object. The drive becomes a powerful constellation and appears subjectively and symptomatically obvious only when environmental failures interfere with the smooth functioning and development of the self. Kohut's metapsychology does not confront the slippage of meaning in his conception of drive. His conceiving of drives as an integral part of the self–self-object configuration suggests that his drives are closer to motivational systems than to forces exerting demands on the psychic apparatus. He also uses the concept of forces with a changed meaning, but does not define what he means by them. His conception of aggression is clinically based on what he calls "experience-near" descriptions. The experience of the subject provides the main tools for theoretical elaboration. It is also difficult to distinguish these formulations from a basically frustration-aggression orientation.

How did Kohut conceive of aggression in his "experience-near" mode of theorizing? Kohut distinguished between healthy aggression in infancy and maturity and pathological aggression. The first function of early aggression, in decisive departure from the kleinian model, is assertiveness: "Stated in descriptive terms: the behavioral base line with regard to aggressiveness is not the raging-destructive baby—it is, from the beginning, the assertive baby, whose aggressions are a constituent of the firmness and security with which he makes his demands vis-à-vis self-objects who provide for him a milieu of (average) empathic responsiveness (1977, p. 118). Not unlike Winnicott, Kohut (1977), saw "elemental aggression" as existing from the beginning in the service of establishing a rudimentary self that needs healthy aggression to define itself. This is nondestructive aggression which has a developmental line of its own. Under normal circumstances it develops "from primitive forms of nondestructive assertiveness" to mature forms of assertiveness at the service of specific tasks. Once the goals of the task have been achieved, it subsides (pp. 120–21). Destructive aggression is not a primary drive but a "disintegration product" resulting as a response to empathic failures of the self-object that are experienced as injuries to the self. Resistance and negative transferences are responses to actual empathic failure on the analyst's part or to revivals of childhood experiences of empathic failure (pp. 114–15).

Ordinary maternal failure may bring about rageful manifestations. However, "the child's rage and destructiveness should not be conceptualized as the expression of a primary instinct that strives towards its goal or searches for an outlet" (1977, p. 118) Infantile aggression is nondestructive and at the service of maintaining the link to the self-object. When the psychic configuration established by this link to the self-object breaks up through persistent empathic failure the assertive component transforms into rage. Thus, what looks like a destructive "drive" is no more than the "disintegration product" that appears when the self–self-object psychic configuration breaks up (p. 119). The function of the assertive elemental aggression is "in the service of the establishment of a rudimentary self and, later, of its maintenance" (p. 120).

Parens's formulation has also been compared to that of Kohut's (1972) notion of narcissistic rage. Rage in this understanding is a consequence of the disillusionment within the matrix of archaic narcissism by a significant self-object (A. Ornstein, 1998). Kohut ascribes such rage reactions to forms of narcissistic pathology, particularly in patients who are rage and revenge-prone. Kohut also emphasized a view of aggression as provoked by events in the patient's life, rather than as a form of innate discharge. These other forms of aggression are under the control of the ego, but are only noted as more mature forms of aggression in comparison to narcissistic rage (Shane and Shane, 1982).

Kohut then went on in the further development of his ideas to formulate a twofold notion of aggression, one the form of destructive rage that is always motivated by an injury to the self, and the second a form of nondestructiveness, which is part of the basic assertiveness of the rudimentary self and is mobilized under conditions of optimal frustration (Kohut, 1977). Thus, he postulates two developmental lines of aggression, one as an integral constituent of healthy assertiveness, and a second destructive line that emerges from the nonoptimal frustration coming from an unempathic environment (Shane and Shane, 1982). This approach was echoed in Stechler's (1985, 1986, 1987; Stechler and Halton, 1987) formulations regarding destructive and assertive aggression. Both Kohut and Parens describe different forms of aggression, both hostile and nonhostile, which undergo different developmental vicissitudes. For both, nonhostile aggression is primary and hostile aggression a secondary or reactive byproduct of frustration.

It is worth noting that contemporary intersubjectivist studies of infant development are more preoccupied with establishing the parameters of the mother-child intersubjective dyad, particularly aspects of affective communication, than in exploring the vicissitudes of aggression. In this they seem to follow Kohut's lead, whose interest in aggression faded in the face of his emphasis on empathic attunement. Stern (1985), whose text provided a major landmark in intersubjectively oriented studies of development, pays little attention to aggression—the term is not even mentioned in his index—in contrast with the comparatively vital role it is accorded by other developmentalists (Meissner, 1989).

Parens himself leans more heavily on the contributions of Rochlin (1973), who also proposed that hostility and destructiveness result from injured narcissism and humiliation, and that aggression arises specifically in defense of the self. In Rochlin's view, it is not only rage and revenge that are provoked by such injury, but also lesser forms of hostile destructiveness expressed as anger. Degrees of excessive unpleasure do elicit in both normal and disturbed individuals the entire range of hostile destructiveness from mild anger to rage and violence. But clearly Rochlin is not trying to define the nature of aggression, but defining one of the most significant motivational factors that enters into the mobilization of aggression, the injury to narcissism.

McDevitt

Another approach to this form of destructiveness was provided by McDevitt (1983) in his discussion of the development of object-directed aggression. He argued that neurophysiological precursors of such aggression are innate and exist from the beginning of life. From the very beginning, they express unpleasure in a form of affecto-motor discharge signaling distress and thereby are placed in the service of adaptation. McDevitt described the emergence and evolution of this form of destructiveness in the subphases of Mahler's (Mahler et al., 1975) separation-individuation process. Both libidinal investment in and aggressive reaction against the mother begin in the differentiation subphase when the infant begins to be specifically attached and differentiated, usually at about five months. The infant's progressive detachment makes it increasingly necessary for the mother to restrain his carefree and often dangerous exploration of the outer world, particularly in more active infants. The infant reacts, struggles against the mother's restraints, and even begins to hit, bite, scratch, and kick her.

This reaction is often more intense when the mother's restrictions seem unduly punitive or restrictive. The infant's capacity to direct anger at the mother parallels his development of a more lasting libidinal cathexis, and the capacity to experience anger in a more consistent and organized fashion. As in Parens's understanding, these reactions did not occur spontaneously, but were related to a variety of unpleasurable restrictions and frustrations of the infant's activity. Further, when the cause of the unpleasure was removed, the anger disappeared, so that the infant's anger at this early stage was short-lived, stimulus-bound, and limited to the specific concrete situation.

Only gradually, probably in response to continuing prohibitions and the eliciting of their own anxiety, these rageful behaviors were modified by ego influences throughout the practicing subphase and increasingly underwent displacement, restriction of aim, sublimation, and libidinal fusion. Anger would quickly be displaced onto a doll or turned against the self or inhibited, and the corresponding behavioral aggression expressed. It might also be manifested as negativism or provoking the mother. The patterns of such aggression slowly became characteristic for each child and each mother-child pair. The infant's anger at this stage did not reveal any deliberate intent to hurt; rather, the infant seemed oblivious to or even surprised by any hurt that happened to be inflicted on the mother or another child. This suggests that the intent to inflict hurt is not part of the original aim of the aggressive act, but rather the primary motivation is to eliminate an obstacle or change an unpleasant situation. The inflicting of pain is secondary. This understanding of the use of aggression would be consistent with our formulation.

Nonaffective discharge of destructiveness. Parens describes his second type of aggression as "nonaffective discharge of destructiveness." This form of aggression arises spontaneously from birth and prototypically takes the form usually of sucking, chewing, and feeding. The aim is to destroy and assimilate the object. This impulse originates somatically and is cyclically activated by vegetative processes. Other manifestations of nonaffective destructive aggression would include fourteen-month-old Bernie swinging a pull-toy and hitting Candy, but remaining unaware of having struck her. Parens concludes that Bernie's object of discharge was to swing the toy, not to hurt Candy. He had no "intention" to hurt her. The destructiveness was incidental to his excitement with the toy.

Aggression in this form is put to the service of self-preservation, and is not aroused by unpleasure, except, one would think, the unpleasurable sensations associated with hunger or thirst. Parens's view that such behavior is an expression of an aggressive drive has been variously challenged. Lichtenberg (1982), for example, would regard such behaviors simply descriptively as sucking and chewing patterns, without any need to appeal to an underlying aggressive drive. The Shanes (1982) launch a frontal attack on this category, stating that it postulates associated destructive fantasies in the infant which reveal the intent to destroy. They challenge Parens's data supporting this category and argue that it is most unlikely that the level of cognitive development of the young infant allows for the production of such complex mental processes as are involved in the intention to destroy an object. Gedo (1982), by the same token, charges Parens with a confusion of the consequence of the infant's chewing or sucking behavior with its purposes. Clearly, the infant's chewing destroys the food-object, but Gedo questions whether this is in fact its purpose or goal. Thus, Parens's view regarding what constitutes aggression seems to be based on the a priori assumption that all behavior, even the chewing and sucking of infants, must be powered by an instinctual drive.

To these objections Parens (1982) replies that he does not attribute complex destructive thoughts and intentions to the neonate. There is a problem in imputing motives to neonatal behavior, but there is also admittedly some point at which intentionality enters the motivational structure of any behavior. It is worth noting for our purposes that Parens stipulates here a form of aggression which is destructive, whether intentionally or not, but which is also dissociated from the usual affective states associated with destructiveness. Even so, in our view, Parens confuses activity that might be destructive in outcome with aggression as such, a conception we would find theoretically retrogressive. In our view, the activity would be aggressive because of its characteristic of overcoming obstacles and not because of its destructiveness. The activities in this category do not require an aggressive capacity, unless the activity runs into an obstacle that requires overcoming for the activity to accomplish its end.

Pleasure-related discharge of destructiveness. In this third form of aggression, an antecedent unpleasure-related hostile destructive impulse (e.g., a sadistic impulse) is displaced or undergoes delay of discharge. This requires the developmental structuring of the libidinal object, which takes place some time after the first year (cf. McDevitt). It does not arise spontaneously but usually is provoked by a reaction to frustration. This category has two modalities. The first, present from the second half of the first year of life, expresses itself in children's activity of seemingly gleefully smashing things. Analysis of different instances of this behavior led Parens (1979) to conclude that it did not represent "destructiveness for its own sake" but rather pleasure-in-function during periods of mounting excitement (p. 118). The second modality appears at the end of the first year of life and has three features: "destructiveness" discharged in association with "pleasure" affects and which seemed to appear "spontaneously" (p. 118). Careful observation of the children left no doubt about the destructiveness. But the dynamic processes involved suggested a preexisting condition for its emergence, the existence of "an intrapsychically registered antecedent" of psychic pain or sufficient unpleasure. The aggressive actions were not spontaneous but calculated, suggesting that they were under the growing ego's capacity for control and delayed actions. Parens gives the example of Candy, a fourteen-month-old who had been hit harshly by Donnie three days earlier. She "calculatedly unleashed destructive impulses toward Donnie" (p. 119) in a delayed reaction. This behavior, an antecedent to sadism, suggests that, under certain painful early life experiences, "the degree to which hostile destructiveness is mobilized and attached to self- and object-representations, by the indelibility of these earliest cathexes, that sadism becomes automatized in the psyche" (p. 120). This aggression is not primary, that is, a drive in need of discharge, but the result of internal ego "dynamics." In conclusion, for Parens, aggression is a nondestructive drive in need of discharge in the service of self-assertion, control of the environment, and mastery. Destructive aggression requires ego mediation.

Lichtenberg (1982) translates this form of destructiveness into "affective-action-patterns reactive to situations perceived as frustrations, and to individuals perceived as aggressors" (p. 221). In these terms, the motivational component is frustration, and aggression is made synonymous with the combination of action-and-affect. The behavior here is provoked rather than innate, and takes the form of transforming, after some delay, a previously experienced passive infliction of unpleasure into a more active effort to master previous trauma. Thus, Parens's view would be somewhat at variance with the traditional notion that aggression fused with libido is in itself pleasurable and does not require any underlying traumatic or unpleasurable experience (Shane and Shane, 1982). In our view, however, sadism is linked to overcoming an obstacle to libidinal pleasure; we would accept the possibility that the overcoming would be secondarily pleasurable by reason of attaining the object or pleasurable on its own terms. It is aggressive, however, only in terms of its motivation and function of overcoming whatever obstacles are involved.

Nondestructive aggression. Under this last category of aggression, Parens (1979) includes forms of assertiveness, control, mastery, curiosity, efficacy, and general competence in relation to dealings both with the environment and within the self. The aim of this form of aggression is in no sense destructive in itself, but when it is blocked it can produce a reaction of hostile aggressiveness, as in his first type of aggression. This form of aggression was present in all eleven normal infants observed from eight to sixteen weeks. It consisted in a "type of pressured, driven, exploratory activity during periods of wakefulness and physiological and psychic comfort" (p. 25).

Spitz (1957) had long ago suggested that the infant's capacity to say "no," usually expressed by about fifteen months or later in the phase of anal libidinal development, not only plays a significant role in distinguishing between self and non-self, but is related to identification with the aggressor, reflecting a mutually hostile relation between infant and mother. In the wake of such identifications, the external obstacle posed by the parental "no" is internalized and metabolized in the form of an aggressive capacity in the child now available for other uses (Tähkä, 1988). But, as Tyson (1994) notes, there is still a question of whether the aggression in question is itself hostile or nonhostile. The aggression in identification with the aggressor is not with the person of the aggressor but with his or her aggression, which may be hostile and destructive or not depending of the nature of the aggressor's aggression. The aggression in question may be nondestructive aggression as described by Parens. Tyson comments further:

> It becomes important to distinguish among three kinds of "no"s—
> "no" as a product of imitative processes, "no" that results from
> identification with some kind of aggressive expression of the
> mother, whether hostile or nonhostile, and "no" that expresses
> the child's intention to oppose or not to comply with another's
> wishes, an intention that may arise from many sources.

The first "no," in the course of imitation, does not have any oppositional intention but reflects the degree to which the child feels himself to be a part of the caregiver, whom he imitates in various ways. The second "no" derives from the shift from imitation to identification and may or may not be defensive. As an indication of the child's intentional opposition, the third "no" employs the previously acquired capacity to say "no" in the service of self-object differentiation and subsequently for other purposes as well. (pp. 297–98)

Parens's (1979) illustration for this type of aggression was little Jane, who at three months and nineteen days attempted to control the spoon her mother used to feed her. A few minutes later she looked around first at her mother, then at items on the floor. She then turned her attention to a set of plastic rings on a string and explored them, mouthing them and soon vocalizing some sounds. Her face expressed a "great deal of pressure," leading Parens to infer that she was "working" at assimilating the rings. After an interruption, Jane returned to the rings. Parens observes: "Notable is the intense, work-like affect—the constancy of the effort she invests in exploring the rings and the inner-drivenness of that activity. Much energy seems to be invested in the exploratory mouthing, pulling, and pushing of the rings. . . . her arms and lifting of her torso, and her legs are activated as well; indeed her entire body is involved in her effort. Her facial expression and entire body posture indicate the tension of, and the large effort invested in the protracted activity" (p. 24).

He concludes that Jane was driven "to gratify the push from within to assimilate, control, and master her visual experience" and the "inner-outer environment" (p. 25). For him, these urges are not the child's unfolding ego functions but the result of the aggressive drive activity, and energic and motivational id activity. This activity is compelled, not elective, pushed "by some inner force which fuels it" (p. 29). Parens concludes from these observations that this activity in small children "is fueled by aggression which has an inherent nondestructive current and which does not require neutralization by the ego" (p. 38). Aggression, therefore, is not inherently destructive as postulated by classic psychoanalytic theory.

Gender differences. Parens (1997) also notes that boys and girls differ very little in aggressive behavior in the first two years of life. There is a shift, however, early in the third year, in which boys begin to manifest a greater degree of phallic aggression and a greater degree of physically aggressive behavior. He does not take this to mean that girls are less aggressive than boys beyond the third year, but the increase in phallic aggressiveness seems to play a role in the masculinization of boys. But, as he comments, "It would be a serious mistake, however, to assume that girls are not amply endowed with aggression and that they are biologically not assertive (nondestructive aggression) or that they are less capable of experiencing and expressing hostility, hate, and rage (hostile destructiveness) than boys" (1997, p. 256).

There are suggestions from child observation studies that gender differentiation with respect to aggressive behavior may be influenced by social factors, showing greater tolerance for masculine aggression (Condry and Condry, 1976; Harris, 1998). Mayes and Cohen (1993) have provided further documentation of this aspect of parent-child interaction and its influence on the development of aggression. Fosshage (1998) also comments on the influence of parental management of childhood aggression as exercising a significant influence on the emerging patterns of experiencing and managing aggression. Galenson and Fields (1989) cite a case of gender disturbance in a male child related to maternal intolerance of his aggressive behavior.

Divergent Opinions

Some of Parens's critics do not accept his last category as a true form of aggression: Gedo (1982), for example, charged him with confusing aggression of this kind with mere purposefulness. In his view, only the forms of unpleasure-related destructiveness and pleasure-related destructiveness can be included in a psychoanalytic theory of aggression. For Lichtenberg (1982), this category becomes a form of "perceptual-affective-action patterns of assertiveness with efficacy and competence pleasure" (p. 221). He further argued, somewhat unfairly, that Parens virtually ignores the evidence supporting an interactional and interregulatory matrix between the infant and his caretakers, especially in the first six months of life. Research based on early infant studies seems to lean away from the notion of aggression as a primary drive present from the beginning of life, as Parens stipulates. Further, evidence from the study of reactions to experimental strange situations as devised by Ainsworth (1969; Ainsworth et al., 1978) indicate that so-called disorganized/disoriented strange situation behavior is not only predictive of psychopathology in middle childhood and adolescence, but such disorganized attachment status is also frequently associated with high levels of aggression (Hesse and Main, 1999).

These conflicting trends have led Stechler (1985, 1987; Stechler and Halton, 1987) to propose a twofold pattern of development, one involving the capacity for assertion, the other that of aggression. In this formulation, assertion involves an "inherent tendency to be active, to reach out, and to engage the world" (1985, p. 537). He maintains that nowhere in this orientation is it necessary to invoke an underlying aggressive instinct providing the driving force behind these behaviors. In contrast, aggression derives from a different biopsychological subsystem, which involves a self-protective mechanism whose purpose is to defend the individual against threats to its biopsychological integrity.[3] Even the young infant can be provoked to strike out against or attack a presumed source of threat. This protective-aggressive system is primarily dormant and reactive, in contrast to the activity-assertion system, which tends to be more active. From the very beginning then, these two subsystems differ with regard to their origins, their functions, and their associated affects (Stechler, 1985, 1986; Stechler and Halton, 1987). It seems clear that this category runs directly in the face of more traditional approaches to aggression within psychoanalysis, which regard it as inherently destructive. Therefore, a number of commentators on Parens's work have declared that this particular category of aggression is not aggression at all, at least in any traditional sense (Lichtenberg, 1982; Gedo, 1982; Meers, 1982). We would not regard it as aggressive by reason of its purposefulness, but by reason of its role in overcoming any obstacles to such purposive intent.

Certainly, the role of assertiveness or nondestructive aggression has been recognized for some time. Hartmann et al. (1949) established the distinction between destructive and nondestructive aggression, and Ives Hendrick (1942, 1943a, b) amplified the latter into a form of ego-mastery. Even newborn infants can show a form of oppositional behavior—e.g., refusing the breast or bottle or later refusing to swallow food, and still later pushing away from the mother in the process of separating and individuating (Levy, 1972). At what point such behavior becomes intentional remains an open question.

The evidence at this juncture does not support a hostile or destructive intention in the infant's mind, but seems to suggest impulses of a nonhostile and nondestructive kind (Tyson, 1994).[4]

Comparison has likewise been drawn to Kohut's (1977) view of aggression in which he sees aggression as a constituent of the child's assertiveness, which under normal circumstances is transformed into the assertiveness of the mature adult self. Thus, for Kohut, "nondestructive aggressiveness is . . . a part of the assertiveness of the demands of the rudimentary self and it becomes mobilized . . . whenever optimal frustrations (nontraumatic delays of the empathic responses of the self-object) are experienced" (pp. 120–21). Destructive rage, in contrast, is always motivated by injury to the self. Thus, like Stechler and other infant researchers, Kohut postulates two developmental lines of aggression: nondestructive aggression as a constituent of healthy assertiveness, and a second line of destructive aggression emerging secondarily out of excessive frustration in an unempathic environment. Like Parens, however, Kohut also sees both of these as forms of man's basic aggression.

Along similar lines, Fonagy et al. (1993) focus on the normal and abnormal functions of aggression in the protection of self-representation and identity. Turning away from portrayals of aggression as inherently destructive, they center their attention on the mother-child dyad, and point out that "[f]orceful self-expression in infants, such as the toddler's insistence on pursuing a specific activity or having a particular toy, is often mistaken for aggression. . . . However, the child's *aim* is not to cause harm, but to realise a goal; this gives pleasure both through the fulfillment of a wish and through enhancement of the child's sense of effectiveness" (p. 474)—a view consistent with our own. However, despite their disavowal of destructive theories of aggression, they go on to say: "In contrast, both healthy and pathological aggression involve the intent to harm (in reality or fantasy), and tend to be accompanied by unpleasant affects, such as anger, fear or frustration" (p. 474). The former part of their statement is congruent with our view in that the effort is directed to overcoming an obstacle. The latter statement points to the difference with our view in which there need be no intention to do harm, consciously or unconsciously. On our terms, such harmful intentions and the dysphoric affects that may accompany the action are not due to aggression, but to other frustrations, conflicts, and subsidiary motivational concerns that reach beyond merely overcoming the obstacle.

WINNICOTT

In reply, Parens aligns himself with other theorists such as Winnicott, Greenacre, Mahler, and Spitz, who address themselves to positive and constructive forces of growth or activity in the organism. In one of his seminal statements on the role of aggression in development, Winnicott (1969)[5] postulated a positive structure-building function of aggression in the mother-infant dyad on the part of both participants. He viewed aggression as a healthy and constructive aspect of the infant's intense early involvement with the mother that facilitated psychic growth, both individuation and separation. In his view, to understand aggression one must take into consideration the moment of development and the child's immaturity and the environment that provides for the child's needs.

Developmentally, Winnicott finds three stages. In the first early stage aggression is not integrated and the purpose of aggressive actions does not include concern for the effects of an action. The baby is ruthless in his love of the mother. Aggression here is a necessary component of love, or, in Winnicott's words, the baby "does not yet appreciate the fact that what he destroys when excited is the same as that which he values in quiet intervals between excitements" (1958a, p. 206). Destruction is incidental. The aggressive motility needs to exert itself in the environment and "needs to find opposition," "something to push against" for the individual to begin to exist and experience itself as real, creating the occasion to discover the "Me" and "Not-Me" aspects of reality. For Winnicott, it is the aggressive component that helps to establish the "Not-Me" external object (1958a, p. 215). The final result, when things go well enough, is the establishment of a "Me," and the sense of being a true self. For this achievement to take place the libidinal object and the object that provides opposition has to be "an external object, and not merely a satisfying object" (p. 217). Thus, in Winnicott's conception, aggression at the earliest stage of life is the foundation on which a true self is built in the context of a good enough object, that satisfies and resists the child in tolerable ways. Aggression is needed for the capacity to love and to establish a relationship with the object.

In relation to his objects the infant searches for gratification to bring about peace of body and mind. There is no primary destructive aggression toward the object, as in Klein, but there is "a theoretical greed or primary appetite-love, which can be cruel, hurting, dangerous, but which is so by chance" (1984, p. 85). The child cannot exist without the object, but when it perceives that some manner of gratification that may be cruel or hurtful might endanger the object, begins to experience frustration. This constitutes a developmental step and provides the basis for the emergence of the function of fantasy. Winnicott believes that the mediatory function of fantasy in relation to objects does not permit pure aggression as a behavior. At first the fantasies are omnipotent even when the behavior involves ordinary aggression toward the object. The fantasies and perceptions that the object might be hurt bring about a restraint in aggressive behavior and a replacement of the omnipotent fantasies by object-related fantasies and behavior: "the infant becomes able to be destructive, becomes able to hate and to kick and to scream instead of magically destroying the world. This aggression is object related and comes alongside with gratification and tender relations" (1984, p. 98). Aggressive behavior is possible insofar as the object survives it. To which we would add: aggressive behavior aims at overcoming the obstacles to possession of the object.

The child finds two mothers in his mother. One is the object mother who has to be found for the infant "to survive the instinct driven episodes which have now acquired the full force of fantasies . . . " (1984, p. 103). The other is the environmental mother whose special function is to be herself, in empathic acceptance of the infant's spontaneous gestures. Reactive aggressive behavior appears when the object mother fails to withstand the infant's primary greed and its unintentional destructiveness, or when the environmental mother fails to respond to the child's gestures. The aggressive behavior has a signal function as a social or antisocial communication of distress, requesting help to alleviate the pain caused by the object's failure. Actual destructive behavior is always—in Winnicott's view—a child's demand for acknowledgment that he has suffered a deprivation requiring amendment. This conceptualization sees aggressive behavior as a way of reestablishing contact with an object.

Another stage is reached when the child's progressive psychic integration permits appreciation of the mother as an object. Concern for the object, Klein's depressive position, appears. The child's guilt "refers to the damage which is felt to be done to the loved person in the excited relationship." In health the infant can bear the guilt with the help of the mother and moves toward constructive giving and mending. "In this way much of the aggression is transformed into social functions." If these efforts fail, the aggression reappears now in the form of internal or external harmful activities. However, if splitting as a defense separates the good from the bad aspects of the object, "love loses some of its valuable aggressive component, and the hate becomes the more disruptive" (1958a, pp. 206–07). In the final stage the child becomes a total person, involved in relationships, triangular configurations, and the ensuing conscious and unconscious conflicts. Aggression here is entwined in conflict and in the efforts the individual makes to disentangle from the anxiety it evokes.

So far, we have described the aggression which in Winnicott's terms is an inseparable component of the excited love of a child seeking satisfaction of needs and an external object in order to constitute itself as a self who is a "Me" in relationship with people and the world that are "Not-Me." When this process fails, the true self goes in to hiding and under the cover of a false self the "individual exists by not being found" (1958a, p. 212). The positive result depends on "good-enough mothering," the indispensable environmental factor to permit aggression to achieve, in conjunction with love, the creation of the core of a psychically alive person. Aggression as reaction to frustration has to do with environmental impingements and the child's reaction to it. The problem with impingement is that the child is so involved in reacting that it cannot experience its own impulses and therefore interferes with the emergence of "Me" (1958a, pp. 216–17). Winnicott observes: "In this case there is no fusion of the aggressive and erotic components, since the 'Me' is not established when erotic experiences occur" (p. 217).

Winnicott (1958b) offered a most original theory about hate, the most significant aggressive "affect." Winnicott agrees with Freud that hate is an ego affect, not an instinctual affect, for a whole person or object. Winnicott asserts that a mother hates her baby before the baby is capable of hating her (p. 200). He gives a long list of facts that prompt mothers to hate their babies. This is important for the baby as long as the mother is capable of tolerating her hate without doing anything about it. The baby needs it, "he needs hate to hate" (p. 202). In a later paper, Winnicott (1969) linked hate to the capacity to use an object as conditioned by "the acceptance of the object's independent existence, its property of having been there all the time" (p. 88). Hate mediates the emergence of the capacity to use an object. This happens when in development the omnipotent child during object-relating destroys the object in unconscious fantasy. The actual survival of the object gives it a very particular value, that of having outlasted the destruction. Now hate and love can be together and the object keeps on living. This has to do with becoming real in early stages of development. The survival of the object follows a paradoxical pattern: "becoming destroyed because [they are] real, becoming real because destroyed" (p. 90). This pattern appears in the treatment of patients with early disturbances when positive changes occur, not because of interpretation but on account of the analyst's actual survival after the patient's hateful attacks.

Along with Winnicott, other theorists sought to rationalize the constructive aspects of aggression. Hendrick (1942, 1943a, b), for example, spoke of an instinct to master or work, and Hartmann (1948) addressed himself to neutral ego energies. Parens finds difficulties conceptually in trying to separate the force that aims toward adaptation and mastery from the force that leads toward defense and destructiveness. He defends Hartmann's concept of neutralization on clinical grounds. In the case of regressions from more neutralized or sublimated forms of drive expression to less sublimated or neutralized ones, he sees the concept of neutralization as more advantageous, since it maintains the common conceptual link between these different forms of aggressive expression. This implies a relative reversibility between levels of drive differentiation, between neutralized aggression and hostile destructiveness. He suggests in addition that it may be that the neutralized aggression that Hartmann addresses may actually be aggression which was inherently nondestructive and had been transformed into a form of hostile destructiveness as a result of the experience of excessive unpleasure (Parens, 1982). More recently, in support of these views of the positive nondestructive role of aggression, Fosshage (1998) added:

> To be able to become angry and to avert a perceived threat or hurt can both protect the individual and self-cohesion as well as enhance feelings of power. In augmenting exploration and assertiveness in overcoming obstacles, aggression can increase our sense of efficacy. . . . Aggression as one pole of aversiveness can serve multiple functions. *In regulating our interactions and attachments with others, aggression serves vitally necessary self-protective, self-delineating, and self-restorative functions.* (p. 47, emphasis in original)

We can add that the overcoming of obstacles as the characteristic motivational theme of aggression can embrace all of these motivational themes—averting threat, augmenting exploration, self-assertion, self-restoration, self-protection, and yes, even willful destruction and sadistic hurtfulness, can all be encompassed under the rubric of overcoming an obstacle of some sort. Further, as the process of development moves ahead through its progressive stages and levels of achievement, the nature and quality of the obstacles encountered by the developing organism change and become increasingly more complex and involve different and more evolved capacities of the organism in order to gain competitive advantage and adaptive satisfaction. The aggression of the newborn in gaining access to the breast is of quite a different order than the toddler competing with a playmate for possession of a desired toy. Thus the meaning of the overcoming of obstacles is by no means univocal, but analogous in all its shifting and multiple contexts of meaning and expression.

And as the meaning and complexity of these contexts of obstacle-overcoming evolve and multiply, the organism itself in virtue of its own inherent development experiences increasing capacity and personal resources for negotiating means and adaptive achievement of goals and ambitions. As the child develops through infancy and childhood on into adolescence and early adulthood, the meaning and contexts of aggression, both with regard to the nature of obstacles encountered and the adaptive capacities and resources of the individual to overcome them, undergo progressive elaboration and amplification. As is the case with all aspects of psychic development, in both normal and pathological aspects (A. Freud, 1965) the developing organism, along with its inherent capacities for action and adaptation, undergoes constant change, one aspect of which is development of the capacity for aggressive motivation and action.

Section III

Clinical Perspectives

Chapter 8

Aggression in Phobic States

In this chapter we wish to extend the implications of our view of aggression to the analysis of phobic states as seen in both classic childhood phobias and in adult phobic conditions. Our purpose is to demonstrate the applicability of our theory in a specific clinical context.

EARLIER APPROACHES

The role of aggression in the genesis of phobic symptoms and phobic states has been viewed as a well-established finding of psychoanalytic research. Fenichel (1944) summarized the classic position, in which phobic formations were involved in defenses against both libidinal and aggressive impulses and employed a variety of defenses, including regression, repression, reversal, projection, and displacement. Anna Freud (1977) would later add condensation and externalization.

In general, these formulations attributed the origin of whatever anxiety the phobic phenomenon was defending against to libidinal and aggressive impulses. As Anna Freud (1977) observed, the distinction between anxiety and fear was paramount, in that it was not fear that lay at the root of the phobia, but anxiety. The anxieties can reflect any level of developmental danger—annihilation, separation, loss of the object's love, castration, even moral condemnation. However, they serve essentially as a warning signal against the related intrapsychic danger. While the mechanisms required to create the phobia formation are intended to contain anxiety within manageable limits, so that the internal danger does not become traumatic, the phobic anxiety itself escapes this containment and the ego is to this extent threatened, but now by an external threat rather than an internal one. Thus, oral-sadistic impulses to bite or devour can be transformed into fears of being bitten (Flescher, 1955), sadomasochistic wishes to be beaten and tortured can take the form of fears of dark streets (Brenner, 1959), or other fears of attack or destruction (Bernstein, 1962), and murderous wishes against the oedipal father can become animal phobias (S. Freud, 1909; Rochlin, 1973).

The prevailing view of the place of aggression in the formation of phobic processes sees it as a given. The aggressive instinctual drive serves as an independent source of instinctual danger, to one or another degree in conjunction with, and reinforced by, external realistic factors. In the early classic view, any conjunction with real determinants or situations was not required to explain the phobic phenomenon (e.g., early kleinian understanding of the death instinct), but more recent views would regard a more complex interweaving of developmental and environmental components as integral to any understanding of the vicissitudes of aggression.

In our view of aggression, it is not postulated, but instead articulated within a specifically motivational context. Our hope is that this will permit a more definitively motivational understanding of the role and import of phobic expressions. We will focus on the phobic phenomenon in the case of Little Hans (S. Freud, 1909) and in that of Frankie (Bornstein, 1949; Ritvo, 1965). We will then examine the genesis of phobic symptoms in an adult.

LITTLE HANS

Hostility and sadism were the impulses central to Little Hans's phobia. He wished his father dead so that he would be free to engage in sadistic, phallic acts with his mother and have babies with her. These impulses were aggressive in the sense that they were motivated to overcome obstacles to their achievement. Before the phobia developed, there was little outward show of these hostile and sadistic aims, and what expression they did obtain was so mild as to evoke no opposing response from his parents. The obstacles to achievement of his aims were, presumably, entirely intrapsychic.

Freud (1909) thought of the setting of Hans's phobia as a "battle" (p. 139) between opposing forces within the child's mind: impulses of hostility and sadism on one side and repression on the other. According to Freud, Hans's instinctual impulses strove not only to gain ultimate satisfaction, but also to force their way into consciousness. When the instincts were intensified by experiences of deprivation and erotic stimulation, they gained enough force to partially overcome the obstacle of repression. At that point the phobia "burst out" so that previously unconscious ideas "forced their way into consciousness" (p. 139) in the form of fears of horses biting him and horses falling down.

Prior to the phobia, repression had protected Hans from feeling hostility toward his father and from the fear of castration, the natural punishment for his forbidden and destructive impulses. When these impulses began to emerge into consciousness, Hans desperately needed adjunctive ways to oppose awareness and expression of them. His phobia served the purpose. His fear of punishment for his impulse to bite his father and see him fall down dead was disguised and externalized as a fear of horses biting him. We would go beyond Freud's interpretation and speculate that this projection also served to reinforce the obstacle to expression of his hostile impulses because it was experienced as a genuine threat; at the same time, it served to maintain a sense of safety and a loving relationship with his father, who otherwise would have been the subject of this projection.

Horses falling down were a disguised representation of Hans's desire to penetrate his mother sadistically with his penis and have babies with her. Freud explained the fear attached to horses falling down in accord with his current ideas about anxiety hysteria, i.e., with the return of the repressed *"the pathogenic material was remodelled and transposed on to the horse-complex, while the accompanying affects were uniformly turned into anxiety"* (p. 137, emphasis in original).

In more contemporary terms, we would add specifically that attaching fear to the sight and expectation of horses falling down would not simply be a disguise of his instinctual aim and a displacement as to object. This fear also compelled him to avoid the possibility of witnessing such an event. We would say that his fear of seeing horses falling down served as an additional obstacle to awareness of and expression of his sadistic incestuous impulses. At the same time, this component of the phobia served as a means of preserving a sense of safety in the presence of his mother, safety from knowing and experiencing forbidden impulses and associated anxiety in relation to her. The phobia also preserved his sense of loving security with her.

In a way resembling our own thinking, Freud (1909) also viewed the phobia as posing an obstacle to impulses striving toward expression. He wrote:

> . . . the essence of Hans's illness was entirely dependent upon the nature of the instinctual components that had to be repulsed. The content of his phobia was such as to impose a very great measure of restriction upon his freedom of movement, and that was its purpose. It was therefore a powerful reaction against the obscure impulses to movement which were especially directed against his mother. For Hans horses had always typified pleasure in movement . . . but since this pleasure in movement included the impulse to copulate, the neurosis posed a restriction on it and exalted the horse into an emblem of terror. (p. 139)

Aggression, then, in the phobia of Little Hans was located not in the quality of his affects, nor in the quality of his erotic or hostile impulses, but rather in the interplay of opposing forces. Prior to the phobia, the striving toward consciousness and satisfaction on the part of his impulses was more or less successfully opposed by the obstacle of repression. Aggression enters the picture to the extent that extra psychic effort may be required to break through the repressive barrier. In addition, insofar as his father posed a threatening obstacle to his desire to possess his mother libidinally, additional aggression would also have come into play with the motive of overcoming and getting rid of this now external obstacle. But the hostile impulse toward his father was also threatening and created a fear of losing his father. The aggressive impulses directed at his father, in serving to overcome the obstacle posed by the father to Hans's libidinal desires, thus simultaneously became themselves an obstacle to a secure, protective, and loving relation to his father.

FRANKIE

Frankie began his analysis at age five years; it lasted about three years. In Bornstein's (1949) classic description of his neurosis, there were several symptoms mentioned, including school phobia, wolf fright, and an elevator phobia. The analysis of each of these symptoms revealed the following dynamics.

1. The school phobia: Frankie was unable to go to school because of his fear of separation from his mother. He feared both that his mother would abandon him and that his own hostile impulses would destroy her. On the way to school, he was afraid of being trapped on the bus, afraid he would forget his stop, that he would be unable to open the door, that he would miss his stop. These fears were related to the wish that his sister had been trapped inside his mother and thus never born. Frankie was very sad, feeling that he was losing his mother to his little sister; his longing for his mother was intense. His affects followed the sequence: unconscious anger at his sister and mother, the wish to destroy them, fear of losing his mother, and deep sadness at the thought of losing her, connected with an underlying longing for her.

2. The wolf fright: The wolves were prohibiting figures, similar to the nurse, preventing him from acting on his desire to go to his parents' bedroom to watch and listen. These wishes involved sexual curiosity and evoked sexual excitement by reason of his identification with his mother and father in the sexual act. All these experiences also evoked jealousy and stirred up thoughts about babies being born; this in turn stimulated intense rage, thoughts of revenge, and sadness. The wolves also represented Frankie himself as a castrator of those who produce babies.

3. The elevator phobia: Frankie said, "The elevator might crash down, or the door might not open, and I would be trapped" (Bornstein, 1949, p. 205). The symptom was overdetermined. (a) The elevator-man was father as well as Frankie himself through identification with the aggressor-castrator father; Frankie also feared his own impulse to kill his father. (b) He envied his mother because she enjoyed being thrown up in the air by his father; he feared his own impulse to throw her out of the window for revenge. (c) He feared his wish to participate in sexual excitement with his father: the consequence might be that "We *all* [land] in the cellar" (p. 206, italics added). (d) He feared the pleasurable sensation of being lifted because he associated it with becoming pregnant. Pregnancy reminded him of his loneliness when mother got pregnant with his sister and left him. (e) He feared his wish to become pregnant because it meant losing his penis. He was terrified by his wish to be carried in his mother's womb, to insure

against her desertion, because the womb was a castrating organ. (f) He feared that his desire to have his sister trapped in his mother's womb would result in the punishment of his being trapped in the elevator.

Later in the analysis, Frankie developed a fear of the analyst, reflecting his wish/fear to be kidnapped and carried away by the analyst. All this was related to the "primal trauma" when Frankie was five months old: his night feeding had suddenly been stopped, leading to an intense unsatisfied hunger for milk and affection expressed in screaming for hours.

Frankie was crying out for union; he was trying desperately to overcome the obstacle to his security which was posed by separation. Here we can see that Frankie's longing to possess the mother would motivate a fantasy of aggression action in the sense of overcoming an obstacle, i.e., as expressing the primitive urge to orally incorporate the object in order to overcome the distance of separation. The purpose of the phobic aggression was to overcome the separation and the related displacement by his sister. In addition, the defenses of displacement and projection contained in the structures of the phobias served as obstacles to Frankie's gaining conscious awareness of his hostile impulses toward his sister.

Ritvo's (1965) report of Frankie as an adult in analysis further supports this formulation. Ritvo, in trying to understand the shift from the phobic neurosis to the later obsessional neurosis, obsessive doubting replacing phobic anxiety, implied that the central element manifested in the later obsessional neurosis was the need to overcome the obstacle posed by separation from the mother; this would be consistent with our formulation. In contrast, Ritvo saw the fear that the father might never find his way home as related to Frankie's aggression against his mother and his unconscious, revengeful wish that his mother, who had abandoned him when his sister was born, should never return.

The fear of being trapped in the bus referred to his original death wish against the baby sister who should have been trapped inside the mother and never allowed out. The fear of wolves was the fear of an imaginary representative of the prohibiting nurse and the father, as well as himself with his strong voyeuristic and castrative impulses. He had to fear for the safety of his genitals, if he were to act on his voyeuristic curiosity about the primal scene. The elevator fear was due to: (a) his hostile impulses against his mother and his identification with her; (b) the death wish against his sister and his desire to take her place; and (c) his masturbation conflicts, including fear of erections, fear of losing control over his own emotions, fear of being lifted—all evoking the danger of castration. Ritvo comments:

> Passive wishes in the transference produced reappearance of the wish to be carried passively inside the mother like the sister was carried. Hard upon it comes the old urge to attack the pregnant mother and the baby inside her. These wishes and their retaliatory consequences were of prime significance in the dynamics of his phobic symptoms as a child. . . . The passive strivings toward the father, in reaction to his own competitive, oedipal feelings, belong to a later developmental period when maturation and cognitive development had placed the intellect and mental functioning at his disposal for defensive purposes. These later passive strivings are warded off by the more purely mental operations characteristic for the obsessional neurosis and obsessive character. These same conflicts for which he sought a solution by the formation of phobic symptoms as a child in the phallic-oedipal phase he later tried to cope with by the obsessive doubting about his mind. (p. 14)

Frankie had tried for years to erase all feeling from his interactions with important persons in his life. He practiced this isolation of affect to protect himself against consequences of emotional dependence on them. This isolation also protected him against feelings of guilt for disturbing sexual thoughts or fantasies about his mother or sister, especially during his adolescence. As a child, he was forced to resort to inventing the omnipotent King Boo-Boo to protect himself from the terror of his passivity and destructive impulses, but as an adult he could find more ordinary and appropriate means of containing the current renditions of the older conflicts.

Ritvo (1965) further observed that there were also dream references to unconscious passive wishes for oral and anal homosexual gratification. In such dream thoughts, the old wishes and fantasies of oral impregnation and of being in his mother's womb, as his sister had been, that were so prominent a part of the childhood analysis, seemed to continue to find expression.

The focus of Ritvo's analysis is on how doubts replaced fears. "The doubts contained a refusal to recognize fully that he had reached these achievements. . . . To have accepted that reality . . . would have meant relinquishing his passive longing for protection, his cherished 'womb-type notion'" (p. 30). Frankie enables us to understand not only "how the past is contained in the present" but also how the mode of conflict solution had to undergo alteration because of advances in development. Ritvo's report supports our formulation that the central element in Frankie's childhood phobias, similar to the central ingredient still present but manifested in the later obsessional symptoms, was the need to overcome the obstacle posed by the threat of separation from the mother. It is in this overcoming of the obstacle that aggression played its part in his phobia formation.

CLINICAL EXAMPLE FROM AN ADULT

Paul, a handsome, well-built, twenty-two-year-old college senior, had no symptoms until he applied to medical school. He then became increasingly anxious and preoccupied over his admission. He was accepted, but he experienced no joy from his success. Instead, his anxiety increased, and unusual thoughts began to crowd his mind. The thoughts were related to dating girls and being afraid that he would contract syphilis from kissing or even from some more superficial physical contact. The fear of syphilis became his constant preoccupation. He developed a phobia of looking at his penis out of fear that he would see a lesion there, even though he had never had sexual relations.

He seemed concerned about his ability to function as a physician if he should get syphilis. He reasoned that syphilis affects the brain, makes the individual demented and dangerous, and would lead to two grave consequences: first, the physician might kill his patients, and second, he might spread syphilis to the rest of the world and many would die.

His great ambivalence about going to medical school and leaving his "youth" behind appeared in writings prior to his admission. Every time he tried to write the word "accepted," he would automatically substitute "excepted."

Paul was the oldest of two boys of a middle-class family. His brother was four years his junior. His mother was a devoted housewife and mother, extremely overprotective, who had raised him as her favorite, her "golden boy." The whole family entertained the highest expectations of him and had great hopes for his future. Up to that point, he had satisfied his mother's expectations by his achievements and excellent behavior. The father was a professional man who also doted on his son and made a point of being close to him. The brother was much less involved with the family. Both parents were very much invested in the son's becoming a physician. The patient had always been a model child. He remembered his childhood as a good experience. He was a bit of a loner and never very close to any of his classmates.

He had two important memories from childhood. The first was his playing with a marionette and in a moment of frustration shaking it so hard that he "killed it"; the other was when he fantasized himself as Tom Sawyer and set out to find a girlfriend. He selected a girl and experienced tremendous feeling for her, but never approached her in any manner. He seemed, by far, more invested in wanting the same feelings of love and freedom Tom had felt. Tom was an orphan, not encumbered by parents; he could devote himself to an adventurous life of constant mischief far removed from the restrictive and obsessive world in which Paul's parents lived.

Paul felt he had never been involved in the outside world and perceived going to medical school as his entering "THE WORLD." In that world, one had to take care of oneself, compete constantly, and be in charge of peoples' lives (which meant one could kill them). Furthermore, one had to have real sex (intercourse) instead of just "making out" or exaggerating about how much sex one was having. For him, real sex meant the possibility of killing the woman, "like a marionette."

The treatment revealed a profound fear and hatred of women and of their power to engulf him and dominate him. He traced this fear to his mother, who had been greatly idealized by the family, in particular by the father. The father described the mother in adoring terms, claiming she was "snow-white pure, a true angel."

But the treatment revealed another side of the mother. She could be extremely sweet, but, if things did not go her way, she could be aloof and removed or, suddenly, she could go into a rage, furiously calling Paul a "dirty bastard." In those moments, which he dreaded, she would turn, in his words, "from an angel into a demon." On those occasions, he would be terrified of her and, as he learned during the treatment, furious with her but unable to recognize it. Instead, he found himself having frightening thoughts of smashing things or killing people. The thoughts always frightened him and he was able to see that he had had them since he was a little boy. He made sense of his memory of "killing" the marionette by linking the destruction of his toy in a moment of irritation with his then unconscious murderous wishes.

Much discussion went into Paul's discovering the murderous desires he had for his mother and how he saw her death as the only means of his being free from her oppressive overprotection, her constant fear of his being harmed or getting sick. He felt his mother had "squashed" him and "loved him to death." On the other hand, he felt that his father was his only source of affection, and he was terrified that if he left home, he would lose his relationship with his father. The clinging feelings included fear and revenge because he remembered bitterly how many times he had wished to go out on his own, to be adventurous like Tom Sawyer, and his parents had forbidden him to do what he wanted.

He improved in the course of the treatment and finally was able to go out with girls and, with much fear, even kissed one. His fear of syphilis did not return in its original form, but expressed itself as anxiety each time he focused his vision on a word that started with "s." He had to read those words as quickly as possible, making sure that he did not spend extra time in looking at them.

Paul's main phobia had not yet disappeared. He was still unable to look at his penis out of fear of finding a syphilitic lesion there. However, it was at this point in his treatment that he began for the first time to talk about genitals and how ugly they were; he became aware of how frightened he was of both female and male genitals. As for the male organ, he feared it could certainly kill the woman. He insisted that he was a big fellow and very strong and that he could kill a woman in the way he had killed the marionette when he let himself go as a child. He produced many sadistic fantasies of beating two or three people at the same time. It was not long before he could express how afraid he himself was of being killed or maimed.

At this point, he had a frightening dream.

> I am in the den of my house. There is a table whose top is supported by a single column. Around the column there is a snake coiled. I am not sure if the snake's head was at the top of the column or at the bottom. Next, I wanted to catch the snake which was now coiled around the table on the floor in front of me.[1] I wanted to catch it by the back of the head or the neck. If I could grab him there, he would be unable to turn his head and bite me. I may have been afraid of the snake wrapping around me and

> squeezing me or strangling me. My mother was present during this part of the dream. She was able to easily grab the snake in the way I wanted to. I wanted to grab the snake so it could not harm me. I may have made some timid and quickly withdrawn attempts. I was pretty sure I couldn't do it. When I looked at it again, it was moving aggressively toward my neck. With the snake near my neck, I became so frightened that I woke up.

Paul connected this dream with the fear of his mother's affection (squeezing and hugging and kissing him to death) and his fear of sexual intimacy, of killing and being killed. He realized how the penis is used to express love and affection and how afraid he was of it all. For the first time he was able to fantasize openly about intercourse, but was still afraid to talk about penetration.

This was a critical dream anticipating the disappearance of his phobia. He finally was able to look at his penis and later on to have intercourse with his girlfriend. The other phobic symptoms had already vanished. From this point on, the treatment focused more on the character problems of a severely obsessive personality.

We can consider this case as a medical school phobia. It has the descriptive characteristics of intense sadistic, murderous, and sexual wishes toward the parents, which filled Paul with anxiety, along with an intense need for parental protection. Mixed in his conflicts is the fear of his own impulse to remove the parents who had posed for so long as obstacles to his desires to be freed. The fear of syphilis protected Paul against killing or being killed by women. It also protected him against the threat of medical school and separation from his parents, because one cannot be a physician if one has syphilis.

Paul's illness was precipitated by his wishes and by his fear of growing up, leaving home and parents, and beginning to do now, with the approval of the parents, what was forbidden when he was a child, i.e., to go out into the world, to leave home, and to have sex. What, then, were the components of his intrapsychic conflict? As with Little Hans, hostility and sadism were the impulses central to the patient's pathology. Since childhood, he had wished his parents and his brother dead (he wanted to be an orphan like Tom Sawyer) and was convinced of his physical power to kill (he had "killed" the marionette). To protect himself against his wishes, he had submitted in docile obedience and had reinforced the defenses against his murderous desires with severe obsessive defenses: reaction formation, isolation of affect, rationalization, and repression.

Paul also had intense sadistic sexual impulses toward his mother: to murder her and punish, even kill, her in intercourse. These impulses were severely repressed and overcome by an intense idealization of a pure and angelic mother who had to be adored and whom he could not marry or with whom any expression or even feeling of anger was forbidden. Unconsciously, he had assumed that all these defensive maneuvers and his submission and renunciations would keep him protected forever; that his homosexual submission to his father would grant him the right to remain a child forever, protected by his father against any demand that would break the precarious psychic balance he had created for himself.

Before the phobia developed, Paul's minimal expressions of hostility, like those of Little Hans, did not create any major opposition from his parents or from his own conscience. His admission to medical school, however, forced his sadistic impulses to consciousness. Now he had to leave home, have sex, face the world and the grown-ups, and stop being a child—in short, he had to renounce the passive security which had reinforced the repression of his sadistic sexual and murderous impulses. Both impulses returned with full force to his consciousness.

In this case as well, previously repressed ideas "forced their way into consciousness." Repression gave way to intense murderous and sexually sadistic impulses. The patient's fear of looking at his penis—the murderous organ—protected him against further awareness of his rage against destructive women. The fear of syphilis protected him against full awareness of his situation, i.e., the feeling of being betrayed by his parents and the concomitant murderous anger toward them. The phobia was an expression of the fear of the punishment he deserved for his impulses, as well as protection against the threat of having to leave home. Admission to medical school threatened to force him out of the passive security which had reinforced the repression. This disruption became the obstacle to be overcome by his aggression.

PHOBIA: A MODEL FOR UNDERSTANDING ITS FORMATION

A phobia is a symptom indicating intrapsychic conflict. The manifest affect dominating the symptom is fear. The situation or thing feared is not dynamically significant in itself, but as an object of symbolic displacement and an externalization of an intolerable mental conflictual content. The phobia is a compromise formation that makes this psychic situation relatively more tolerable. The components of the compromise are simultaneously contradictory motivations: to obtain an object of libidinal or narcissistic investment and to avoid the intrapsychic danger posed by its attainment. The creation of the phobia provides safety in this situation, which has been assessed as dangerous, by displacing and externalizing one of the conflictual contents. The dangers against which the phobia defends are castration, loss of the object, loss of love, or loss of self-esteem. As a generalization, we could say that these are dangers which threaten to disturb the state of well-being. We could conceptualize these dangers as presenting an obstacle to the maintenance of well-being in terms of body narcissism, object attachment, secondary narcissism, and ego-superego equilibrium.

Although the phobic symptom may include the avoidance of particular situations and things, the phobic structure does not include any external action on the part of the individual. Even when reality may pose some threat to the phobic individual should one of the forbidden wishes be expressed, this is not the significant danger. The dangers which contribute to the formation of a phobia are entirely intrapsychic.

Our understanding of aggression in its role in the formation of a phobia requires that the aggression in question be viewed not only as the effort to overcome an external obstacle, whether person, thing, or situation, but more particularly as an effort required to overcome internal psychic obstacles. In ordinary psychoanalytic language, this activity is involved in the organization of psychic defenses. The aggressive nature of the defenses was graphically illustrated by Anna Freud (1936) when she described the appearance of resistance to following the fundamental rule: "This means that the inroad of the id into the ego has given place to a counter-attack by the ego upon the id" (p. 14). The intrapsychic battle is set out: "Were it not for the intervention of the ego or of those external forces which the ego represents, every instinct would know only one fate—that of gratification" (p. 47).

In our view, aggression comes into play only at that point at which an action or state of psychic equilibrium, which is otherwise naturally, easily, or comfortably effected, is inhibited, impeded, or otherwise counteracted by an obstacle. Any of the mental processes of ordinary mentation, from an image to a thought or fantasy, to an impulse, or to some form of motivation, can serve as an obstacle. Thus the role of aggression in the formation of defenses generally may take the form of creating or imposing a barrier or a countering mechanism to the unimpeded expression of an instinctual drive, or to the free imposition of superego standards, prohibitions, or punishments, or to the conscious acknowledgment of a dreaded (fantasized or real) interpersonal situation. Such a defense mechanism is aggressive, in our view, insofar as it is called into play when the unimpeded expression of the drive or other psychic force would create an obstacle or impediment to other psychic aims or objectives (usually, but not exclusively, associated with the ego). In this sense Hans's impulse to hurt his father, motivated by the need to eliminate the obstacle the father posed to Hans's libidinal desires for his mother, interfered with and posed an obstacle to his loving attachment to his father. The defensive displacement of his impulse from his father onto the horse involved the use of aggression in order to overcome this latter obstacle, which carried with it the threat of the loss of the father or his love. Aggression, by the same token, can also come into play when an additional degree of effort or intensity is required for the drive to gain expression or attain its object. In the face of a defensive barrier, whether repressive or otherwise, an additional degree of intensity or effort may be mobilized as a consequence of motivation to overcome the defensive obstacle and gain satisfaction.

This description suggests that aggression is frequently at work in ordinary psychic life. In normal circumstances it operates silently and unobtrusively, aiming at maintaining adequate psychic satisfaction. Aggression becomes overt and behaviorally obvious when the obstacle posed to some motivation requires overt action on external objects. However, aggression may be neither overt nor behaviorally obvious, as in the case of phobic symptom formation.

In view of these considerations, a phobia may be conceptualized as the final result of a series of defensive maneuvers to overcome a situation in which incompatible needs or wishes and their anticipatory fantasized actions can be neither resolved nor renounced. Each wish, and its derivatives, poses an obstacle to the fulfillment of the opposing wishes. In the above example, Paul's wish to be passively dependent was set in opposition to his destructive wish to hurt and destroy women. The passive side created an obstacle to any more assertive adulthood; the destructive wishes prevented his comfortable passivity and dependency.

Alternatively, one obstacle posed by one wish is overcome by the first level of defense, the repression of the idea. Repression is at the service of preventing representational awareness, which, once achieved, requires that the represented satisfaction be obtained, compelling the subject to act. This conscious representation becomes in and of itself an obstacle. To remove it, aggression draws on the defensive maneuver of repression. The other side of the wish brings the repressed material back to consciousness.

The next level of defense is the disguise of the idea by displacement onto an apparently innocent object. The wish persists and reappears in relation to the object of displacement, which now has to be avoided. The defenses do not work properly because the ambivalent nature of the wish does not permit full repression. Each new aggressive-defensive move against a wish that, in its present form, cannot be renounced and therefore has become a new obstacle creates the need for further aggressive internal action to overcome the obstacle which refuses to disappear. Finally, a significant portion of the life of the individual has to be constricted to keep the intrapsychic dangers repressed and to substitute for them a more tolerable and manageable external threat.

The analysis of the role of aggression in conflict and defense with regard to phobia formation deals primarily with conflicts of defense. The same analysis may not be equally applicable to all contexts of conflict, e.g., conflicts of ambivalence (Kris, 1984). Conflicts of ambivalence involve divergent rather than convergent opposites and are resolved through mourning rather than through aggressive action. In such conflicts, aggression would not be involved in the internal dynamics of the conflict as such. The conflict may pose an obstacle to other objectives, e.g., resistance to free association, and may thus elicit an aggressive response.

We can point to certain advantages to our conceptualization of the psychic formation of a phobia. It permits a developmental and dynamic understanding of the vicissitudes and interplay of contradictory needs and the progressive and aggressively (in our terms) motivated defensive efforts aimed at maintaining psychic balance and self-protection. This approach may offer a basis for meeting Anna Freud's wish to understand the role of aggression in development and character structure formation.

In phobia formation, the symptom emerges as the result of a progressive narrowing of choices, forcing the individual to resort to condensation and externalization as final defenses (after attempts at regression, repression, reversal, projection, and displacement). These two defenses condense in a particular object or circumstance the motivation to fulfill a variety of unmanageable wishes and to locate them external to the self. In this way, even when the phobia elicits intense anxiety, the sense of self is protected and self-equilibrium may be maintained.

Another advantage of our view is that it facilitates establishing connections between the representational world of objects and the obstacles posed by their original real or imaginary qualities to awareness of and action based on internally experienced wishes. This concept of phobia formation gains in motivational, circumstantial, and object specificity what is missing from a theory of aggression as a biological drive.

Chapter 9

The Role of Aggression in Sadomasochism[1]

INTRODUCTION

A person who enjoys hurting a loved object is, by definition, sadistic. The individual's hurtful actions, hostile words, destructive and humiliating behaviors, and their accompanying affect of satisfaction, led Freud and present-day psychoanalysts to conceive of sadism as a manifestation of an aggressive instinct or drive. One consequence of our revision of the understanding of aggression is that it requires a distinction between on the one hand sadism and masochism, regarded as affective and motivational states, and on the other the aggressive capacity. In this sense, sadomasochism may or may not involve aggression, but the determining influences have to do with the circumstances and meaning of the behavior and its relevant context, not with anything inherent in sadistic or masochistic actions themselves. The motivational understanding of sadism also proposes a core unconscious fantasy operative in the complex sadistic psychic activities and external behaviors.

We will review the classic theory of sadomasochism, specifically as expressing aggressive drive components and dynamics—a view connecting sadomasochism to aggression as one of the specific vicissitudes of the aggressive drive. We will also briefly consider more contemporary modifications of the classical theory that have moved closer to the view we are proposing.[2] We will then consider three clinical cases in which the implications of this shift in psychoanalytic perspective regarding sadomasochism and its relation to aggression are exemplified, and conclude with some specific conclusions concerning our view of the role of aggression in sadomasochistic clinical contexts.

TRADITIONAL AND CONTEMPORARY THEORIES[3]

The terms "sadism" and "masochism" were coined by a professor of psychiatry at the University of Vienna, Richard von Kraft-Ebing (1840–1902). Kraft-Ebing's groundbreaking *Psychopathia Sexualis* (1886) described with detailed case reports all sexual perversions. He had found sadism and masochism, well described as human sexual behaviors and desires, in the fictional writings of the Marquis de Sade and Leopold Sacher-Masoch, whose names became for Kraft-Ebing synonymous with sexual pathologies that find excitement and satisfaction in either inflicting or suffering pain, humiliation, and submission. His vivid case histories were descriptive, but offered no motivational basis to explain these perversions.

Freud appropriated Kraft-Ebing's terms and introduced significant theoretical modifications in them. His first mention of the terms is in *The Interpretation of Dreams* (1900): "There is a masochistic component in the sexual constitution of many people, which arises from the reversal of an aggressive, sadistic component into its opposite. Those who find their pleasure, not in having 'physical' pain inflicted on them, but in humiliation and mental torture, may be described as 'mental masochists'" (p. 159). Freud had extended the concepts of sadism and masochism from applying to desires and behaviors of some sexually perverted individuals to the "sexual constitution" of many; he had introduced the notion of reversal as a transformational mechanism, and enlarged the concepts to encompass mental suffering alone. This sliding of meaning from the original significance given to the terms by Kraft-Ebing was to continue in Freud's own theorizing and in the work of present-day theoreticians to the point that sadism and masochism remain confusing terms in psychoanalytic vocabulary (Maleson, 1984). The blurring of the terms' meaning stems from the different theoretical levels Freud used to conceptualized them: metapsychological, developmental, structural, and mental dynamics as represented by the core fantasies which he made explicit for masochism but left undescribed for sadism.

Metapsychologically, Freud linked sadism and masochism to the aggressive drive, at times fused with the sexual drives, at others separated from it. Early on, Freud (1915) considered sadism as primary, as aggression directed against an object, and masochism as the turning of aggression upon the self. Later, after the introduction of the death instinct, he postulated a primary masochistic impulse preceding sadism and contrary to the pleasure principle (Freud, 1920, 1924). Since Freud conceived of drives as continually active, by implication sadistic and masochistic impulses must be continuously present at a certain level of the psyche. Developmentally, they appear most obviously in some psychic organizations such as oral-sadistic and anal-sadistic phases of development, while they are less visibly present in other psychic levels of organization, particularly in the polarities of passivity-activity so directly linked in Freud's thinking to masochism and sadism. The superego may sadistically oppose the ego's libidinal wishes and place the ego in a masochistic situation. The aggressive instinct, mediated by the identification with the parental imagos, may exert its sadism upon the submissive ego (Freud, 1923). Dynamically, the mediation of fantasy life, in particular sadomasochistic fantasies, can organize the internal scenes of sexual desire and satisfaction. For Freud, the prototypical masochistic fantasy was that of being beaten (Freud, 1919a).

Most psychoanalytic writers have not challenged the metapsychological connection between the aggressive drive and the complex psychic and interpersonal interactions elicited by the interconnections of the pair sadism-masochism. Many studies have enlarged the applications and implications of sadomasochistic derivatives, as Freud himself did in relation to the structural theory (Freud, 1924). Maleson (1984) pointed out that "wishes to desexualize the term (when not used to denote manifest perversion) have in large part been an outgrowth of approaches made from the standpoints of ego and superego analysis, object relations theory, and studies of narcissistic and aggressive vicissitudes" (p. 332), perspectives made possible by Freud's 1923 and 1926 theoretical revisions, which in the end confuse the meaning of the term even more by intermingling levels of abstraction of many conceptualizations.

The traditional psychoanalytic approach to sadomasochism, whether as perversion or character trait, tends to link aggression and sadomasochism, preserving the original connection in Freud's early formulations. The perversion thus took the form of deriving sexual pleasure from inflicting pain or humiliation on another person (sadism), or having pain or humiliation inflicted on oneself by another (masochism), and these were even regarded as nonneurotic aspects of sexual foreplay (Freud, 1905b): "The sexuality of most male human beings contains an element of aggressiveness—a desire to subjugate; the biological significance of it seems to lie in the need for overcoming the resistance of the sexual object by means other than the process of wooing" (pp. 157–58)—a view echoed more currently by Kernberg (1991). The sadistic components, in the form of physical abuse, torture, rape, or other ways of inflicting pain or humiliating the love object, were regarded as forms of aggression thought to be fused with libido. Freud (1915) originally regarded sadism as primary, masochism secondarily deriving from sadism by turning the aggression against the self, but later reversed the sequence, postulating, along with the death instinct, a primary masochistic impulse (Freud, 1920, 1924).

Subsequent applications broadened the implications and applications of sadomasochistic derivatives. Reik (1941), for one, attributed perverse gratification not so much to the experience of pain itself as to other motivations of victory, power, and self-assertion that introduced greater complexity to the motivational substructure of sadomasochism and gave greater play to defensive aspects. Blum (1995) also noted the combining of defensive and adaptive functions in these configurations, and the compensatory character of fantasy reversals— "the vulnerable child becomes the invulnerable hero or irresistible heroine" (p. 43). These developments of the theory soon found further application to the analytic situation. Menaker (1942) focused on dependence and submission of the analysand to the analyst as expressions of a masochistic attitude, and correspondingly, the relative assumption of dominance, power, and authority by the analyst as sadistic.[4] The analyst, in these terms, is thus put in the sadistic position of dominance, while the analysand falls into a masochistic position of dependence and submission. She also broadened the implications of masochism by recognizing other hidden gratifications, and by connecting it with defensive and, particularly, self-preservative functions of the ego (Menaker, 1953).

These same components could take the form of character traits, based on sadomasochistic wishes, daydreams, fantasies, drive derivatives, ranging from the perverted to the relatively normal (Blum, 1995; Brenner, 1959). Conscious and unconscious gratifications can be found in a variety of behaviors—sarcasm, teasing, joking, and passive-aggressive behavior—in addition to sexual activity. These traits and behaviors were regarded as representing blended derivatives of libidinal and aggressive drives in varying degrees that become sadistic when directed against objects and masochistic when directed against the self. In all these forms of sadomasochistic expression, the part attributed to aggression pertains to the wish to hurt, humiliate, or cause pain to another—all destructive and damaging in tone and intent and driven by a biologically based and inherently destructive impulse. The theory we are proposing calls for a very different emphasis; insofar as we view aggression as nonhostile and nondestructive, the hostile aspects of sadism are not specific to aggression, but require other motivational components for explanation.

Berliner, in a series of articles (1940, 1947, 1958) focusing on the consequences of internalization of painful object relations for formation of the masochistic character, proposed that traumatic oedipal relations with a parent who hates and acts sadistically toward the child are causative prerequisites for formation of masochistic character. The child will submit and "accept the hatred as if it were love" (1940, p. 326) and "introject the hostile object in order to save it as a love object" (1940, p. 327). The self-destructive impulses, then, are not those of sadism turned against the self, but the internalization of the destructive impulses of the hating love object. The aggression directed against the self is that of the love object. The sadism of the masochist results from the identification with the sadism of the love object. The sadism against others is merely identification with the sadistic object and his or her actions. For Berliner what is primary is the search for parental (or other) love, not sadism or masochism (1958). He concluded that "masochism is the hate or the sadism of the object reflected in the libido of the subject" (1947, p. 461). Sadism is not primary (1940, p. 32), the search for love is (1958, p. 46). Aggression may appear as unconscious hostility stemming from the hatred of a hating object. Aggression may take the form of insisting on obtaining love from the object at any price, even if more suffering is inflicted. This position anticipates one aspect of the theory of aggression we are proposing, that is, the urgency implied in certain psychically intended actions to achieve their goal, which, in Berliner's understanding of sadism and masochism, is parental love. The obstacle in this case, in our view, would be the inability to obtain that love.

Brenner (1959) saw in diverse manifestations such as sarcasm, teasing, joking, passive-aggressive behaviors, and sexual involvements the blended derivatives of the sexual and aggressive drives organized as character traits with their respective sadomasochistic fantasies, wishes, and overt sexual enactment in the case of a perverse character. The hurtful components of the character are derived from the biologically and inherently destructive aggressive drive.

Other more recent reconsiderations of aggression have attempted to divorce aggression from drive theory, but tend to preserve the classical perspective linking aggression with threat or danger. Grossman (1991) considers developmental sources of sadomasochistic phenomena to include many factors; the decisive factor, however, is "whether the aggression is turned against the self because of love, fear of object loss, or threat from a feared, powerful person or, instead, because these dangers have been internalized" (p. 35). Thus, actual relations with an object are involved in the control of the aggression and its turning against the self. But we would question the model of turning aggression inward to explain masochism. In our view, what is turned inward is the hostile or sadistic intent displaced from the sadistic object. The masochistic stance is a form of denial of any hurtful motives—adopting the victim posture becomes a way of denying, defending against, or minimizing one's own hurtful or sadistic motivation. Better to be a suffering victim than a hurtful victimizer. Any hurtful intent is thus disavowed and the only hurtful components remain with the sadistic victimizer. Aggression may play no role in this configuration at all.

The consequence of our theorizing for the understanding of sadism and masochism is that it does not require the postulation of an aggressive drive to explain the motivational and affective sources of sadomasochistic acts and fantasies. The determining influences for aggression become linked to the motivational and affective components of sadomasochistic instances depending on the role of obstacles and the stimulus conditions of the circumstances at the moment when the behaviors occur.

Sadism appears, in this manner of theorizing, not merely as intrapsychic or external activities elicited by the added psychic effort to overcome obstacles—this would be aggression in our view. The modalities and dynamics of sadistic behaviors, fantasies, and wishes are determined by other complex and multidetermined motivational sources. The aggressive component of any sadistic behavior concerns only that added effort required to overcome the resistance of the obstacle. In the background of those multilayered motivational processes, in strictly intrapsychic terms, there seems to exist in sadism an internal obstacle, namely, profound self-doubts about being lovable and acceptable as an object. Most sadistic behaviors and wishes represent efforts to overcome this insurmountable internal obstacle that often takes the form of a firm conviction. The intrapsychic situation created by this internal obstacle calls to action, in moments of proportional intrapsychic or interpersonal stimulation, the intervention of the biologically rooted aggressive capability to carry out external or internal actions aimed at overcoming this obstacle. The person uses whatever means he deems necessary to obtain what is desired from objects at hand or attempts to force the objects to give it. The repetition of sadistic actions and fantasies is only a measure of the continuous but ineffective effort to overcome such internal obstacles.

CLINICAL CASES

Case 1

Mrs. S illustrates the psychic situation of a person whose sadistic fantasies complement her masochistic behavior. She is a person incapable of saying no regardless of what is demanded of her. The only exception to this inability appears when the request conflicts with her moral standards and she finds herself in conflict with her principles and beliefs. Even in such a circumstance her capacity for fine discernment of moral situations gets narrowed by an almost automatic submission to introjected parental imperatives. Her compliance is carried out in a cheerful disposition with the feeling that she can do it. Examples of this behavior rank from sexual submission to instantaneous compliance with the request of a superior or friend. If she is dating, as soon as the man suggests that he wants to have intercourse, she begins to disrobe, even if the place and circumstances are not appropriate for the act. In this manner she has found herself having sexual relations in public buildings, parks, cars, and friends' homes. If someone asks her for money, a book, or food, she gives it at once. As a result of this behavior, she is always greatly overworked and running to replace what she has given to others. What is most noteworthy about her behavior is the mood in which she carries it out. She is there and at the same time not there. Her attitude is cheerful and cooperative. She claims she enjoys very much what she is doing and not infrequently she volunteers her availability, if she assumes the other person wants her. In spite of this visible, almost manic, offering of her person, people around her complain that, even when she does well what they ask her to do, they sense she is not fully involved. Her lovers reproach her that she is not present during intercourse, despite her explicit orgasmic response. Her boss claims he has a very good worker, but that he feels there is something missing in their working relationship.

Her fantasy life is another matter. Frequently during intercourse and while masturbating, she imagines herself bent over a file cabinet, while several very excited men wait in line to penetrate her vaginally from behind. She cannot see their faces and she has to submit passively to their sexual act. She is forced to do it. They would not allow her to move. She seems to be mistreated, but in the fantasy she enjoys the men's actions. In fact, her orgasm responds to that moment in the fantasy rather than to her sexual activity at the moment. At times she enacted some of these behaviors with a lover. She would ask the lover to pin her down and to make believe he was forcing himself on her. At other moments she would ask him to tie her down with a rope as a "joke," something he did reluctantly several times. She had orgasms in these experiences without the help of the fantasies.

The analysis uncovered that, together with the masochistic components of her behavior and of her fantasies, there were sadistic fantasies and behaviors that had not been previously available to her. She remembered destroying her toys and books as a latency child during moments of great frustration with her parents. At other times she destroyed furniture or her parents' wall pictures and porcelains. She recalled fantasies of wishing for her rival classmates' deaths, and feeling both joy and remorse when one of them died in a car accident. Finally the analysis brought to light her wishes to kill the analyst, beating him up or penetrating him with a knife. She laughed with pleasure, imagining the fright of the analyst while she was killing him. After the prolonged analysis of several of these fantasies, the patient concluded that she was greatly enraged and had been covering up her rage with her submissive and cheerful disposition. The origins of the rage were traced to the intense fear of her extremely strict and overdemanding parents, in particular her mother, and their persistent demand that she never be afraid of anything. Both parents had defined themselves as special human beings, quite superior to their neighbors in every aspect. Part of their superiority was to indicate that ordinary pain did not make them suffer. Such a philosophy of life prompted the father to beat the children on their bare bottoms and legs with a leather strap, while requiring that they did not cry.

In retrospect, Mrs. S grew up in a situation in which she was constantly required to carry out immediately and without protest the excessive and exhausting demands of her parents. She experienced hostile and destructive wishes toward them that had to be suppressed and repressed. To obey she had to use isolation of affect, repression of her better judgment, as well as reaction formation manifested in her cheerful disposition. The joint working of these defenses, creating her pattern of automatic obedience, worked, up to a point. In moments of excessive stress, her hostile and murderous wishes became uncontrollable, prompting her to destroy objects precious to her parents as a displacement of the wish to destroy them. She also felt affection for her parents that was directly linked to the shared family pride of being superior to everyone in their community. She identified with their narcissistic stance and felt her own narcissism enhanced when, in obeying, she became like them, a superior being. As a result, she had a pathological attachment to them, a mixture of masochistic submission to their control together with a secret hope that, if she controlled herself well enough, they would love her. Deep in her heart, she was terribly afraid that only her actions, not herself, could elicit any affection. Thus her cheerful disposition was the false-self facade covering up intense wishes for personal recognition and powerful wishes to destroy, to rid herself of her parents. As a child she fantasized being a *free* orphan.

When the beatings by her father began, at latency, the psychological domination her parents had exerted upon her became libidinized. There was a secret sexual pleasure, connected to childhood fantasies about violent sexual relations, in being pinned down and beaten by her father. There was also a tremendous rage and wish to kill him that had to be repressed at all cost. The prohibition against crying or complaining facilitated not only the isolation of affect but also a state of being absent from herself to avoid awareness of the simultaneous experiences of pleasure and murderous rage. For her, the best revenge toward her parents was not to be fazed by anything. This, she felt, was the greatest triumph she ever had. It made her superior to them. In the end, therefore, her greatest, and most hidden, pleasure, never separated from concrete reality and actual effective work, was to be master of it all, the one who had the final power, even if it was at the cost of not having room to be herself.

The raging battle between parents and child created obstacle upon obstacle. Their demands became an obstacle to her wish to have parents who attended to her. Hostile and destructive wishes appeared aiming at overcoming the obstacle posed by the parents' constant demands. These wishes had to be immediately repressed out of the double fear of losing the objects and of being punished. However, the hostility also became an obstacle in itself, because continual stimulation of persistent parental demands required an additional defensive shift, the affective dissociation and automatization of obedience, which became her dominant masochistic trait. The masochistic submission, however, implied a sadistic narcissistic triumph, of being superior and never fazed by anything. In this way she had power over them—a Pyrrhic victory, but a significant one with respect to her narcissistic equilibrium.

Case II

Mr. G is forty years old, single, and quite successful as a freelance cartoonist. His work combines a superb sense of humor, artistic skill, and a sharp intellect. He has been in continuous psychotherapy once to twice a week since graduating from college, i.e., for eighteen years. Despite being quite intelligent and unusually in touch with his feelings, he has remained resistant to any deeper form of treatment. Insight means little to him. He does, however, care very much about the support he receives from his therapist, and in that context he can be thoughtful about his feelings and his behavior, with some benefit. His feelings of hopelessness, depression, and rage are of such intensity and duration as to cause him frequent and intense suicidal preoccupations and urges. He believes he would long since have killed himself were it not for his therapist's concern and help.

He was an only child and suffered a marked learning disability, one that he continues to cope with. In grade school he was thought to be mildly retarded, but in high school his actual brilliance began to be recognized when teachers became aware of his relative disability in mathematics and science. Physically he was awkward as a child and not popular. His mother felt deeply sorrowful about his disability and his painful awareness that he did not fit in with other children. She tried to make up for it by showing him that she loved him deeply, seemingly exclusively, and she thought him wonderful in every way.

They were very close. He grasped hold of his mother's view and feelings toward him and never let them go, even though as he grew older he found that he truly was not by any means the utterly superior boy, then man, that his mother believed him to be. In fact, he saw himself as a pitiful failure. So his belief about himself became unstable, ricocheting between the irreconcilable extremes of shameful, hopeless disability and innate greatness.

His father was a gruff, utterly self-centered businessman who talked with his son only about his own prowess and his son's being well advised to try to follow in his footsteps. When displeased with his son or under the impression that punishment was in order, he descended on him with powerful criticism and physical abuse. The patient hated his father from early on, becoming conscious in midchildhood of wanting to kill him. At the same time he loved his father and could not give up on the possibility that his father might somehow come to appreciate him.

In his late adolescence and adult life sadism and masochism were interwoven in his relationships with women. Despite active dating and unceasing efforts to find a woman to love and be loved by, no romantic relationship came close to working out. Women found him humorous and conversationally engaging, but they could not sense any capacity for deeper emotional relating on an enduring basis. Furthermore, he was very critical of the women who might have been willing to make a life with him. He tended to overwhelm women with his humor and sharpness, as well as with the intensity with which he pursued them. The same qualities pervaded his sexual efforts with them. He was accomplished at getting women to give in to his sexual advances despite their initial protests, and he was equally accomplished at providing intense and prolonged genital stimulation. They generally responded afterwards with objections that he had overwhelmed them, and he never understood that their intense pleasure did not mitigate their feeling of being violated.

His direct sadism took the form of convincing many women to allow him to tie them to the bed, thus submitting to a condition of even greater helplessness in response to his stimulating them. But he did not carry out this activity to the full extent of his wishes. His fantasy was to prolong the stimulation, with the use of objects such as feathers, to the point of driving the woman into a state of sexual anguish. But he often did stimulate them into multiple orgasms beyond their endurance, not stopping when they more or less begged him to.

Another form of sadism found expression in his window peeking. His need to engage in this activity was for years beyond his control. He would stake out the bedroom windows of various women, some of whom he dated, masturbating while watching them undress. In the process he experienced having power over the women, a power they could do nothing about because they did not even know they were being used sexually.

His sexual sadism was inextricably combined with masochism in that he always felt that he was shunned by the women, found to be lacking, even laughed at. Reality gave little support to these feelings, except that no woman persisted in wanting a relationship with him. Their refusals of dates or not returning his calls were grounds for intense feelings of rejection, being made a fool of, and being found out as sexually ineffective. Episodes of impotence reinforced these feelings and fantasies. He yearned deeply for their sexual favor, and he hated them deeply for not receiving it. Among the most masochistic of his experiences were his peeking through windows to witness sexual intercourse, feeling greatly stimulated but not masterful, instead feeling left out, humiliated, while the other man triumphed in virtue of the woman's ecstasy in giving herself over to him.

Associations and dreams convinced the therapist that Mr. G's sexual sadomasochism was rooted in the intensity of his oedipal conflicts. He was uninterested in all efforts to work therapeutically to gain insight, and he remained unaware of his sexual interest in his mother. But he clearly was devoted to her as the most wonderful woman in his life—pretty, intelligent, and kind. By contrast, his macho oaf of a father held no reason for gaining his respect. He found him intrusive and emotionally stupid. Yet his parents got along well, were a real couple in love. He could not make sense of this.

It was in relation to his father that another facet of his sadomasochism was lived out. He was more or less continually at war with the world and the fates that frustrated him. A policeman stopping him for speeding, a salesman who presented an unreasonable attitude of nonhelpfulness, an auto mechanic who failed to fix the problem with his car, and all others who similarly bothered him were experienced as part of an overall program to "fuck him over." He was not psychotic, but he experienced fantasies of this sort as if he believed them. He pitched into them with fervor because they fit his sense of himself and what life was destined to be for him. When his body was afflicted, e.g., when he injured his knee or broke his ankle in athletic endeavors, he experienced it as "God is fucking me." In frenzies he would rage, "Go ahead, God, fuck me some more!" Often he would accompany these outbursts by motioning in the direction of his anus. By himself, he would accompany his rages with violence toward his possessions, once smashing his car window, another time kicking a bureau drawer to pieces. With store clerks and others who had the misfortune of frustrating him, he would begin shouting, creating a scene, while cleverly putting them on the defensive so that they would try to mollify him by acceding to his wishes. Thus he repetitiously lived out his murderous rage toward his father, while simultaneously experiencing himself as the masochistic victim of his father's sexual assaults. This insight was eventually achieved through associations to his father, finally with recovery of his memory of childhood rages at his father in which he would, when by himself, shout out, "God, I hate you God, fuck you God!" He was able to understand that he used the frustrations of everyday reality to feel abused so as to unleash his pent-up fury.

While his pathology was extreme and insight quite limited, Mr. G had many strengths and successes, and he steadfastly managed to avoid using the therapist in a sadomasochistic transference. He held on to the therapist and the therapy as his only hope for survival and a resource for somehow improving his life. In a limited way he did achieve considerable modification of his sadomasochism, though it remains a potential for disrupting his life, given any precipitating misfortune.

When Mr. G began his treatment, he fit the description of the "exceptional" patient provided by Freud (1916). In his immature narcissistic and oedipal fixation, his need was to maintain his sexualized narcissistic image of himself. While reality presented frustrations to achieving this, the most important obstacle was internal in the form of narcissistic depletion, an inner depletion that has intensified with successive years of nonsuccess. This inner narcissistic depletion was founded in the innate disabilities that were apparent from an early time in his life. In addition, Mr. G's mother misled him into thinking of himself as especially gifted (thus betraying his trust in her); furthermore, reality inevitably cruelly countered his illusion, and his father subjected him to abusive humiliation.

Mr. G's sadomasochism was a response to his need to maintain a sexualized narcissistic image of himself. In identification with his internal image of his sadistic, dominating, self-centered father, he conducted his own grandiose behaviors in abusing and intimidating others. He extended his efforts for omnipotence and oedipal triumph and revenge through his sadistic sexual practices and window peeking. In identification with his mother's passive acceptance of the father's behavior, he submitted himself to all the injuries dealt by reality, defining them as God's fucking him. In this, too, he rescued his sexualized grandiosity through experiencing himself as the object of God's special sexual attentions.

He began his therapy wanting treatment but not insight, placing the whole therapeutic burden of not killing himself on his therapist's caring for him. In this way, from the beginning, he was able to make the therapist his victim. However, since the therapist did not put an obstacle to being cast in this role, in accordance with our understanding of aggression in the analytic situation, no aggression was involved despite the unconscious hostility and control expressed by the patient in this victimization. The patient's mother compensated for the narcissistic injury of his learning disability and awkwardness by exalting his value and telling him he was wonderful, rather than helping him deal with his defectiveness. He accepted this narcissistic illusion of grandiosity. Thus the obstacle posed to his narcissistic equilibrium by his disability was overcome by compensatory grandiosity. As such, the employment of grandiosity can be seen here as serving the aggressive purpose of overcoming that obstacle. But this aggressive defense never worked well because his sense of inferiority reappeared with any occasion that put him to the test, even if it was only a policeman with a traffic ticket.

His remaining very close to the mother, who provided the narcissistic compensation, also failed to remove the obstacle of his feeling inferior with women. He could fascinate and overwhelm them with his humor, sharpness, and sexual excess, but could not relate to them or convince himself that he was an adequate male. To deal with this terrible inferiority, he had to employ a compulsive and barely controllable need to be the greatest possible sexual stimulator for the woman regardless of her suffering. So for him the woman was simultaneously an obstacle to his sexual narcissistic equilibrium (which depended on grandiosity) as well as an opportunity to reestablish his equilibrium by overcoming the obstacle she posed. This he accomplished by placing her at the service of his sadistic compulsion to control her—the obstacle—by subjecting her to excessive and overwhelming sexual stimulation and taking pleasure in her fruitless protestations and helpless erotic responses. Hence the obstacle posed by his sense of inferiority was overcome by these sadistic acts which served the purpose of convincing himself of his sexual powers.

The same dynamics of the obstacle of narcissistic vulnerability being fended off by aggressively overcoming the obstacle—in pairs of inferior-superior, powerless-powerful, impotent-hyperpotent, rejected-accepted—seem to apply to his window peeking and his relationship with his father. In his window peeking, the women were rendered helpless victims of his concealed power to vitiate their supposed sexual disregard for him. Despite the obstacles they were felt to pose, he triumphed in making them unwittingly serve his sexual pleasure. In this way, as a means of overcoming the obstacle, his window peeking is understood in our terms as aggressive. His father's nonrecognition and devaluation of him were experienced directly at the hands of the father and in displacement with anyone or any inanimate object that frustrated his narcissistic equilibrium. The narcissistic murderous rage elicited by moments of narcissistic depletion was expressed in displaced acting out with inanimate objects as well as in casual encounters.[5] The aggression aimed at overcoming these obstacles took the direct form of verbal and nonverbal hostile, controlling, often destructive actions, accompanied by murderous rage.[6]

Case III

Ann was first referred with her husband for couples therapy. Their marriage of fifteen years was in process of breaking up. They had three children, a boy and two girls. The patient was employed as a nurse—at the time head nurse in an ICU. Her husband was a successful lawyer. The problem in the marriage was that Ann's husband was a rather primitive borderline man who was abusive, demanding, and infantile—temper tantrums were common. He was unfriendly and antisocial even to the point of paranoia. When he lost his temper, he lashed out destructively—throwing food on the floor if he did not like it, breaking furniture, beating his wife, punishing the children severely for little or no offense, and so on. His behavior made life in the family a continual hell—no holiday was unspoiled, having any social life or friends was impossible, and the tension and resentment in the house were monumental. In addition, although he earned a salary in the six-figure range, he was stingy, refusing to buy even essential things for the house or the family. Ann was forced to use her own income to pay for the upkeep of the house, for food and clothing for herself and the children. The couples therapy did not last long; he could not tolerate the idea that he might be a contributor to the family problems in any way, and when it became clear that he would have to examine his own behavior, he refused to come.

In the process, it became clear to Ann how impossible and pathological her husband's behavior was and how her own pathology played into his sickness. Over the years she had submitted to his disruptive and infantile behavior without complaint or resistance, and had accepted this as her lot in life. Whatever effort she made, whatever degree of self-effacement and sacrifice, it was never enough to stem the tide of his precipitous rage and bizarre attitudes. The cost to her was a more or less chronic depression and a collection of obsessional anxieties and symptoms. She continued to see the analyst in weekly psychotherapy that was gradually intensified and finally converted to psychoanalysis.

Her own psychic life was a torment of depression riddled with intense anxieties. Almost everything she did was discolored by obsessional doubting and a sense of impending doom. These symptoms had come to the fore around the birth of each of her children. Over and above the depression, she was thrown into an agony of doubt and anxiety over caring for the infant. She was afraid of hurting the child, of dropping or drowning it, of making a mistake in feeding the baby, afraid of infecting the child in breastfeeding, poisoning it with bad milk from her breast, harming it psychologically by her handling or interaction with the child. If the child became ill, she suffered a paroxysm of anxiety and guilt, fearful that she had caused the illness, taking extreme precautions, obsessing over any medications that had to be given or other procedures the doctor might recommend. Visits to the pediatrician were occasions of soul-searching and agonized guilt, fears that she would be found to be inadequate, that she would be charged with being a bad mother who was doing damage to her children. All of these anxieties had to be dealt with by obsessional devices, rituals, endless checking and rechecking to make sure everything was in order, preoccupied cleaning and sterilizing. It was a wonder that she and the children survived at all.

She came by these traits honestly enough. She was raised in a small town, the oldest daughter in a family of four children—she had a younger brother and two younger sisters. Her father had a small business; he was a gruff, quiet man who never said much, never spent much time with the family, kept to himself, and devoted his efforts to the business. There was little capacity for enjoyment—the family took no vacations, never went anywhere to visit relatives or see anything. The father never took a day off; he worked from early in the morning until suppertime, many times working late. When he came home, he retreated behind his newspaper. There were times when he seemed to become even more negative and antagonistic to the world around him, almost paranoid. The result was that he had no friends, the family had no friends, and no social life.

Ann's mother was a paragon of masochism, not a quiet masochism since she complained noisily every step of the way. She never confronted her husband, crossed him, or complained to his face about the quality of life he imposed on the family. But she clearly suffered mightily from it, hated it, struggled with a murderous rage, and complained about and endlessly bemoaned her horrid fate to her oldest daughter. All through her years of growing up, Ann's parents lived a life of emotional separation. They slept in separate beds, sat in separate rooms, rarely spoke to each other. In the face of her mother's unending complaints, Ann enlisted as her mother's savior, the one who would bring joy into her mother's tortured existence. The cost was endless agony and anxiety. For example, since her mother was constantly threatening suicide, when Ann got on the school bus in the morning, she did not know whether she would find her mother facedown in a pool of blood when she got home in the afternoon. She could remember the anxious worry she carried with her through the day, and the apprehension, almost to the point of panic, that she felt as the bus approached her home. At the same time, the mother's praise and her constant refrain that she would be lost without her little angel were music to Ann's ears.

Ann's marriage choice was disastrous. She met her husband soon after graduating from nursing school. He was tall and handsome, on his way to a successful career. She fell in love, idealized him beyond all recognition, and was swept off her feet. She felt that this was her one and only chance, that no one would ever be interested in her again and that she had better grab at the opportunity; otherwise she was doomed to eternal spinsterhood. The marriage was difficult from the first. He resented her working, and when children came, he resented them as well. They took her time and attention, and cost him more money. He refused to involve himself in any of the childcare or childrearing. They were her responsibility, and as far as he was concerned, her job was to keep them out of his way. He insisted that she pay for their upkeep, and any extra expenses were the subject of endless complaints and at times explosions of temper.

In her analysis Ann came to an increasingly deeper understanding of her parents' pathology and how it affected her life. In her girlhood her father had been an object of admiration for his obvious intelligence and what she saw as his hardworking dedication. Gradually she saw how selfish, isolating, stingy, and rigid he had been. It began to dawn on her how similar he and her husband were. A sidelight to this issue was her difficulty in dealing with her then early adolescent son. He was failing in school, was recalcitrant and rebellious at home, and seemed headed toward a delinquent outcome. Ann felt helpless to deal with this situation. She could not set appropriate limits, and any limits she tried to set were easily abandoned or overridden. Ann came to see that she was creating a copy of her husband's pathology in her son. This realization horrified her and brought home the realization that if she did not change, she would be ruining her son's life as well. Much of the analytic work centered on her conflicts in dealing with this situation, on her difficulties in setting and reinforcing limits, on the elements that gained some hidden and unconscious gratification from her son's delinquent behavior. These disciplinary problems did not arise with her daughters; somehow Ann was better able to deal with them in a reasonable and effective way.

An identification with her father played a strong role in Ann's own personality. This became much clearer after the marriage broke up. Her husband left her with the custody of the children and refused to provide alimony and child-support payments. While he was on the scene, the blame could be laid at his door; but after he was gone, it became clear that there was a part of Ann that could not take time off, that found reasons to work extra hours and weekends, that could never find time for a vacation—all too reminiscent of her father. But Ann's identification with her mother was an even more powerful theme that overshadowed all others, especially with regard to her mother's masochism. Like her mother, she was the uncomplaining and self-sacrificing victim of a cruel fate. Suffering was for her an ideal, a noble expression of the human spirit. The idea of standing up for herself or of becoming assertive or aggressive on her own behalf was quite foreign to her mindset. Better to be the patiently suffering martyr than to take control of life and try to achieve a better outcome.

It was not difficult for her to see the pattern in her mother and how dramatically she carried it out in her own life. But it was only with great difficulty that she could acknowledge her rage at her mother. This came to light through an obsessional symptom. She began taking the precaution of washing her hands before writing a letter to her mother, afraid that some germ she might have contacted in the ICU would be transferred to the paper, would infect her mother and cause her death. Exploration of these "poison pen" letters led to recognition of these feelings and the aggressive conflicts involved in her depressive and masochistic stand. Her sense of herself as victim derived from the identification with her mother, reinforced by her defensive need to escape from the destructive and murderous wishes that reflected the power of her hostile impulses and wishes.

As these elements were clarified and worked through, Ann began to deal more effectively with her life and responsibilities. After picking her way through the difficulties of the divorce, she began to put together the pieces of her life. Her capacity to deal with the children, especially her son, improved considerably, and led to a striking change in the behavior of the children. The son settled down, completed high school, and was accepted at a good college, even though it wasn't Harvard. This was due in large measure to Ann's ability to take firm stands and set clear limits. Along the way Ann eased out of her depression, and for the first time began to see that she could find happiness and satisfaction. The quality of her work improved, particularly as the result of her gaining control of her tormenting obsessional worries over whether she had done something to her patients that would kill them or that she might have done something inadvertently that would cause her to be sued and her life ruined.

During much of the analysis, she suffered from severe depressive episodes usually related to some disappointment or painful emotional event that she could not face head-on. One such event was the occasional visit from her mother. Her mother's unending complaints, self-pity, and fault-finding attitudes would drive Ann to the point where she could not deal with her rage at her mother, and the outcome was usually depression. Another variety of precipitant was related to her difficulty tolerating painful feelings. For example, when her son was preparing to return to college at the end of the summer vacation, she became obsessed with the idea that he would have a heart attack and die. This threw her into a paroxysm of anxiety and anguish. She and the analyst decided that the real problem was that she could not tolerate the pain of the sadness at his leaving and the rage at him for abandoning her. It was easier to shift into an obsessional worry that some harm would come to him.

Ann's case, in addition to other aspects of this pathology, best exemplifies the intergenerational transmission of sadomasochistic traits based on parental identifications, particularly the intense neurotic attachment and identification between mother and daughter. The combination of her father's rather sadistic and paranoid orientation and her mother's intensely masochistic pattern carried over into the patient's own family and into her relations with her husband and children. She managed her intolerable and intense rage, manifested as barely repressed wishes to kill her mother and her children, by severely obsessional reaction formations and by adopting a persistently masochistic and victimized position. The intermingling of masochistic and narcissistic themes suggests the degree to which these patterns became adaptive and served basic defensive needs to mitigate and avoid the underlying rage. The dominant identification with the mother was primarily an identification with the masochist, serving to fend off hostile and destructive impulses, and taking the form of a pathological ego ideal carrying with it significant narcissistic rewards. The identification with the sadistic father played a minor but important role as part of a configuration disturbing to her ego ideal, thus prompting her to revert to the masochistic position.

SADOMASOCHISM IN REVISED PERSPECTIVE

Our intention in this chapter is to offer an understanding of sadomasochism that is opposed to an explanation based on the workings of an aggressive drive fused in various degrees with a libidinal drive as the determining source of character traits and behaviors. Instead we propose a motivational theory capable of encompassing developmental and dynamic processes, in which aggression is put in the service of overcoming intrapsychic, interpersonal, and external obstacles interposed between an intended psychic aim and its achievement. The aim may be the satisfaction of a need, the fulfillment of a wish, the expression or avoidance of an affect, the maintenance of narcissistic equilibrium, the attainment of a particular type of object relation, or some other objective more specific to each individual. Once any of these aims acquires the form of a mental representation about its fulfillment, there is an urge to carry out the action to obtain it. Any intrapsychic, interpersonal, or external interference with that action becomes an obstacle. Aggression, as we define it, must be called on to overcome the obstacle. This aggression has at its disposal all the resources of the organism, from physical actions to defense mechanisms, to persist in the effort to achieve the action as portrayed in the mental representation of the aim. This may require the participation of several defense mechanisms and the capacities of the self-as-agent. In this view, as stated in the introductory chapter (chapter 1 above), aggression is not a single drive force, but a capacity called into action by the persistence of the motivational aim under the stimulus conditions interfering with its achievement (Rizzuto et al., 1993).

In sadism and masochism there is an indispensable interpersonal dimension in reality or fantasy. If one person inflicts pain or humiliation, another has to suffer and be humiliated. In this respect sadism and masochism appear as a complementary pair, not only at the interpersonal level, but also at the intrapsychic level, where sadistic inclinations alternate with masochistic ones, revealing the common source of both positions. The same phenomenon occurs intersystemically, as illustrated by superego judgments that humiliate the person in front of himself.

The above three cases reveal the intergenerational replication of sadomasochistic traits and behaviors pointing to parental identifications, as well as superego formations resulting from normal and neurotic attachments to the parental figures. They also suggest the significance of intergenerational disturbance in regulating narcissistic self-appraisal leading to the formation of an exalted, yet not quite believable, self-ideal. The parents presented to the growing children greatly inflated representations of their beings. Mrs. S was described as "capable of anything," Mr. G as beloved and "wonderful," and Ann as "a little angel" her mother could not do without.

In our view of aggression, the sadistic components of these cases call the aggressive capacity into play in order to overcome a specific obstacle, namely the obstacle posed by internal masochistic inhibitions proscribing destructive wishes, fantasies, or specific sadistic behaviors against the mother (e.g., poison pen letters), children, and patients (e.g., fear of killing). It is worth noting that these hostile wishes are not in themselves aggressive, but only become so to the extent that they might require overcoming certain obstacles, internal or external. The identification with the sadist would then have a different implication than identification with the aggressor. The masochistic defense is aggressive only insofar as it overcomes and fends off the obstacle of unacceptable sadistic wishes and impulses and their derivatives.

The three cases reveal the persistent components of sadomasochism: intertwining identifications, object relations, and narcissistic themes in the formation of sadomasochistic character traits and behaviors. As a result, sadism and masochism are—in different degrees and levels of pathology—potentially involved in all aspects of human relations and intrapsychic fantasies. These components can manifest themselves clearly in sadomasochistic sexual relations. In these cases, however, narcissistic and aggressive motives readily come into play, and often seem to prevail. The circumstances involved in provoking particularly these aggressive motives often lie in overcoming obstacles posed by the limitations of generational, oedipal, and personal boundaries.

With regard to generational boundaries, the themes of big and small, power or lack of it, reappear in infinite variety, enmeshed in intense feelings of self-enhancement or self-devaluation. Self-devaluation evokes intense feelings of hostility and wishes to turn the tables on the humiliating object, to make it feel small and powerless, or, in the extreme, to destroy it. Awareness of these wishes may lead to the formation of many defensive configurations as protection against the needed and hated object. In addition to our analysis of phobia formation (chapter 8), it seems that the formation of sadomasochistic character traits requires the existence of similar traits in at least one of the parents. In other words, sadomasochism is not an exclusively intrapsychic formation, but is influenced developmentally by the object relations context.

The wish to transgress oedipal boundaries leads to a narcissistic inability to accept defeat. The need to pursue, in displacement, a desired and ambivalently held oedipal object, fueled by childhood fantasies of violent and torturing sexual relations, as the only way to obtain satisfaction, may lead to the most bizarre sadomasochistic enactments (window peeking to watch a partner in intercourse). They are sought as psychic proof that the subject has the power to overcome the oedipal obstacle, if he so wishes, thus obtaining the oedipal object and overcoming inhibitions against satisfaction or control of the object.

The narcissistic inability to accept the limits on one's wishes imposed by the object or society motivates the aggressive transgression of personal boundaries. The sadist needs to overcome every resistance (obstacle) of the object, to obtain some specific response that would satisfy the need to be responded to, to be accepted in the way he wants to be accepted, to be sexuality validated in the way he deems indispensable. The response, the acceptance, and the validation are interpersonal measures aimed at obtaining an experience that can be used to overcome intrapsychic convictions of being unlovable, unacceptable, and sexually inferior, which persistently bring about narcissistic disequilibrium. These feelings and wishes may accompany, but are not the same as, aggression. The "proof" never works, bringing about intense rage and destructive and hostile wishes toward the object that may become enacted and factually hurtful.

In sadomasochistic sexual relations, there is a certain synchrony between the sadistic and the masochistic partners, leading in sexual union to a compelling, frequently driven, intimacy. The analysis of the dynamic components of such intimacy reveal that the satisfaction obtains from the overcoming of several obstacles. First is overcoming the resistance of the object, who, being perceived as a displaced frustrating oedipal object, is expected to resist; then there is overcoming of the refusal of the object to respond in a precise and specific way, capable of overcoming, or so the sadist believes, the internal obstacle posed by doubts about being acceptable, lovable, potent enough. It is this component of the narcissistic disturbance of the inner world of the sadist that poses the most unremitting urgency to repeat sadistic acts. Finally, there is the need to show one's power and disregard for moral norms, social conventions, and even the law. Hostile feelings, actual wishes to hurt and destroy, contempt for the object, need to humiliate it, to overpower it, emerge as the cumulative result of the original failures, as well as the repeated inability to overcome the internal obstacle posed by the self-doubts, regardless of how many times the sadistic actions are carried out.

The masochist, in turn, has complementary obstacles to overcome. Similar doubts about being lovable, likable, sexually acceptable, fueled by a dim awareness of hostile, destructive, humiliating wishes toward the displaced oedipal object, call for defensive moves. Past idealization of suffering and the narcissistic enhancement provided by the ego ideal, under conditions of submitting to pain, overcome the obstacle posed by the wish to act sadistically toward the object. In this manner, the masochistically idealized suffering, as proof to oneself of one's own goodness, synchronizes with the sadistic pleasure of the sadist in inflicting narcissistically enhancing suffering on the other. A synchrony of narcissistic needs, even if highly defensive, provides a particular type of sexual intimacy, a sense of special union.

Our understanding of sadomasochism removes it from the realm of aggression as a drive, to place it as the result of developmental and psychodynamic vicissitudes. The emphasis falls on the internal dispositional factors, both developmental and concurrent, in conjunction with eliciting external stimulus conditions and contexts as providing the motivational components. The explanation of sadomasochistic behaviors, including fantasies, lies in an appeal to these internal and external factors rather than to a putative antecedent drive. The developmental factors that facilitate the formation of sadomasochistic character traits or pathology are linked to the inability to overcome the obstacles posed by the narcissistic injuries of ordinary or pathological development. The hostile, destructive, murderous wishes, or wishes to humiliate evoked by the frustrating objects, call for aggressive defensive moves to be able to keep the object and its love, as well as to maintain narcissistic equilibrium. When circumstances are particularly frustrating or injurious, and the parents themselves have marked sadistic and masochistic traits, the combined working of intrapsychic defenses and identification with the parents create the occasion for the emergence of sadomasochistic traits. Aggression is present inasmuch as progressive intrapsychic, interpersonal, and external obstacles emerge that, if not overcome by aggressive intervention, would severely threaten relational bonds and narcissistic equilibrium.

Chapter 10

Aggression in the Analysis of a Male Hysteric

The study of aggression in the analytic process is less a matter of focusing on specific episodes of aggressive action than of discerning the role of aggression in the course of the individual's life history and psychic development, and tracing their derivatives as they find expression in the analytic relation and process. The theory of aggression as motive locates the roots of aggression in the patient's motivational life, including the developmental history and past and present interpersonal involvements and relationships and their motivational components. In the clinical perspective we are advancing in this study, the emphasis on aggression as a motivational component draws the explanatory focus away from an impersonal drive operating as an inexorable psychic force, impinging on the patient's psychic apparatus and demanding either pathological expression or adaptive management, to the constellation of personal influences, relationships, and motivational configurations that provide the context and motivational substructure for aggressive behavior or lack of it. Our approach embraces aspects of both a one-person and a two-person perspective, but without engaging that controversy, we would at least emphasize that the experience of, vicissitudes, and therapeutic engagement with aggression inevitably involve the patient's interaction with other individuals, even as the motivational dynamics take place intrapsychically. The critical interaction in analysis, of course, is with the analyst.

A major consideration for many patients, from the point of view of our understanding, is not the excess of aggression but the lack of it—or often enough the distorted and at times perverted employment of aggressive capacity for pathological or neurotic purposes. The distinction between aggression and the affects attending it becomes paramount—more often than not, the threat posed by intense affects of anger and rage deter the patient from the effective and meaningful utilization of aggression in the interests of personal advantage or life attainment. The present patient was a young man whose analysis centered largely around issues related to aggression and whose case history tells the story of a gradual progression from a self-destructive, angry, and hostile use of aggression to a more positive, productive and constructive use that benefited him and his life circumstances. The analysis lasted over four years and was conducted on a five-session-per-week basis on the couch.

PRESENTING COMPLAINTS

Larry was referred for analysis by his previous short-term therapist. His coming to therapy was triggered by traumatic disruption of a relationship with his girlfriend, but this was superimposed on more chronic difficulties. His relationships with his family had been difficult and quite tense since he began graduate school. Moreover he suffered from long-standing emotional difficulties. He was shy and insecure, and had difficulties in relating to people generally. He was constantly tense, anxious and worried. His anxiety was at times nearly incapacitating, particularly when he was called on to perform—in class, or when he had to make some form of presentation, or when he had to consult professors or advisers. At such times he would literally shake with anxiety, sweating profusely and feeling that he would surely bungle what he was doing or make a fool of himself. He would begin to stammer, could not organize his thoughts, forgot important things that he knew well otherwise, and generally deteriorated in his level of functioning.

This was also the case in his relations to women. He felt awkward and embarrassed asking girls for dates, feeling sure that they would turn him down, or that they thought him funny or ugly or repulsive. He could overcome his doubts and anxieties up to a point, but as the relationship became closer or sexually more intimate, his difficulties escalated. He became obsessed with the idea that he could not perform sexually, frequently experiencing the humiliation of premature ejaculation. These fears pervaded all of his thinking about women and sex and served as proof to him of his sexual inferiority and inadequacy. A few months of psychotherapy convinced him that his problems were deep and long-standing, and he was referred for psychoanalysis.

He was evaluated in several face-to-face interviews. He was in his early twenties, short in stature but sturdy and well-built. His manner was at first noticeably tense and his speech somewhat pressured and punctuated with nervous laughter. His level of anxiety was obviously high. Even so, he was able to relate with apparent warmth and spontaneity, expressed himself fluently and with some insight—and despite his anxiety left a rather good impression. Despite the at times incapacitating anxiety, he had maintained a rather high level of achievement academically. In the last interview, he was even able to show some humor and warmth, and seemed well able to respond to the analyst's questions and a few trial interpretations. His symptomatic picture was consistent with a diagnosis of anxiety hysteria and his personality seemed structured along the lines of male hysteria with an admixture of obsessive-compulsive features.

FAMILY BACKGROUND

Larry's involvement with his family was chronically troubled and turbulent. He was born the youngest of three brothers and an older sister in a Jewish family. As his father's business prospered, the family moved, when Larry was about five years old, from a relatively lower-class section of the city to a more affluent middle-class neighborhood. This was a definite turning point in the family history from hard times to better times, from life in a more or less ghetto-like atmosphere of an almost exclusively Jewish neighborhood with close family ties and many relatives to a more diverse and better-off pattern.

Mother

As the analysis progressed, the first important figure to emerge with any clarity was his mother. Without doubt her influence on him was powerful and decisive. She ruled the roost, a dominating and intrusively controlling Jewish mother. When Philip Roth's *Portnoy's Complaint* came out, Larry remarked on the strong similarity between Portnoy's mother and his own. While Larry saw his father as weak, ineffectual, compliant, and as giving in to whatever demands were made on him and never having his own way in family matters, he saw his mother as dominating, controlling, intrusive, undercutting, critical, devaluing. He saw his own birth as a way of satisfying her maternal needs in the face of her declining fertility, providing her with a new baby to fill the empty nest. His next-older sibling was seven years older. He was thus conceived as her toy, her plaything, intended for her amusement and gratification—and by implication as a counterbalance to her narcissistic depletion and depression. Larry had an intense wish to fulfill this gratifying function, but also an equally if not more intense resentment that he was regarded by her and by the family as the "baby." His attempts to express or assert himself were met by amused smiles and laughter and comments that what he was doing was "cute." He resented attempts to treat him as a child, even, or especially, when circumstances called for it.

Larry's mothering experience was colored strongly by his mother's anxiety and guilt-ridden hyperconcern. She was a constant worrier, typically imagining the worst and most dreadful possibilities. Her caretaking was obsessive and was focused most clearly in toilet-training. Larry was toilet-trained early, put on the potty at regular times and left there until he did his job. Performance on the potty was very much a performance for his mother's pleasure; pleasing her was gratifying, but carried overtones of having to please and having to submit to her wishes. To encourage his urinating and defecating, mother would tickle his penis—with obvious masturbatory and seductive implications.

Their relationship was markedly dependent and close. He clung to her and as he grew older was beset by fears of losing her. When she would leave him for any time, he would have terrifying fantasies of her being killed in an accident and never coming back. Such separations in his early years were accompanied by screaming and crying, and his mother responded with excessive concern and placating maneuvers. His childhood efforts centered around gaining her approval and building a close, protective, intimate, and special relationship. Despite his resentment, he effectively made himself her baby. He directed much of his attempts at "cute" behavior to her. He would make up special secrets, which he would tell only to her, with the specific objective of excluding his father and siblings from this special relation.

Larry invested a good deal of effort in gaining his mother's affection and attention. All through his latency and early adolescent years, he tended to retreat from the anxious and uneasy world of his peers, coming home from school and retreating to the security and specialness of home and mother. He would engage her in conversation, telling her all the interesting things that happened to him, making up stories to keep her involved in the face of his perception that adults were not much interested in his child's world. He felt he could never compete with or be as interesting or worthwhile as his big brothers or sister. He complained that in his efforts to engage her he always seemed more involved and invested than she did. Often when the telephone would ring, his mother would interrupt the conversation to carry on a trivial and unimportant dialogue with a friend of hers. These interruptions infuriated Larry, a resentment that was revived by occasions when the telephone in the analyst's office would ring and he would interrupt the session to answer.[1]

Larry clung to the imagined specialness and exclusivity of this relationship as a protective haven against the threats and inevitable defeats awaiting him in the outside world. This pattern lasted into his high school years.

While his persistent striving for closeness and approving attention from his mother was a predominant theme throughout Larry's development, there was also a countertheme expressing the opposite side of his powerful ambivalence. He came to regard his mother as inconsistent and unpredictable. He would tell her things that he thought amusing or interesting, and without apparent reason or warning she would become anxious and worried. She was controlling and intruded into every corner of his life. He saw her as possessive, demanding, castrating. She interpreted everything in terms of its effect on her—either for or against her. If Larry did not get a haircut, he did it to hurt her; if he did get a haircut, he did it for her sake. Everything that was not congruent with her wishes became an attack against her. Everything that was not exactly as she wished or expected became a calamity, a catastrophe. And there was no distinction between great calamities and small. They all elicited the same response of hurt, tormented self-pity, and outraged injustice; she was a helpless victim, tormented by the selfishness, lack of gratitude, carelessness, thought-lessness, stupidity, stubbornness, and willfulness of her children. While he bitterly complained about her behavior, it became increasingly clear that he played his own part in eliciting and provoking this pat-tern of interaction.

While his later relationship with his mother remained intensely ambivalent, Larry longed for a closer relationship and understanding between himself and his father, but it always seemed that his mother was interfering and keeping them apart. She would break into their conversations, change the subject when their conversation turned to subjects of their interest and not hers, etc. He saw her more and more clearly in the course of his analysis as an extremely neurotic, anxious, and troubled woman. This was an important appreciation for him, since he had formed his own self-image as weak, defective, unlov-able, and hurtful—an impression that had enabled him to blame him-self for all of these difficulties. He began to see that his mother had problems of her own. Gradually his ability to stand on his own grew and with it the ability to become less reactive and involved in her neurotic behavior.

The inescapable tension of involvement versus noninvolvement formed a major dimension of his analysis, and displayed itself in dis-guised and displaced ways in other aspects of his experience. Involve-ment meant surrender to his mother's obsessive, worrisome, and guilt-provoking anxiety, but it also meant having her attention and a privileged and special involvement with her as the defective child, the helpless baby who needed to be protected and hovered over with anxious concern. To be uninvolved meant rejection and isolation, being cut off from all contact and all affection. Larry felt trapped between these unhappy alternatives, but he was gradually able to recognize and face his fears. Particularly difficult for him to recognize was the gratification he derived from her anxious and obsessive concerns about him. His weakness and defectiveness was *the* special secret they shared. Even more unavailable, however, was the intense rage and resent-ment that discolored his relationship to her, not merely his anger at her controlling intrusiveness, but the deeper rage at her frustrating his oedipal wishes and infantile longings. Obviously this at times mur-derous rage posed a significant obstacle preventing his taking a more aggressively assertive and autonomous stance in relation to her.

Father

While Larry's father was the major source of support for not only the immediate but also the extended family, he was relatively passive and permissive at home. How his father could support the whole family, and where the money came from, remained a source of mystery and wonder all through his childhood. But at home he clearly saw his father as a weak and ineffectual man controlled and dominated by his mother. Mother ran the house and made the decisions, and father had no other choice but to comply and give in to her. One of the constant enigmas for Larry was how his father could be so shrewd and successful in business and respected in the community when he was so weak and ineffectual at home.

In his childhood memories, his father was distant and remote figure. There were no memories of close contacts with his father: he complained that his father never paid any attention to him or spent time playing with him. The father's role was complicated and confusing in Larry's mind from the beginning. Mother and father would often argue. In these family fights, Larry rarely, if ever, saw his father coming out the victor. Mother always won, always had her way. She was the powerful, controlling, dominating one; father was the weak, vulnerable, manipulable sucker who got taken and was pushed around by mother and the family, and who had no say of his own. Larry's special relation with his mother also became a testing ground for his oedipal wishes to exclude and defeat his father. If his father could take mother off to bed, then little Larry could take her away from father through these confidences and special secrets. It was especially humiliating when mother would divulge these little secrets to father, treating them as "cute" and "amusing."

But his father's weakness was a constant disappointment to Larry. He wished desperately that his father were stronger and particularly that he would stand up to his mother and not let her control everything. But his father never did. He always gave in and let mother run the show. Larry's fantasy was that father could really have made it big, become a powerful business tycoon, if it had not been for mother holding him down and preventing him from taking the big gamble, the one fantastic speculation that would have made him rich and powerful, the risky investment that would have spelled the difference between ordinary moderate success and the big time. He felt that mother held him back and kept him from this success because, if father became rich and powerful, her own influence and strength would be threatened. In Larry's eyes, mother had to keep father under control, to keep him down.

While Larry felt angered by his father's inability to put his mother in her place—and despised his father's weakness—he was also angered by his mother's continual interference in his relationship with his father. He had a strong yearning for greater closeness to his father; yet father was an enigma that he could not understand. The yearnings involved homosexual wishes and fears. Larry recalled occasions when friends visited the family and he would have to sleep with his father. He feared that father would roll over on him in the morning and kiss him, just as he rolled over on mother.

In Larry's mind his regressive wishes to remain his mother's special dependent and defective baby were paralleled by his thinking of any moves toward greater maturity or independence as attacks on his father calculated to defeat and humiliate him. Both of these currents in his thinking had to be thoroughly worked through in the course of his analysis. He gradually became more aware of these infantile wishes and fears, and came at one point to a showdown with both his parents. The confrontation was generated over his vacation plans to go on a long car trip with his girlfriend. The family was horrified and mortified. The scandal of traveling unchaperoned with a girl was too much for mother. Mother launched another all-out attack. Larry saw her as the protagonist and the struggle as a last-ditch battle for survival. Everything was at stake. He felt that his father was basically sympathetic to his cause, but was controlled by mother. Mother threatened to completely disown him if he went on the trip. Larry hung on desperately, thinking in his despair of calling his analyst for advice and support, but finally was able to withstand the onslaught. When it was clear that he would not budge, his parents begrudgingly gave in: father immediately sat down and wrote several checks to cover expenses for the trip. Larry was torn by his intense wishes to be on good terms with his parents, to give in to their wishes, to be their good little boy—and at the same time to free himself from their domination and control, especially his mother's. The risk was twofold. He ran the risk of losing his mother's affection and being rejected by her, and he ran the risk of defeating and humiliating his father. Father's writing out the checks was the terms of surrender, a humiliating defeat as Larry saw it.

Closely related to this wish for his father's approval, there lurked a deeper and less accessible fantasy. Larry felt that, in having a child in their advanced years, his parents had wished for another daughter. He attributed this wish to his father, more so than his mother. His birth, then, had been a disappointment to his father. Larry felt inadequate to meet the standards set by his brothers, and cherished the fantasy that if he were only a girl he could then have found approval and affection in his father's eyes. To be a boy meant having to compete with his brothers, on their terms. His older brother Joe had been the personality boy—the social success—and his brother Harry was the family genius. How could little Larry be expected to match their performance? He could find no way to be a success on his own terms. Had he been a girl, things might have been different; as it was he was nothing but a defective male child, doomed to inevitable failure.

Larry's Siblings

Larry's oldest brother, Joe, was eleven when Larry was born. In his childhood years, Larry idolized Joe. He was the big brother who was admired, popular, who knew what to do with girls. Joe was the family playboy. He never studied, had many girlfriends, was constantly dating and going to parties. Joe's frivolous ways caused his parents a good deal of anxiety, but in Larry's eyes they were the hallmark of the cool and smooth "operator" who knew how to get what he wanted, especially from girls. For Larry, Joe was everything that his father was not. Joe knew his way around, was popular, the slick manipulator who could get his way. He could have any girl he wanted. Father was none of these things. They would share a fantasy game—that Larry was Joe's son. Larry felt that he would much rather have had Joe for a father than his real father, who seemed so clumsy and weak.

Larry's older sister played a minor role in Larry's early family experience. She was ten years older and much taken up with teenage concerns, friends, dates, boys, and other activities outside the family. In the analytic material, she came through as a pale shadow of her mother, but her interaction with her youngest brother was minimal, not even babysitting, as one might have expected. Even in more adult years, when she was married and lived in another part of the country, relations between Larry and his sister were distant.

The other brother was Harry, who was seven years older and

played a most significant role in Larry's life, second only to his parents. Harry was the family genius. His scholastic performance was consistently brilliant; he was an intense and dedicated student. He poured his energies into schoolwork, and in contrast to Joe, had few friends and dated very little. The picture Larry painted of him was that of a serious, withdrawn, angry, contemptuous, severely obsessional and highly intellectualized and moralistic adolescent.

Larry's relationship with Harry over the years was difficult and highly ambivalent. He clearly idolized Harry and greatly admired his intelligence and accomplishments. Harry set an incomparable standard that Larry sought to emulate; but he also felt this to be an impossible task, that he never could match or even approach his brother's performance. He also strove to gain a closer and friendlier relationship with him, but this too seemed impossible. Harry did not seem to want to have much to do with his baby brother. In childhood games, Harry would play tricks on him so that Larry would be made to look or feel foolish or stupid.

Sometimes Harry and his friends would trick Larry and run away, leaving him alone. In the school years, Larry's greatest delight was when he could get his brother to teach him something. At times he would try to get Harry to help him with his school assignments, but usually any help was accompanied by severe criticisms and comments that left Larry feeling that he was just too stupid and incapable of ever doing anything. Larry recalled, for example, that he showed Harry his bar mitzvah speech—one he had written himself—and asked Harry for help in improving it. Harry tore up the speech and wrote another, saying that Larry's effort was worthless and stupid.

Their relationship was intense, ambivalent, conflictual. The sibling rivalry was intense, and terribly threatening for Larry. On the one hand he admired his brother and wanted to emulate him, but any alliance with Harry meant subjugation and humiliation. Whatever the flavor of their childhood relationship, Larry projected the image of Harry as his childhood nemesis. Consistent with his inability to feel and express his anger, it took a considerable amount of work in the analysis before Larry could deal effectively with this relationship. He gradually drew a portrait of his brother's rather sadistic and demeaning treatment of him. As might easily be imagined, it was only in the transference that many of these feelings came to light. We will see more of the transference development later, but an important part of it was Larry's feeling that his analyst was out to get him, to criticize and put him down, that he would sooner or later use anything Larry told him against him, particularly any of his foibles, peccadilloes, or secret thoughts about his weakness and inadequacy. He was convinced that, no matter how kindly or considerately he was treated, one day without warning and without reason the analyst would turn on him and tear him apart. These feelings went back at least in part to his relationship with Harry. His feelings about his analyst were clearly related to memories of Harry leading him on by asking him questions, and then unexpectedly springing the trap on him and ridiculing his foolishness. Larry expected the same of his analyst, and of others in his life. This aspect of the transference was highly overdetermined.

THE FAMILY BABY

The image of his specialness and defectiveness was carried on into childhood. Around the house he continued to be the "baby." His pranks were laughed at and his naughtiness excused as "cute." He continued to be close to and dependent on his mother. He dreaded spending any time away from her. Larry was unquestionably a bright and precocious child, and quickly learned to mimic adult mannerisms. He recalled wanting to dress like an adult, wanting a checking account of his own when he was seven, trying to order drinks in a restaurant, etc. The family treated all these as "cute escapades."

Thus Larry was surrounded by adults—people who knew more, could do more important and interesting things than he could, could take initiatives that he could not, were allowed privileges and gratifications that he was not. He resented his lot—that of the baby of the family—and strove mightily to act in adult ways. These childhood attempts were obviously inappropriate, and turned out to be merely attempts of a child to mimic and ape the antics of his elders. Inevitably they provided a source of amusement and condescending interest for the adults around him. He complained of feeling like a midget, as if he were the possessor of an adult mind trapped by accident in a child's body. As a child, he wanted desperately to be treated like an adult, but he was not. And as an adult, he wished to be and be accepted as adult, but continued to feel that he was still a child. There was a curious quality to this perception of himself, as though he felt himself forever doomed to being a child. He seemed to have no operative concept of development, no appreciation of himself as growing up and developing his capacities through time, and thus little by little becoming an adult. In growing up, he absolutized the disparity between himself and his elders. He was small, weak, incapable, bumbling, ignorant, and defective, and would never be anything but that. *They* were strong, capable, effective, smart, and adult, and it seemed that they were always so. And as a young adult, he clung to the same self-image, while the adults around him—his professors, mentors, fellow students, bosses, even his analyst—seemed unrelentingly adult and powerful.

This attitude carried over to Larry's life concerns; he could not envision himself becoming more proficient and capable in his professional work. It was as if in his mind he was unskilled and ineffective and others around him were knowledgeable, effective, and capable. There was little concept of his own ability to learn and to develop skills and capacities, and to become as proficient as the older and more experienced professionals who surrounded him. There was no concept of his being able to change and grow in the analysis either. He seemed to cling to the notion that he was defective and inadequate, and that there was no possibility of changing this state of affairs. Any attempt to do so or any thoughts that such might actually be taking place were deemed illusory.

THE ANALYSIS

These broad lines of his history allow us to discern the patterns and themes characterizing his neurosis and character. But these acquired added meaning and depth in the light of material emerging gradually in the course of his analysis, particularly in the variations on the theme of aggression in its varying guises and vicissitudes. The major vehicle of therapeutic change, as we will argue, was the activation of the aggressive themes in the transference and their gradual resolution by his encounter and interaction with the analyst's own therapeutic aggression mediated through the therapeutic alliance.

This analysis, like all analyses, was multifaceted and complex. Our interest here is in the vicissitudes of aggression as they played themselves out in the course of the analysis. The themes of defectiveness and powerlessness, so pervasive in his developmental history, came alive in the analysis, particularly in the transference. The major analytic task was transformation of his aggressive capacities from self-defeating and pejoratively self-demeaning channels into more adaptive and constructive ones. His aggressive enactments fell into three discriminable areas, namely the sexual area, the career area, and the analytic relation. Within the analytic relation, aggression came to display itself differentially with respect to the three components of the analytic relation—transference, alliance, and the real relation (Meissner, 1996b). Correspondingly, the analyst's aggression came into play within these same components of the analytic relation in interaction with contributions from the patient. We will discuss these components separately, but with the constant reminder that they are mutually interactive, contemporaneous, and intermingled in the ongoing flow of the analytic process. They can (and we believe should) be distinguished and differentiated, even though they are concurrently interactive and parallel components of the analytic relation.

Analytic Themes

The analytic themes centered around issues related to Larry's image of himself as defective, a doomed failure, dependent, and powerless—all reflecting conflicts over aggression and to a considerable extent narcissism.

If there was any theme that dominated Larry's analysis from beginning to end, it was the theme of his defectiveness. There was no area of his life and experience that it had not touched and within which it had not worked its malign and often devastating influence. He was convinced that he was doomed to be inadequate, weak, dependent, without strength or power, that he could never grow up to be a man and stand on his own feet. Larry tried desperately to find ways to compensate for these overriding and inexorable inner feelings of defectiveness and inadequacy. He tried to act like an adult, but he had little or no idea of what that was all about. He tried to find ways of making himself more interesting or of making himself seem worthwhile. His conviction was that anything he had to offer was worthless and of little value to the adults around him. As he had as a child, he kept a record collection, but always felt that it was worthless and inadequate, because it did not have every conceivable record in it. He would experience strong impulses to run out and buy up every record he could afford, just to make his collection less defective. He saw such possessions as mirroring himself; they were defective and inadequate, even as he was. The magical wish was that somehow by building them up and making them bigger and more complete he could manage to build up his own inner sense of emptiness and incompleteness.

The projection from the inner to the outer world affected his whole experience. He could take care of nothing, could make no investment in preserving or maintaining things he owned. His car was in a constant state of disrepair. His apartment was a mess. It was as though he had to put everything in a state of defective functioning or disarray, for it was only in that context that he felt comfortable. He constructed the world around him to fit the inner image of himself. His car would not start properly and was literally falling apart because it belonged to him—that was as much as he deserved or could expect. Anything valuable that he received was sure to be destroyed in his hands. His parents bought him an expensive stereo rig, and he was convinced that it was too good for him, that he would mess it up, that he would not be able to take proper care of it, that he would quickly break it and reduce it to a state of uselessness and defectiveness.

The same set of convictions permeated his work and professional activity. In school he was constantly convinced that he was going to flunk exams, fail courses, and that if he were called on in class to answer any questions he would blunder; if he spoke up in classes or seminars he would make a fool of himself and let everyone know how little he knew and how stupid he was. In his professional work he was nearly paralyzed at every step. If he had to make a telephone call, he would put it off and agonize over his fear of messing up the negotiation and making all sorts of foolish mistakes. If he had to write a letter he was convinced that he would be unable to do it, unable to say the right things, etc. It can easily be imagined that these preoccupations with failure and the conviction of messing up became even stronger in proportion to the importance or significance of what he was trying to do.

Presenting a report was a paradigmatic situation of assured failure. To begin with he had great difficulty in negotiating with other colleagues and peers. His fears of making mistakes and appearing like a foolish little kid and his concomitant anxiety made this procedure very difficult for him. He felt that he was an incompetent child, interfering in adult business, messing around. Up to a point they would be amused and condescending, but then they would be angry at him and would attack him in retaliation. In formal presentations, he felt like a small child, playing an adult role for which he was not ready and not suited. Because of his short stature, he had to look up at other participants. Looking up at a chairman or corporate officer was like looking up at some great and powerful figure. He constantly felt that they would see through him at any moment, see that he was ineffective, stupid, that he was carrying out a charade of being an economist, that he didn't deserve to be involved in such important matters, and they would humiliate him and cast him out ignominiously. These feelings were directly related to similar feelings and fears that he had had in relation to his father and brother Harry.

Such humiliating discovery would finally reveal his worthlessness and defectiveness. In order to overcome these obstacles to his self-esteem, Larry resorted to deceit and subterfuge. He constantly felt that he was deceiving people, pulling the wool over their eyes, and that any moment he would be found out and unmasked. This pattern permeated all his relationships. He felt it in school when talking to his professors, when talking to other economists and lawyers, in his relationships with women—and not surprisingly in his analysis. He persistently expressed the feeling that he was messing up the analysis, that he wasn't able to do it right, that the analysis was after all going to prove once and for all his defectiveness. He was especially concerned about free associating, constantly complaining that he couldn't do it, that he was just messing things up. When he experienced a relatively free flow of associative material, he would declare that it was just wasting time; "bullshitting" was his term for it.

There were several interesting aspects to this inner sense of defectiveness. One was that Larry fantasized that the end result of his weakness and incompetence and impotence was to be suicide. There was no other way out; it seemed the inevitable and inexorable consequence, born out of irrefutable logic, that he should have to kill himself. He was doomed to failure, and it was simply mistaken and misguided to think otherwise. His fantasy was elaborated in relation to the analysis. He fantasized that one day his analyst would turn on him and tell him the farce was over, that there was nothing left for him but suicide.

Throughout the analysis, he struggled with his wishes to be passive and dependent. These wishes formed in fact the other side of his preoccupations and fears that the analyst would attack and hurt him. The opposite pole to his guarded suspiciousness and constant fear of attack was total submission and unquestioning subjugation. He could find little ground between these drastic alternatives. He felt himself becoming increasingly dependent on the analysis and increasingly involved in it. The only way he would envision this was in terms of complete surrender. This meant handing himself over to the powerful analyst who could do with him as he pleased. The alternative was attack, struggle, confrontation, the analyst destroying him or his destroying the analyst. It took many months to work through these paranoid anxieties. As his conviction that the analyst would attack him and tear him apart receded, his wish to gain a close, loving, passive, and submissive relationship with him came into prominent focus.

He recalled an occasion when he had been away from home for one summer at camp. He had been very unhappy at camp, unable to make any friends among the other boys, unable to join in their childish games, and keeping himself more or less an outsider. At the end of camp, he was offered an opportunity to join some of the older boys and counselors on a canoe trip. But he knew his mother would want him to come home. The canoe trip would have meant a step away from her, an adventure away from his childhood dependence, a more grown-up and independent undertaking. He was frightened by it and could not accept it. He had to retreat to the safety of his clinging dependence on his mother. The canoe trip became a sort of paradigm for his difficulty in the analysis. Was he going to be able to embark on the adventure that analysis offered him—the opportunity for greater independence and maturity and the capacity for adult functioning? Or would he cling to his self-appointed condition of defective dependence? He saw himself as desperately needing the analyst to support him and help him. He felt intensely dependent, as he had felt fearfully dependent on his mother. He felt the need to have the analyst as his powerful protector to whom he could submit himself in loving subjugation. He had recurrent dreams about the analytic situation, in which he and his analyst would be talking face-to-face, not as doctor and patient, but as good and close friends. Or they would be lying on the couch embracing and fondling each other. Besides the homosexual content in these dream fantasies and wishes, there was also the threat of complete submission to the analyst's power, which could then be capriciously and viciously used against him, and against which he had no defense.

Another important aspect of his concerns over dependency was his feeling that the analyst might become dependent on him. The analyst, for instance, might depend on him to be cooperative, a good patient, one that didn't cause any trouble or didn't argue or resist in any way. The wish to have his analyst dependent reflected his desires to be powerful himself, not to be in the position of submitting, but of having the analyst submit to him and obey his wishes. These wishes were highly erotized, and were associated with parallel wishes for women to submit to him sexually, as well as to his latency and adolescent fantasies of having boys submit to him sexually. He feared that if he showed any independence or any will of his own in the analysis, the analyst would not be able to handle it. He would become anxious, or upset, or hurt and depressed. Larry tried assiduously to avoid any objection, or questioning, or confronting of any of the analyst's observations or interpretations. Behind this behavior, there lurked the image of his father. Any moves on his part toward greater independence within the analysis were seen as against the analyst, as putting him down, as putting his value and competence in question, as making him feel worthless and humiliated. Similar issues pervaded his relationship with his mother. The transference was cast in the same extreme form that it had been toward his mother and father: the alternatives were complete subjugation, which he hated and reviled, or destructive hostility, which he feared and avoided. It was extremely difficult to find a workable middle ground in which he could express himself and take his own independent position without attacking or destroying or humiliating or defeating the analyst— or alternatively being attacked, defeated, and humiliated by me.

The issue of power versus powerlessness was central to Larry's experience. Every relationship, every context of relating to or dealing with other people, became a field in which forces of power and submission played themselves out. The alternatives were clear-cut and decisive—either mastery and power or complete submission and powerlessness. He recalled as a child feeling helplessly submitted to his parents' power. But the opposite side of that coin was that, when his parents capitulated and gave in to his wishes (as they frequently did, for example, in his tantrums when they were about to go out for an evening), he felt a frightening sense of power over them and that he was bad and demanding for making them do something against their wills.

The power issue carried over into his relations with authority figures. He saw them as powerful and dangerous, felt that they could turn against him at the least warning and hurt him in some unforeseen way. He was frightened of policemen, professors, judges, older colleagues, superiors, even the landlord—anyone with decision-making capacity that could affect him in any way. He saw others as powerful, and himself as powerless. Along with this concern with power, he was extremely sensitive to any infringement on his rights or freedom. The loss of freedom was a chronic complaint that he brought forth in multiple situations, not merely the sexual. He could not envision himself as an active agent with capacity and potency to set goals and accomplish them. The notion of cooperation or collaboration was completely foreign to his way of thinking. His was a master-slave morality of the first order.

This came to a major focus in the analysis. Larry saw the analytic situation as a power struggle, in which the analyst was the powerful aggressor, and he was the powerless and helpless victim. The analyst was a dangerous opponent who was lying in wait, ready to pounce on him and destroy him. He was afraid of the analyst's "shooting him down" or "putting him down." The issue was raised in many contexts. As he saw it, the analyst determined the appointment times, the days off, the vacation periods. Larry saw himself as having no say in these matters, his only recourse being to accept and submit to the analyst's decisions. Any sense that for the most part these issues were as far as possible negotiated was completely alien.

The question of power remained a live issue throughout the entire course of the analysis. It was extremely difficult for Larry to accept the idea that the analysis could be a cooperative venture, in which he and his analyst could work together toward a resolution of his difficulties, and in which he could take an active, responsible, and determining part. Only gradually, as this issue was worked through, did his obsessive anxiety diminish, so that he was able to make his own decisions about taking time away from the analysis—as his job sometimes required—or even feeling more comfortable when he arrived a few minutes late. His tendency to erotize this aspect of his experience was unmistakable. He saw the power dichotomy in terms of winning the analyst over and gaining the same sort of special, intimate, confidential relation he had with his mother. Losing out in the power struggle meant being "fucked over." Rather, as a poor, weak, and defective baby he had to be protected and taken care of and given special consideration. Larry worked at re-creating the quality of special defectiveness and helplessness he had had with his mother in the analytic situation. When it became clear to him that the analyst was not going to respond as his mother had, he was both frustrated and angered—but also relieved. It was only at this point that the basis for a firm therapeutic alliance could be constructed.

Woven into the fabric of this analytic tapestry, like a constantly recurring leitmotif permeating and coloring every corner of the picture, was the theme of aggression—specifically, in accord with our theory, as a basic motivational pattern related to the facing and overcoming of obstacles, in the analysis predominantly psychic obstacles. Larry's conflicts over aggression—the need to control it and suppress it and avoid any expression of it—were a major source of difficulty for him. We have already seen some suggestion of the manner in which conflicts over aggression came to play such a significant role in the sexual sphere. He was driven on the one side by his intense phallic wishes and desires; yet on the other side he was inhibited and impeded in the expression of these sexual wishes by his fears and anxieties. The idea that sex was destructive and hurtful derived from his mother. In true "Jewish mother" style, every action on his part that deviated from his parents' wishes or that smacked of independence and self-assertion was interpreted as an attack on his parents, as calculated to hurt and disappoint them. Larry's mother had also charged that Larry's "bad" behavior would be the cause of his father's death. His disobedience, she declared, would give his father a heart attack, so that Larry would then be responsible for his father's death. Larry's defense against the threat of harmful destructiveness was to keep himself the weak, helpless baby, even though at the same time he bitterly resented and felt angered and hurt by being treated as such.

He continually saw himself and tried to portray himself as inadequate and defective. He recalled that as a child his favorites were the *Wizard of Oz* stories. He thought of himself as being like the Tin Man or the Scarecrow: they were defective as he was and like him doomed to failure. Any accomplishments or attainments had to be kept hidden. Successful performance was "showing off." He could not think of himself as a capable adult, but clung to the image of the baby who only played at being an adult. When a baby did adult things, he was showing off, and his performance was only fit to be smiled at or laughed at and treated as "cute." Any successful performance was "too much," it was "going too far." The image was that of losing control and bringing about unexpected, unforeseeable, and inevitably disastrous consequences. Any degree of self-assertion or aggressive effort and striving to overcome obstacles and accomplish goals was discolored by fears of destructiveness and retaliation. His neurotic behavior was clearly in the service of several closely linked objectives—avoiding destructive consequences, minimizing competition, and preserving the dominant fantasy of his defectiveness. He worked at making himself a failure. His flight from aggressive competition was tied tightly to the latent competition and rivalry with his brothers. As a child he had avoided such competition because he was certain to be the loser. As an adult he continued to avoid it: to be better than Joe he would have to be a supersuccessful lover; to be better than Harry he would have to be supersmart. If he could not attain those exalted standards, there was nothing left but failure. It was again the logic of extremes—all or nothing.

The threat of aggression was demonstrated graphically in a dream. In the dream a tough-looking guy was in a building packing large amounts of money into boxes. He was carrying a gun. He had just robbed a bank and was packing the money for his getaway. Larry was standing outside with a gun in his hand. The man came out of the building and Larry was terrified. He thought that the guy would shoot him, so he threw away his own gun and started running. The dream was a reflection of his waking experience. He was always throwing away his gun, denying and hiding any aggressiveness or assertiveness out of fear that someone would attack him in turn. Beyond that was the fear that if he did not throw away the gun he might himself go too far and thus become the agent of destruction.

The close linkage between aggressive assertion and sadistic wishes to hurt and destroy set in motion a projective defense that contributed to certain more or less paranoid attitudes. Larry's world was a world populated with enemies. All around him there were strong, powerful figures ready to pounce on him and do him in. He often felt people were criticizing him, or laughing at him behind his back. Frequently in the course of his analysis—even remarkably late in the course of it—the feeling would burst upon him that the analyst was snickering at him and laughing behind his back, as though he thought what Larry was saying was inconsequential, boring, stupid, or laughable. At every step he expected attack from powerful forces surrounding him, in the analysis and without. He felt that people were out to get him, that they were just looking for the first opportunity to put him down, to show him up, to make his weakness and defectiveness apparent. He was constantly in fear of being "shot down." Any assertion or independence was an invitation for others to attack and destroy him. This was one of the most difficult aspects of his treatment. For him to trust meant putting himself at the analyst's mercy. He had no assurance, and every expectation, that the analyst would take advantage of his vulnerability and "put him down."

The world around him was hostile, threatening, and controlling, a world of mothers and brothers. He saw himself as a helpless victim, a pawn in others' hands. He felt himself to be ugly and repulsive. He had frequent dreams in which people were disgusted and repulsed by him. They would either treat him with contempt and disgust or else attack him and chase him. The police were always after him, a circumstance reinforced by his occasional flirtation with illegal activities, such as selling pot. Such devices were obviously calculated to give some real substance to the fears and anxieties of his fantasies. In his dream life he would look in the mirror and his face would be covered with repulsive bugs that he couldn't pull off. He even described occasions when he felt the same when he looked at his face in the mirror while awake, as though there were ugly and deforming growths and scabs. He felt he smelled bad, recalling his worries about the smell of his own feces. He constantly worried about smelling badly in public and especially on dates. He associated his bad smell with his tendency to perspire heavily, especially when he felt anxious.

Clearly Larry saw the world in terms of hostile and armed confrontation. His was the Swiss defense—no one would ever attack a worthless and defenseless noncombatant. But unlike the Swiss, he had strong impulses to act aggressively himself. His own wishes, repressed and denied, were strongly hostile and were expressed in terms of fantasies of domination and forcing others to submit to his will—sexually and otherwise. The least act of assertion was redolent with the wishes and fantasies of such phallic, sadistic, destructive, and dominating impulses. He expected the attack from others that he wished to launch himself, but was too afraid to even attempt. It took several years of clarifications, interpretations, and working through of these feelings in the analytic setting before he began to see that the grim and ominous colors with which he had painted his world came from his own brush. This realization was gained at first in his relationship to me, and then gradually in the other areas of his activity.

The logic of extremes played itself into this context too. If there were any slight disproportion in any of his relationships, he would view it as one of total domination and submission. If he was not completely in control of what was going on, he felt himself to be at

the mercy of those around him and thereby vulnerable to their attacks. He thought in all-or-none terms. One was either on the top, or
on the bottom. The only way to assure himself that he was not on the
bottom was to try to put someone else on the bottom. He felt people
were always trying to do just that to him. Only gradually could he see
that in fact not only was there no evidence that anyone was trying to
put him down, but in many instances the only one putting him down
was himself. This became clear in the analysis: on a number of occasions, he acted out attempts to get the analyst to criticize or ridicule
him, to be intrusive and controlling as his mother had been, and thus
validate his expectations. When he saw what was afoot in these episodes, he began to realize that he had often done similar things, not
only at home, but in his work and other aspects of his life. By playing
the weak and submissively compliant role, he had literally invited
others around him to take advantage of him; he had maneuvered
them into the dominating position. Then he could feel resentful and
rebellious, angered and bitter at his lot in life as the worthless and
defective underdog, who could have no expectations of success, recognition, or reward. The prophecy was self-fulfilling!

We are emphasizing in this discussion the ways in which aggressive themes were interwoven in Larry's development and in the defensive and dynamic patterns that found expression in his analysis.
Underlying many of these dynamics were profound and troublesome
narcissistic issues, reflected dramatically in the dynamics of the "exception" as demonstrated in Freud's (1916) formulation. This dynamic
centered for Larry around his self-concept as defective and inadequate.
His defect and the circumstances of his early life experience could be
seen as establishing him as an "exception" to whom considerations of
privilege, special treatment, and satisfaction of his desires were due
as a matter of course. More detailed discussion of these issues, however central to the dynamics of the case, would draw us far afield.
However, one important connection cannot be overlooked. The narcissistic entitlement related to his position as the deprived and disad-
vantaged "exception" provided the core motivational context for his
resentment and for the mobilization of his aggression in the interest
of redeeming his injured and narcissistically defective sense of self.
The dynamics of the exception syndrome thus provided some of the
fundamental components constituting the inner psychic obstacle for
the overcoming of which his aggression was called forth. This took
the form of his need-wish to be special, powerful, masterful, in con-

trol of his life, its circumstances, and of anyone with whom he had involvements of any significance.

Accordingly, the women in his life should want to sleep with him without any hassles and willingly submit to his perverse sexual wishes. He should get all A's without bothering to study. When he sat down to write a paper, it should be a masterpiece. His colleagues and professors should have automatically recognized his talent and applauded him for it. The difficulty, of course, was that when he tried to write or perform in the classroom or in consultative situations, his performance did not measure up to these standards of genius. In his mind they were thereby merely more evidence of his inadequacy and failure. If you can't be the best, you are doomed to be a failure. You were somebody special, or you were a failure. There was a unique paradox concealed within this perverse narcissistic logic. For Larry there was an investment in and a commitment to failure. His high narcissistic expectations set the stage for failure. When his work was not recognized and proclaimed as the work of a genius, he took this as proof once again of his inferiority and failure. The paradox for him was that failure was success. To be weak and defective, after all, was the basis of his specialness. His weakness and failures confirmed and demonstrated his defectiveness, had also made him a special child who deserved special attention and consideration. The special attention and treatment were continued and preserved by maintaining himself in the position of the baby. He became the family prince. He commented: "Even if you lose, even if you are beaten, you're still the prince!" In this distorted logic, success and failure had become blurred and confused. Success had become failure, and failure had become success. Success had come to mean power, strength, hurtful destructiveness, cold hard egotism, loss of love, isolation, and attack from other hostile and powerful antagonists. Failure had come to mean safety, protection, loving care, specialness. Failure had become Larry's strength. It was his avenue to being babied, being allowed to get away with things, being given special privileges and special consideration.

His resistance to any modification of his sense of himself as defective, inadequate, and special was stubborn as rock. Only little by little did it wear away, under the persistent pressure of deepening interpretations and the analytic process. At first his attitudes did not seem to budge, but it gradually became more and more evident that in one or other area of his life he was beginning to function more adequately. He began to be able to speak up in class without embarrassment or overwhelming anxiety. He was increasingly able to converse with and consult professors without a feeling of panic and predestined failure. He was slowly and by infinitesimal degrees able to function more effectively in his work. He became increasingly comfortable with the consultation situation, and even began to enjoy it. As we shall see, his severe anxiety in sexual matters also began to diminish and finally disappear. In all these areas, his increasing capacity to mobilize his aggression in the interest of overcoming obstacles and adaptive functioning was noteworthy. The inhibiting fears and convictions of weakness and inadequacy gave way to an increasing capacity to overcome the obstacles to effective self-expression and self-assertion. Ever so slowly, he began to accept the possibility that he could make the analysis a success too, that it need not turn out to be a failure. As he stuck to the analysis over time and began to make it work for him, the disparity between the reality and his fantasy became all the more marked and unavoidable. Such too was the case in relation to his extra-analytic experiences. The gap between the reality of his performance and the doubts and fears of his fantasies became irreconcilable. The fantasy had ceased to dominate and control his behavior, but it became all the more clear that he clung to it in neurotic and willfully stubborn ways.

AGGRESSION AND SEXUALITY

The problem of sexuality was central in the analysis, a catch-all area within which all the conflictual themes were channeled, and which required continual reworking and working through of the basic issues. When feelings of inadequacy and convictions about his weakness and defectiveness had been eroded in most of the other areas of his life, he remained stubbornly convinced that he was doomed to be a failure sexually. His first experiences with girls were hesitant and anxious. He felt awkward, unsure of himself, and could never understand how other guys got to know girls and take them out. Asking a girl for a date was a "trial by fire"—he dreaded refusal, rejection, being told that he was repulsive and no good. Adolescent sexual talk about making girls excited him, but he professed little idea of what that meant or how one did it. Attempts at touching girls or feeling them up were met with rebuffs. He would become terribly anxious, feeling that his attempts were clumsy and awkward.

Alongside this timorous and inhibited pattern of experience, he maintained an active and intense fantasy life. During latency, he had cherished an elaborate fantasy in which he was headmaster of a large school of boys. The boys were all absolutely submissive to his will. In the school they were all naked, and Larry lived in an apartment at the top of the school. He would bring the boys there and play with them sexually, and they would submit completely to his sexual and largely perverted wishes. About this time he and Piggy, the kid next door, started playing with each other, and Piggy would passively accommodate himself to any of Larry's sexual wishes. The extent of the actual activity is uncertain—probably little more than mutual masturbation—but for Larry this was the realization in fact of his fantasy. The activity lasted for only a few months.

When Larry came into puberty, the fantasy did not disappear, but instead of only boys in the school, there were also girls. Masturbation fantasies pertained to certain girls to whom he was attracted, but whom he was afraid to approach. He would fantasize them without clothes and completely submissive to his wishes. Most exciting were the fantasies of fellatio—getting a "blow job"—and anal intercourse. In the fantasy he was domineering and powerful. He could tell the girl to "strip and suck"—and she would immediately submit to his commands. Essential to the fantasy, however, was the idea that she was forced against her will; so powerful was he that she could not resist his wishes. Along with this there was a sadistic streak. He would imagine himself tying up these naked girls so that they were helpless, then beating them, whipping them, screwing them, and having them suck his penis.

The difficulty was that, however exciting the fantasies, they intruded on his attempts to relate sexually. As he became increasingly intimate with a given date, he also became increasingly tense and anxious. He began to think of the real girl in terms of the slave-woman of his fantasies. Every conversation became a seduction. Every movement placed him on the threshold of rape. His mind was flooded with preoccupations: Would she do it? Would she surrender herself to him? Would she "strip and suck"? The overpowering fear was that she would. His fantasies might become a reality, as they had with Piggy. He longed for and dreamed about a girl who would take

Piggy's place, who would become his sexual slave and fulfill his every whim. Every girl he met became an instant candidate for the position. At the same time, the prospect filled him with anxious dread, trapped between the fulfillment of his desires—making him the powerful and destructive phallic aggressor—and the fear of failure—preserving and confirming his weakness and defectiveness. With every girl, and in every least contact with girls, he was caught between his anxious wishes to sexualize and to desexualize, to succeed or to fail, to play the man or the child.

He was convinced that wanting sex was reprehensible and evil. His parents would not approve of sleeping with girls. It was something he had to be devious about and conceal. And the girls might find out what he was thinking and what he wanted to do to them: then they would know that he was perverted and dangerous, and that he should be repulsed and avoided. If he made any move in that direction, he would be found out and be doomed to sexual failure. He felt the urge to leap in and get the whole thing over, but at the same time dreaded coming too soon, ejaculating prematurely in his pants so that then the girl would know that he was a weak and defective male and could not control himself.

As we worked on these problems in the analysis he became increasingly able to relate to girls and finally developed a rather intense sexual relationship with Janet. All of his sexual fears were again focused in this relationship. He could not believe that she was really interested in him or that she could care for him. His view of himself as an outsider found its way into a dream. In the dream they were in a motel room. Janet was in bed with another man, and Larry was forced to sleep in a chair. He sneaked over to the bed and watched while Janet and the man were lying naked in the bed. The man was very good—"screwing and eating" her. Janet looked up and saw Larry, but didn't stop. The man kept screwing for the longest time, and Janet was having intense orgasms. Larry felt inadequate and lonely—left out. Then Janet came to him and tried to console him. He was dejected and just wanted to cry. "How could they do this to me?" He recalled his feelings of being left out and lonely when his parents were in bed together. How could his mother go to bed with his father and leave Larry alone? How could they leave him out?

In Larry's view sex was something that girls submitted to even though they didn't want or like it. They had to be forced or tricked into it. If a boy had relations with a girl, it was something that he got away with by being sneaky or devious. It did not take long to discover that this attitude derived from his mother. For her, sex was something men did to women, something women had to accept as part of their burden in life, that in sex boys hurt girls even if they don't know it. Mother and son shared the fantasy that sex was aggressive and hurtful and destructive. Larry's comment:

> She's a woman with a lot of anger. She's terrified of her emotions. When my grandfather died, she almost cracked up—she was still crying a year later. She took it harder than my grandmother. She sees everything as hurting her. I could never understand it. She can't let people live their own lives. She thinks her children grew up just to hurt her. That's just the way she puts it. My whole life is based on that. I grew up with the feeling that I could really do damage. The scariest line is "How could you do this to me?" She used it often—not just for special occasions. How could boys do such things to girls? And the grimmest part is that she never gives up. That was part of her sitting *shiva*—to grow up was to kill Mother.

Larry's sexual life was dominated by his image of the relationship between his parents. To allow oneself to love a woman was to become vulnerable and weak, to be taken advantage of and exploited, controlled and domineered. Sex was not based on love but on power. The only sexuality he could conceive of was the sexuality of brute force, sadistic subjugation, phallic aggression. The alternatives were forcing the woman to submit or being subjugated and controlled by her. His ambivalence was displayed on both sides of this dilemma. His aggressive and sadistic wishes to force women to become his sexual slaves were matched by his fears of hurting them by this form of hypermasculine attack. His wishes to be passive and dependent were matched by his intense fears of vulnerability and weakness. It was a trap out of which he could not find his way.

His relationship with Janet was shrouded in Larry's mind with clearly oedipal concerns. He feared that she would try to control his life, would pull him down so that he could no longer be free and independent, that he would be trapped into having to please her and submit to her whims and her control, as he had so often seen his father having to give in to his mother. For a time he tried to fend off his tender and loving feelings for Janet, but they were soon evident. He found them threatening. To allow oneself to feel and to admit love for a girl was to put oneself in a vulnerable position. He wanted to keep himself in the position of being able to play at sex—without accepting any deeper or more meaningful commitments. Loving a girl meant marriage, restriction, responsibility, being trapped, helpless, and vulnerable.

The fear and longing for his mother lay behind these concerns. At one point he dreamed that he and Janet were lying together naked. He moved his bowels, and Janet wiped his behind. She asked him if he wanted Vaseline rubbed on his penis. He remembered that the night before Janet had been playing with his penis and had "beat him off." He had felt passive, as though she were just leading him around by the penis. The associations moved to the scenes with his mother, when she would rub his back, and he would want her to play with his buttocks and fondle his penis. Beyond that were the memories of sitting on the potty and of her stroking his penis. His mother had led him around by the penis, gotten him to do her bidding by playing with his penis. In relationship to Janet, he felt like a helpless baby that she could play with and do with as she pleased.

Castration anxiety was a strong component in all of these fears. Not long after he had begun to sleep with Janet, he dreamed that he was sleeping with a huge black woman with large sharp teeth in her vagina. He first recalled his first visit to a prostitute at about fifteen. He remembered being frightened and unable to get an erection, and wanting her to give him a "blow job." The woman had a large dog and he was afraid that the dog would bite off his penis. A second memory was of a time in college when a friend of his, whom he saw as a strong male figure, suggested that they get some women. Larry was reluctant but went along because he didn't want to seem afraid or weak in his friend's eyes. The two women arrived, one white and one black; Larry got the black. He remembered that his friend had laid his girl and screwed her in a matter of minutes, but Larry didn't know what to do. He had trouble getting an erection, then couldn't penetrate, and finally came prematurely all over her belly. His friend and the other girl sat watching him, and his embarrassment and shame were mortifying. He felt like he was a little kid who had messed his pants, and everyone could see that he was a defective, messy baby who couldn't control his bowels or his penis.

Another association in this context, related to premature ejaculation, was his feeling that intercourse was like running to the toilet when he had to go as a child. He felt that there was little sense of separation in his mind between bedroom and bathroom. As a child he would wait until he couldn't hold it any longer, then run for the bathroom, so that he could go quickly. Then his mother would be pleased and proud of him. The problem, of course, was that he would sometimes mess his pants. The association with premature ejaculation was clear, as was also the conclusion that wetting his pants, like coming too soon, was proof of his defectiveness and inability to control himself.

The aggression in Larry's sexual escapades was directed to overcoming the supposed resistance to sexual activity on the part of the women. It served an added function in overcoming the obstacle posed by his sexual anxieties and his sense of himself as sexually inadequate. The violence and peremptoriness of his sexual demands were in another register efforts to overcome the obstacles posed by his persistent attachment to his mother and to break free of her controling influence. Along a parallel track, his efforts to deal with his parents' attitudes regarding sex took the form of increasing confrontation and deviation from their wishes.

But we are getting a little ahead of the story. As we continued to process this sexual material, little bits of doubt or questioning began to arise in his recountings. At times it was not altogether clear that the women were acting as sexual slaves submitting unwillingly to his demands. The possibility had to be considered that they might be interested in having sex, that they might want it and even engage in it quite willingly. This might imply that they did not view him as repulsive and want to reject him, but that in some degree they might find him attractive and the idea of sex with him desirable. This ran counter to his basic convictions about himself, but he came gradually to accept the possibility. As this appreciation took hold, the necessity and pressure behind his sexually aggressive and sadistic approach began to diminish so that sexual activity became less a matter of power and submission and more a matter of mutual satisfaction and pleasure.

These trends found their way into his relationship with Janet. As the analysis progressed she became his primary sexual object. The relationship had its ups and downs, but over time Larry became increasingly involved and began to develop feelings of fondness and caring toward her. It took a long time for him to come to the point at which he could say he loved her. The obstacles were not only his longstanding convictions of repulsiveness and unlovability, but his pervasive fears of commitment, of being tied down, of allowing a woman to enter and start running his life, of being forced to submit to her demands and wishes. Larry had episodes of doubt and recrimination when Janet would see other men, or when he thought she might be having sex with other men. But regardless, the relationship developed, and finally he worked up the courage to propose and his proposal was accepted. The marriage turned out to be successful and solid.

From the point of view of the vicissitudes of aggression, at first his aggression was stymied and inhibited. The sense of vulnerability and inadequacy that permeated his view of himself as sexual was defensively organized to keep in check the sense of powerful destructiveness and hateful sadism that had become associated in his mind with any expression of aggression. His sexuality was at that point inhibited and fraught with anxiety. As this linkage was gradually loosened, room was made available for more direct expression of his wishes and fantasies, however perverted and destructive they remained. From a position of anxious inhibition with premature ejaculation, he moved to the opposite extreme in which his sexual aggression found open and prolific expression. The element of rebellious flaunting of these wishes was unmistakable, reflecting his rejection of and rebellion against parental, especially maternal, proscriptions and control. Under the circumstances, halfway measures would not do. It was all or nothing. He was either to remain the inadequate, weak, defective, sexually impaired baby, or he would become the powerful, demanding, forceful, master of any and all sexual objects, who could force them to submit to his least and most perverted wish.

But how did this evolution take place? It is worth noting that the quality of Larry's sexual activity, whether inhibited or predatory, was never directly in question. Rather the focus fell on the underlying assumptions and view regarding himself that lay behind his behavior. From the analyst's point of view, the task was maintaining a neutral perspective and avoiding the constant invitation and pressure coming from the patient to endorse his view of himself or to interact with him in terms that would confirm or reinforce his convictions about himself, that is, to engage in some form of countertransference and/or transference-countertransference enactment. The interpretive process focused on these assumptions, for example his view of himself as a defective baby, questioning the assumption and tracing its origins in his family experience. Gradually the sources and motivations underlying this conviction became clearer, as well as the motivations involved in his need to cling to this conviction about himself. Similar questioning of his self-concept as the powerful, sexually demanding, and sadistic master of his sexual slaves led to a gradual unveiling of its underpinnings, especially on one hand the defensive need to counter the opposite view of himself as inadequate and defective and on the other his rebellious of throwing off the parental, especially maternal, yoke. An increasing appreciation of these dynamics on his part allowed his aggressive capacity to find more adaptive and constructive outlets.

AGGRESSION IN CAREER

The role of aggression in Larry's career trajectory followed an analogous path. When he started the analysis, he was still a graduate student. Anxiety and inhibition pervaded his whole experience. In class he was overwhelmed with anxiety, particularly if he was called on or had to make any sort of presentation. Conferences with mentors or professors were torture—he was constantly convinced that he was making a fool of himself, that he wasn't smart enough to do the work, that they thought poorly of him, that anything he did was of inferior quality. When he wrote papers he was convinced they were worthless and that the professor would reject them out of hand. When a paper came back with a superior grade, he could not believe it, thought there was some mistake, and so on. His life as a student was an agony of anxiety and insecurity, despite the obvious signs of acceptance and even distinction. Despite his anxieties, his level of academic performance remained high.

After graduation, the anxieties continued, now in the context of his professional work and performance. Because of his qualifications and expertise, he was hired by a prestigious firm and increasingly found himself consulted and his opinions solicited. He accepted an academic appointment, which put the further burden on him of teaching and acting as a guide and mentor to his students. By this time, work on his basic anxieties had progressed in the analysis to a point at which he was increasingly able to control his anxieties and doubts and still perform effectively. The anxieties continued, however, and reasserted themselves in countless contexts. He constantly reiterated the familiar theme of his being a little boy playing at adult's business, and that he was not up to the challenge, that he couldn't do the work, that too much was expected and he couldn't measure up. He frequently appealed to his childhood fantasy of having an office of his own and a checkbook from which he could write checks and play a grown-up role. The image of a child playing an adult game pervaded his image of himself working in a real office and doing real adult work. The idea of making decisions and taking responsibility for his decisions and actions was frightening—too adult for him.

Paradoxically, alongside these pervasive convictions, he became increasingly involved in the demands of work, took on increasing loads of responsibility beyond the call of duty, even beyond the call of reason. Not unlike his sexual involvements, his attitude was that he should be able to do anything. His wish for power and control was omnivorous; if he let any opportunity go by, someone else would snatch it away from him and he would be pushed aside and to that extent no longer important. He seemed to have little sense of proportion or of his own limitations. Everything was opportunity, possibility, or a source of power and specialness. Anxieties born of insecurity gave way to anxieties based on undertaking too much and trying to do too much. He could not do justice to the projects he undertook, and to that extent found himself overwhelmed and able to turn these shortcomings against himself in self-accusations of inadequacy and defect. But the driving force was the desire for power and importance. The narcissistic dimensions of this pattern were clear, but there seemed little room for the idea of working out of a sense of interest or deriving pleasure from work activities. The concept that enough is enough was entirely alien to his thinking. Narcissism demanded more and more, and there was no such thing as enough.

The therapeutic task was to help him to see the self-defeating quality of this pattern of behavior and to begin to question the motivational underpinnings. Professionally, his behavior was driven by a competitive need to match or excel the accomplishments of his brother Harry, who had become a quite successful professional on his own. For Larry to call a halt, to say that he had enough on his plate, or that he could plot his own course of accomplishment or path through life, was to accept being second-rate, being less successful than his brother, being the little brother who was less than adequate and inferior. The way out of this dilemma was to become the greedy, ambitious, hardworking power broker, whose reach had to exceed his grasp. He was able to turn his aggression to this purpose, quite analogously to the way in which he correspondingly had directed his aggression into his predatory sexuality. In both cases, as the underlying image of himself as a defective, weak, and inadequate little baby, who could only play at being an adult, began to mitigate, the pattern of hard-driving, intensely competitive, voracious, and predatory expression of aggression also began to soften into a more moderate and balanced picture. Instead of staying at the office until late in the evening, he began to plan his day better and go home at the end of office hours. Instead of greedily grasping at every opportunity that came along, he became more discriminating and selective, paying attention to those that interested him or that seemed more important. His life gradually became more normalized and manageable. This shift became most noteworthy after the birth of his first child, a boy. Larry became a father and he sincerely loved this child, wanted to be a good father, to be the father that he had always wanted his own father to be.

THE ANALYTIC RELATION

Aggression in the Transference

The course of Larry's analysis was by no means smooth and untroubled. From the beginning he was evidently terribly frightened of the analytic situation. He had delivered himself into the clutches of a powerful monster who could control him, force him to submit, turn on him and destroy him—all his fears of vulnerability and attack were raised to a pitch of intensity. He saw the analyst as a Nazi stormtrooper who would delight sadistically in tormenting and bringing ruin upon his helpless Jewish victim. These thoughts dominated his fantasies and dreams. He talked of leaving the analysis, of wanting to bolt off the couch and run to safety, of wanting to get on his knees and beg the analyst to be kind and merciful, begging him not to hurt him. These fears were dramatic and dominated the early phase of his analysis and were accompanied by intense anxiety, almost to the point of terror at times. These fears burst forth almost from the beginning of the analysis, presumably reflecting a transference readiness that had been tuned to a high pitch of intensity.

It quickly became apparent that something had to be done or the analysis would be in imminent danger of foundering on the harsh rocks of Larry's acute persecutory anxiety. It was necessary to intervene actively and somewhat forcefully to attempt to reinforce the therapeutic alliance. Larry needed an ally and some sense of support in order to gain some perspective on his neurotic fears and anxieties. The analyst commented that he did not know what was happening to Larry at that point, but apparently it was something that was frightening him so severely that there was danger of disrupting the analysis. If they allowed his feelings to run their course, they could do him damage; the analyst added that he did not see breaking off the analysis as in Larry's interest, but that they had better do what they could to understand what he was experiencing. By that time enough information about his object relations history was available to suggest some of the roots of his anxieties and distortions. The analyst took the bull by the horns and pointed out the transference elements that seemed to loom so large in his reaction. The analyst suggested that the malignant thoughts and intentions Larry attributed to him were in large measure his thoughts and not the analyst's, that in fact he had no idea of what the analyst's thoughts really were. He also suggested that Larry expected him to respond as his mother had, by being intrusive and controlling and by trying to run his life: but perhaps the analytic situation was quite different, in fact one such as he had never experienced before in any other context of his life. It seemed very difficult for Larry to think of the analysis in terms of a cooperative effort in which he and the analyst might work together to understand his problems and help him to deal with them. The analyst thus took a forceful stance aimed at overcoming the threat to the analysis posed by Larry's distortions and anxieties.

Episodes like this cast light on some of the perils connected with the analyst's aggression in the analytic interaction. This intervention was both confrontative and interpretive. It reflected the impact of the analyst's aggression, aimed here at overcoming the obstacle to the analytic work posed by Larry's transference fears and fantasies. The problem for the analyst is whether his aggression will be channeled through countertransference or through the therapeutic alliance. The confrontational aspect draws the analytic response closer to the countertransference model but does not necessarily involve it. The analyst's intervention was forceful, forcing the patient to attend to certain issues and to take some responsibility for the consequences of what he was thinking and feeling. The question at that juncture was whether the analyst was playing out the role of aggressor to his victim—one possible scenario. But the intervention was also cast in terms of the need to achieve some perspective that would salvage the analytic process and contribute to some better reformulation of the analytic relation and the way in which he and the analyst interacted. This was in the interest of preserving and extending the analysis, ultimately for the patient's benefit. On these terms, the intervention, even though aggressively advanced, was more attuned to the alliance model (Meissner, 1996b). Had the analyst adopted a more parental posture, scolding, belittling, criticizing, or otherwise infantilizing Larry's anxieties, he would have been enacting a countertransference stance. The approach through the alliance, even an aggressive response calculated to overcome obstacles, is quite different.

The acute form of Larry's transference anxiety was channeling into the relation with the analyst anxieties that were overdetermined and derived from several mutually reinforcing sources. Further exploration and rather extensive working through of the persecutory concerns related to his parents seemed to diminish his paranoid fears, but did not eliminate them. It gradually became apparent that there were other determinants of these anxieties, which had not been adequately dealt with, and which little by little came into focus. They had to do with Larry's older brother Harry. It turned out that the decision to undertake analysis was strongly influenced by Harry, who had undertaken his own analysis and advised Larry throughout and supported Larry's decision to do an analysis. In the ancient spirit of his resentment, Larry felt that being in analysis was another manifestation and instance of his brother's trying to push him around and run his life. In undertaking the analysis, he was following Harry's wishes, not his own. The analysis was at that point Harry's, not Larry's.

Larry felt resentment about this state of affairs, but in his typical style reinforced his submission to Harry's wishes and his supposed dependence by continually consulting him about what was happening in the analysis. As he explored his fears and doubts and questions in the analysis, it soon became apparent that the thoughts he was expressing were in fair measure not his own, but were ideas that he had picked up from conversations with his brother. Harry would tell him stories about how analysts dealt with patients, how they tricked them, how they manipulated patients by using certain techniques, how patients became dependent, etc.—all of which fed into and reinforced Larry's paranoid fears. There was obviously no way of knowing how much of this really came from his brother and how much was distortion on the part of Larry himself. The question that had to be settled was whether this was going to be his analysis or his brother's.

He was clearly using his brother as a defense against his own deeper fears that, if he committed himself to the analysis, made it his own, and invested himself in the hard work that it entailed to make it a success, he might not be able to carry it off. He was clinging to the position of dependent little brother—the baby—afraid to take the risk of succeeding or failing on his own. Participation and engagement in the analysis was a direct challenge to his dependent baby status and correspondingly to his sense of specialness.

The focus of the analysis gradually moved away from these anxieties and turned instead to the myriad and multifaceted contexts in which Larry felt himself to be weak and defective and doomed to failure. The contexts were many—we have considered most of the important ones. His depressive feelings had to be worked through in each instance. This was by far the longest phase of his analysis. He increasingly came to see that the basis for his anxieties was not the reality that confronted him, but the elaborate fantasy that he carried in his head. The working through consisted in large measure of defining and demonstrating the effects and implications of his self-devaluation and its related fantasies in so many contexts of his life and activity—sex, work, study, play, etc. The roots of the fantasy were clear and the working through brought us back again and again to the infantile basis of his convictions of defectiveness and helplessness and weakness.

As these issues were gradually worked through, the anxieties diminished in other areas of his experience as well. He slowly developed a rather firm and productive therapeutic relationship. He felt less and less of a distance and difference between himself and me, and more of a sense of his own capacity to do the work of the analysis—freer to advance his own interpretations, to offer his associations without fear of seeming foolish, or being laughed at. Free associating was no longer "bullshitting." The paranoid thoughts seemed to evaporate. They became increasingly rare, and were revived only in minor forms and as passing thoughts with less and less conviction or feeling in them. Such recrudescences seemed to occur in circumstances in which he was called on to perform or produce and in which his competence or ability was being put to the test. The paranoid concerns in the many other parts of his life faded and became increasingly remote in his experience as time went on.

The counterpart on the part of the analyst in the analytic interaction to the transference is countertransference. The point of our discussion is that aggressive countertransference enactments are generally to be avoided. Countertransference reactions are inevitable and perhaps unavoidable, as Renik (1993, 1995) has suggested, but in our view they are to be monitored, contained, and analyzed whenever they become conscious. On such terms they can contribute positively to the analytic process, but we are not in agreement with those who advocate countertransference enactments as a technical tool. In our view it is not the countertransference that is potentially therapeutic, but the capacity to process countertransference disruptions or enactments from the perspective of the alliance (Meissner, 1996b).

Countertransference inducements there were aplenty. Larry put a good deal of his effort in the analysis into trying to convince his analyst that he was defective and inadequate. The analyst's persistent refusal to accede to this view or to deal with him on any such terms posed a decisive obstacle to his continuing to hold on to this pejorative, self-demeaning, and self-diminishing view of himself. His aggression came into play in his more or less persistent efforts to draw the analyst into collusion with him in prolonging this view. But the analyst would have none of it, a response that at first frustrated him but in time became reassuring. The analyst would point out that the effort to maintain a therapeutic perspective (as contained within the alliance perspective) and avoid or overcome the obstacle posed by the patient's transference and/or countertransference inducements calls for implementation of the analyst's aggression. In an alliance perspective, paradoxically, the analyst's aggression can be mobilized to avoid or circumvent countertransference involvement. Larry's adherence to this view of himself and his efforts to convince the analyst of it put pressure on the analyst to bend his expectations or the requirements of the analysis to meet these insistent demands. But the analyst felt that he had to hold his analytic ground in the face of Larry's efforts to pressure him out of it. In other words, Larry's efforts posed an obstacle to effective therapeutic work that the analyst had to overcome or nullify in the interest of preserving the therapeutic context. Perhaps it was the manner in which Larry went about it—with a certain dogged determination and persistence—or perhaps it was the analyst's own obtuseness as a young analyst, but the analyst consistently found Larry's efforts more or less transparent, so that he could remain alert to such potential countertransference traps and try carefully to avoid them.

Aggression in the Real Relation

Aggression found its way into a variety of interactions between analyst and patient that we would regard as pertaining to the real relation (Meissner, 1996b, c, 1999c, 2000b). We are distinguishing the real relation from both transference and alliance as pertaining to those aspects of the analytic relation in which both participants are engaged in real interactions or are subject to real influences that lie beyond the scope of alliance factors. These are all aspects of the analytic relation and are simultaneously and concurrently intertwined and interacting. Thus, while transference, alliance, and the real relation are all concurrently in play, their respective roles in the analytic interaction can be distinguished and separately conceptualized.

If we can recall the earlier episode described above in which Larry was overwhelmed by panic and the fear that the analyst would attack him, so that he felt impelled to break off the analysis, that reaction could be conceptualized as a form of acting out in which his transference fears were being translated into an impulse to give them real expression. If the analyst would have accepted his fears as real and allowed him to act them out in breaking off the analysis, his reaction would have extended the interaction in real terms. This consideration highlights the interplay between transference and reality. Had the analyst acceded to his wish and allowed him to flee the analysis, he would have been acting out something on his own part. While the behavior would be enacted in real terms, we would have to wonder what might lie behind it in countertransferential or other terms. Would the analyst have wanted to get rid of Larry? Would he have been frightened by the intensity of Larry's reaction and so scared off? In fact, he was frightened both by the intensity of the reaction and by his own insecurity in understanding what was going on. Taking a strong stand was directed to overcoming the obstacle posed by his fears and the anxieties posed by his own fears that the analysis was self-destructing, and feeling correspondingly helpless and impotent in the face of it.

A central focus for such interaction in all analyses, not just in this one, is the effort on the part of the patient to actualize transference fantasies, that is, to draw the analyst into enacting some aspect of the transference wish. While Larry's transference fantasies were highly determined by the image of his intrusive, demanding, and controlling mother, elements of a father transference also played themselves out—

more in the positive terms of the kind of intimate and supportive relation he had always wanted from his father but never seemed able to achieve. This took the form of wanting to be on friendly terms with the analyst, to forget the analysis and go out together and have a man-to-man talk over a cup of coffee. This dynamic was driven by other transference fears of the analyst as the judging and potentially dangerous, attacking, and powerful figure who posed a constant threat to him. One way of dealing with these fears was to seduce the analyst into being his friend and confidant; only then could he trust him and allow himself to submit to his analytic control. The wish was also reflective of aspects of his maternal transference—his need to engage his mother in terms of the secrets they could share together was one way he had adopted to overcome his fears and anxieties involved in his relation with her.

A second area of real interaction focused around the issue of time. In the early stages of the analysis, coming on time was an issue fraught with anxiety and concern. For the most part, Larry was on hand a few minutes before the hour was scheduled to start. But increasingly this became a matter of anxious compulsion. He would dawdle until he barely had time to get to the office, then would scramble and make an anxious and uncertain dash to get there on time. If there were any obstacles or delays, like traffic jams, he would become panicked and enraged that his plans were thwarted. The issue of coming on time became another area in which Larry sought to elicit a controlling and parental reaction from the analyst. It was a repeated invitation for the analyst to scold him, to force him to come on time, in some way to punish him for not coming on time. But the analyst made no effort to respond to his lateness and waited for him to bring it up as matter for discussion, taking the position that it was Larry's analysis and that it was up to him to get himself there on time as he saw fit. The analyst expected him to assume that responsibility and to live up to the terms of the therapeutic agreement.

While these efforts to draw the analyst into a more real interaction were calculated to overcome the obstacle posed by the analyst's abstinent stance, the analyst's effort had to be directed to holding to the analytic tack. These enactments posed an obstacle to the preservation of the analytic situation and called into play a response from the analyst aimed at countering these pressures and keeping to the analytic path. Any attempt on his part to control Larry's lateness would have played into his hands and set up a pattern of interaction around the real issue of coming on time. If something might have been gained in terms of the time factor, something would have been lost in drawing the interaction away from the alliance sector and synonymously reinforcing his fantasies of the analyst as powerful, controlling, and demanding.

Aggression in the Alliance

The role of aggression in the alliance is difficult to conceptualize since so much of what pertains to the alliance we tend not to think of in aggressive terms. So much of it seems related to what we do as analysts and how we work with our patients when we are doing our analytic job effectively. The alliance pertains to those aspects of the analytic relation that have to do with the terms and conditions on which patient and analyst can work together to accomplish the analytic task. In this view, the alliance sector of the analytic relation is under constant challenge and pressure both from the side of transference and from the side of the real relation, so that the analyst is constantly called on to exercise himself in the interest of preserving the alliance and thus keeping the analytic process on track. The preceding examples can be read as indicating ways in which aggression can be called into play in resisting these pressures.

One of the salient aspects of analytic work requiring continuing effort and attention is interpretation. It is reasonable to assume that every interpretation is made in the face of some degree of resistance on the part of the analysand, if not on the part of the analyst. The motives for resistance on the part of the patient can be multiple and complex. In Larry's case, hearing and accepting an interpretation from his analyst meant acknowledging and accepting the analyst's legitimate role as interpreter, which meant accepting him as a trustworthy and well-intentioned object, acknowledging the degree of his dependence on him, and developing a sufficient degree of trust in him as a helpful, supportive, and understanding collaborator. Such a view of the analyst ran diametrically counter to his transference-generated view of him as judging, attacking, and potentially hurtful. Time and again in the early stages of the analysis, any attempts on the analyst's part to make an interpretation were met by Larry as accusations, putting him down, criticizing him, trying to manipulate him or force him to accept the analyst's views and take advantage of him. The issue for him at such points was either to submit and become the dependent and clinging child or to rebel, reject the analyst's view of things, and cling desperately to his way of seeing things. Interpretations were generally offered in a tentative form, as suggestions or possible hypotheses. As it became clear that there was little in such a stance that Larry could fight with, he became more aggressive in asserting his own views and positions—making his own interpretations much more in a spirit of competition. He wanted to prove to himself and to the analyst that he could do the analyst's job better than the analyst, that he could beat him to the punch and out-interpret him. The analyst's tack was to accept his interpretation as valid and then to reflect on it with him, developing the pros and cons, the consequences and implications, so that the interpretive process became more a matter of collaborative engagement, a back-and-forth give-and-take. It became a dialogue of assertion and counterassertion, calling into play a mild degree of aggressive effort at each point of move and countermove. One is reminded in reviewing this material of Freud's comparison of the analytic process to a chess game. At the better moments of this process, the exchange even had a quality of playfulness—never without its competitive edge and aggressive implications for both participants.

TERMINATION

This account of Larry's analysis is already lengthy enough. We would just add a word about the termination phase, which was significant. Not unexpectedly, many of Larry's anxieties and fears were brought up again in the context of termination. They were verbalized as fears of regressing after the end of the analysis when he no longer had the analyst and the analysis to fall back on. These fears did not have the same intensity or quality of concern as previously. They were voiced more or less as thoughtful possibilities rather than experienced as anxieties. The analyst responded to them as last vestiges of Larry's wish to be dependent and to avoid having to be responsible for himself and standing on his own feet. Larry was able to recognize that he had indeed accomplished a great deal during the course of the analysis, but was reluctant to accept the idea that he could go on from there and make a success of his life without the analysis. The basic question at that point, in terms of analysis, was whether the work that had been done in the past years was due to the analyst's efforts or whether the effects were due to the part that Larry himself had played in making them a reality. The realization that the analyst had been for the most part on the sidelines coaching, that he himself had been the one playing the game and that he himself was the responsible agent for his own therapeutic success, was an important stabilizing insight.

And so he came to the decision to end the analysis. The decision was itself an expression of aggression on his part, overcoming his reluctance and the obstacle posed by his fears of regressing and being unable to sustain the results of the analysis without continued support and assistance.

Chapter 11

Intensive Psychotherapy of Aggression in a Borderline Personality

Jim Smith began treatment when still a graduate student. His lifelong feelings of depressive emptiness were growing more intense, and he was progressively enveloped by diffuse anxiety. His brilliance and hard work had earned him the high regard of his professors and peers, but he had no truly close friends. Any who did gain some intimacy with him found themselves repeatedly rebuffed, as time and again he withdrew on some pretext into an irritated reserve, often then drawing closer to someone else. His homosexual way of life was in itself nonconflictual. However, he conducted his sexual life only on a casual basis, never in the context of an ongoing friendship or love relationship.

THE PARENTS

His mother was often on Jim's mind, and thinking about her filled him with rage. He liked his father, a semiskilled laborer, and respected his ethic of steady work. But he was also revolted by his father's subservience to his mother, punctuated by episodes of their shouting and actually physically fighting. Usually these were times when his father had been drinking too much. His mother was emotionally quite

227

overinvolved with Jim. Her intensity was always in terms of her own wishes and needs. She rarely recognized him in his own right as a person separate from her. His identity was her identity. While she often became so preoccupied that she seemed to forget his existence, she would just as often approach him seductively with sensuous body closeness, only to push him away in disgust when he responded with an erection. When angry she would declare that she had made him and she could just as well kill him. As a child he believed her. At times she took to her bed in depression, unresponsive to everyone.

Despite all this, his mother remained a compelling figure for Jim. As he said, Jeannie was very beautiful, and it was heaven to be close with her. She gloried in his high intelligence and encouraged his efforts to achieve academically. Although economically poor, she vigorously and successfully gained admission for him in the best schools in the city.

Jim was the firstborn child. When he had just turned three, his mother began having the other children, four more in all. At the time of each delivery, she sent Jim away to live with her childless sister in another state, once for a full year. She claimed that the reason was to ease her burdens. The aunt and her husband were quietly kind, but did not relate well to the boy. He felt desolate, describing these times away from his mother as like being stranded on a frozen desert. Part of the time he managed his isolation with blissful fantasies of being harmoniously close to his wonderful Jeannie, but he could not sustain them.

THE TREATMENT

As twice-a-week psychotherapy deepened over a period of several months, Jim felt increasingly dependent on his therapist. Missing him between hours became urgent, and anxiety mixed with his longing. He grew increasingly angry with the therapist for not being with him enough. He believed this was because the therapist did not really care. The transference evolved into a vividly lived-out projection of his introjected relationship with his mother. His associations ranged back and forth between experiences with his mother and with the therapist. He spoke about her lack of caring, or her seeming to care, only to turn her back on him again, at which he would become enraged. Repeatedly the therapist asked about, or directly noted, similarities between his experiences with his mother and with the therapist. The therapist's clarifications and interpretations effected some degree of cognitive insight—Jim could at least see the similarity. But he could not really grasp the fact that, as experience, his relationship with the therapist was not actually like that with his mother. He could not experience that the therapist consistently cared about him and wanted to know him in his own right. In his experience, he now needed the therapist to care for him continually, not his mother; and because the therapist basically did not care about him, he often disappointed him severely and let him down.

As this combined experience of needing and being abandoned by his therapist and his mother deepened, he alternated between feeling that some of his time with his therapist was wonderfully close, but much of the time, especially between treatment hours, he was left alone in desert-like isolation. He seemed to become unable to use evocative memory for maintaining a sense of being with the therapist. Not only was he often unable to call to mind what it was like to be together with the therapist, but also he could not even at times recall any depiction or image of the therapist in his mind's eye. His excellent academic performance continued apace, but most of the time everything seemed meaningless to him.

As Jim's need for contact with his therapist became increasingly conscious and urgent, his rage with him grew to intense proportions. For two years, he refused to look him in the eye, even to glance at his face. He kept his head down or averted to one side. However, as they worked to retain whatever contact and therapeutic endeavor was possible, he gradually regained some capacity to look at the therapist's face with increasing eye contact. Eventually he was able to explain that he had been so filled with rage that he developed the terrifying delusion that his direct gaze would shatter the therapist's head into slivers of glass.

THE ROLE OF AGGRESSION

In trying to understand the role of aggression in this experience, Jim seemed to be struggling with two issues that required the use of aggression in refusing to look at the therapist. Both derived from the intensity of his desire and need for closeness. One issue was that his desire and need was in itself unbearable when he was in the therapist's presence. This unbearable yearning constituted an obstacle to his allowing himself to be together with the therapist. In order to overcome this obstacle, at least enough to allow continuing treatment, Jim steadfastly averted his gaze, thus reducing the intensity of the stimulation he felt in the therapist's presence. The second issue related to his frustration in not being able to attain the intensity of closeness with the therapist that he felt he needed. On one level, Jim directly hated the therapist because he had failed to fulfill these urgent needs. In this respect his hatred was destructive in nature, but not in our view aggressive. However, on another level his intolerable frustration motivated Jim to wish to destroy his therapist simply to gain relief from the frustration. In our view, it was at this point that Jim's destructiveness qualified as reflecting an aggressive motivation insofar as the destructive fantaasy served the purpose of overcoming the frustrating obstacle by destroying the therapist as the object of his unfulfilled need. His aggressive destructiveness took the form of a delusion that if he looked at the therapist his gaze of hatred would shatter his head.

This delusional form of aggressive destructiveness presented Jim with the dilemma that carrying it into action (by looking at the therapist) would mean destroying him, and that would mean losing him. The result would be to plunge him into even more desperate aloneness. Thus both his destructive rage (derived from frustration) and his aggressive destructiveness (motivated by the need for overcoming the obstacle and gaining some relief) posed further obstacles to his need to preserve whatever sustaining contact he could have with the therapist, contact that, even though insufficient and in some degree frustrating, he experienced as essential for his survival. His means for overcoming this obstacle was to mobilize an aggressive effort to oppose the (delusional) consequences of his destructive urges by forcing himself to avoid the face-to-face, eye-to-eye contact with his therapist that he otherwise greatly desired.

Based on this understanding of aggression, therapeutic work with Jim's survival-based needs and destructive rage were conceived in motivational terms rather than as drive derivatives. The term "aggression" was never used in the therapeutic interchange because it was not necessary in order for Jim to come to full motivational understanding of his use of aggression. Furthermore, while our theoretical understanding of the meaning of aggression guided the process, for Jim any use of the term "aggression" on the therapist's part would have caused confusion because it would have been so difficult for him to understand it without confusing it with the vernacular meaning of the word.

INCORPORATIVE YEARNING

As both his rage and the fear of his rage diminished, Jim was able to realize more clearly the marked degree to which he needed and yearned for closeness between himself and the therapist. However, even though he expressed how painfully he yearned to be close, he grew more and more aloof during therapy hours. Eventually this aloofness was expressed with physical distancing. On entering and leaving the office, he followed a path as far away from the therapist as the contours of the room and the size of the doorway would allow. Whenever the therapist shifted forward a little in his chair, Jim, with a look of fear, pushed himself as far back in his own chair as he could. The therapist commented that it looked like these behaviors expressed a fear of closeness. Jim acknowledged this and worked with it associatively, to the point that he became conscious that he—nearly delusionally—feared that on entering and leaving the office he could fall into the therapist's chest and disappear, becoming totally absorbed in him. Interpretations suggested that his fear might be arising from unconscious wishes for just that kind of ultimate closeness. Here it seemed clear that Jim experienced his need for closeness in terms of being absorbed in the therapist, or, vice versa, the therapist being absorbed in him, as posing an imminent threat of annihilation of either one or both. That is, his yearning for absorption presented a potent obstacle to his and the therapist's survival. In the service of maintaining survival of both, he mobilized aggression to overcome this obstacle, aggression in the form of symptomatically employing a behavioral counterforce to maintain as much physical distance as possible. At the same time, he also aggressively employed the defense of repression in order to avoid internally conscious awareness of the extent of his yearning as well as the annihilatory fear it aroused.

Further associations and related interpretative work led to the emergence of overt cannibalistic urges, which came to full expression in a dream in which Jim was eating pieces of meat and recognized, to his horror, that the meat was pieces of the therapist. Another dream brought further insight into a frightening reversal of the means for gaining such ingestive togetherness: in the dream the therapist appeared in the form of a large-billed bird that was trying to eat him. Further therapeutic work allowed Jim to gain full understanding of how his intense survival-driven need, arising from his extreme aloneness, naturally excited intense, heretofore unconscious, urges to incorporate the therapist into his own body by eating or absorbing him, or conversely to be incorporated into the therapist's body by his eating or absorbing Jim. He was able to understand, with increasing perspective, that the intensity of his need was so great as to bring about experiencing these nearly delusional conscious and unconscious fantasies as if they seemed to present real dangers of destroying or being destroyed by the therapist, thus losing any possibility of togetherness and plunging him back into unbearable aloneness.

In this phase of the therapeutic work, the therapist's view of destructiveness and aggression was much the same as when they had addressed the destructiveness of Jim's head-shattering rage and his compensatory use of aggression in managing it. The paradigm was cast in terms of motivations rather than an appeal to drives, and aggression was understood as central to his life-preserving defenses. It is notable that once his head-shattering rage subsided, there was no further anger involved in his incorporative urges and defenses against them. Aggression took the form of overcoming the obstacle posed to their survival by maintaining both a literal distance between his body and the therapist's as well as a psychological distance by means of repression and an attitude of aloofness. Conversely it should also be noted that Jim further employed aggression in the service of maintaining the treatment. Because his great fear of annihilation through absorption aroused such intense fear of being with the therapist, it seemed that his struggle with the urges to avoid being in the therapist's presence altogether posed an obstacle to his remaining in the treatment he so much needed. He brought his aggression into play in overcoming this obstacle by forcing himself regardless to remain in treatment.

In the working through of this therapeutic achievement, Jim gradually lost his fear of incorporative urges. They no longer threatened loss through mutual destruction, and so no longer presented an obstacle to his experiencing and expressing them. He continued to feel them just as urgently, with consequent reemergence of his rage with the much-too-absent therapist. He began consciously and purposely to translate both his need and his rage into action by cruising in a notorious area of the city where homosexual men engaged in anonymous, indiscriminate sex that risked violent assault. Jim ragefully confronted the therapist with his determined quest for fellatio, saying, "I'll take what I have coming." It was clear that he meant to seize and ingest what he both needed and had a right to; at the same time the danger to which he exposed himself expressed his rage. It was relatively easy to help him see that all this was displaced from his rageful hunger for the therapist, to get the therapist inside, and that the fury arising from frustration of his survival need was being simultaneously acted out on the therapist as well as turned against himself. But that insight was insufficient to protect him from pursuing his dangerous behavior. However, his behavior was not in motivational terms aggressive: there was no obstacle for him to overcome in expressing his need and hate in this displaced action. So it fell to the therapist to mobilize his own aggression in order to protect him. His behavior presented a dangerous threat to his safety. Clarification of the danger proved useless, because he did not care. Aggressively, the therapist confronted him that he must cease this behavior.[1] He forcefully insisted, but did not threaten. Jim was surprised with the force of the therapist's confrontation, and it proved adequate to bring about cessation of his activities.

Deprived of this means of acting out and satisfying his incorporative need and rage, Jim became more purely enraged and suicidal. In this part of the therapy, he experienced nearly intolerable moments in which he could summon no memory image of the therapist beyond a vague inner picture, one that gave him no sense of connection. He could not sense any feeling of being in the therapist's presence in memory. He described very frightening times when he grew convinced that the therapist did not exist. Functionally, he lost use of evocative memory of the therapist and his relationship with him.[2] On one such occasion, he drank heavily and in a rage of aloneness recklessly crashed his car into the side of a river bridge. His suicidal feelings and urges grew more frequent and urgent. The therapist interpreted his loss of memory for the therapist and their relation as resulting from the impact of extreme rage with the therapist so that he lost cognitive and emotional contact with him in his memory. This experience was related genetically to the times in childhood when he was separated from his mother, feeling so exiled that it was like being alone on a frozen desert. On a cognitive level, these explanations made sense to him, but seemed to offer no relief.

In terms of our present perspective, we could say that his functional loss of memory of his sustaining relationship became an obstacle to the preservation of Jim's life. He was helpless to overcome this obstacle, so that the therapist was required to provide the means to do so. The therapist responded to the dangers of his memory regression and self-destructiveness by insisting that at such times he must not act on his fear, rage, and suicidal urges, but must instead telephone him and, when necessary, have extra appointments. He emphasized that in this way Jim would have a chance to learn that the therapist did continually exist, did continually remember and care about him, and actually was available to him. This insistence proved to be an effective use of the therapist's aggression to overcome the obstacle to his treatment. For about a year, Jim did contact the therapist by phone when faced with too much anguish of aloneness, memory loss, hate, and suicidal urges. At the worst times extra sessions were held. By these ways of giving him more supportive contact while maintaining interpretive efforts, the therapist attempted to help him gain full insight and continue working through his aloneness, rage, incorporative urges, regressive memory loss, and suicidal propensity. Genetic interpretations and working through were also focused on his clear transference to the therapist as a seductive and abandoning mother. It would not have been possible to accomplish this work without prolonged aggressive responsiveness to the obstacles to his survival by insisting that he accept the support of telephone contacts and extra appointments.

The therapist's use of aggression succeeded in overcoming the obstacles to therapeutic progress posed by the patient's belief and acting out his belief that his rage could destroy both himself and him. This process, in turn, allowed for the development of Jim's capacity to give full verbal expression to his rage, while at the same time clearly understanding that both he and the therapist remained safe. Now he could involve himself in a working through process, in which he expressed his residual rage over not having his needs for sustaining closeness totally and passively fulfilled. Urgent need was no longer the issue, but deep yearning and wishing remained to be worked through. For example, he spent forty minutes of one hour verbally assaulting the therapist. He hated him intensely and wanted to kill him. He was certain the therapist did not understand what he was going through, that he could not understand how he felt because he did not care. He said the therapist wanted only to collect the fee. He absolutely wanted to kill him, crash into him, drive his car into his house and smash it, rip it apart as though it were canvas. He hated the patient who preceded him and thought she was getting a higher form of caring in analysis than he was getting. He wanted to run over people in the neighborhood with his car and run the therapist over too. He knew the therapist's family was in the house, and he wanted to kill them too. He expressed all this with great intensity, feeling at the time that he really meant it. But with the therapist's persistent attitude of attention and acceptance, he grew calmer in the last ten minutes of the session, saying finally that his problem really was that he wanted to possess the therapist completely, literally to swallow him whole.

In these hours, no aggression was mobilized. There were no obstacles to be to overcome, only rage because realistically he had to settle for a relationship that fell short of his ideal desires, even though it was sustaining enough. He still expressed his yearnings in terms of fantasies of incorporative togetherness. The therapeutic work described thus far culminated in his recounting a favorite fantasy he had held dear since childhood, one that he now fondly attached to the therapist. It had first developed after he learned about slaughterhouses for cattle. What he yearned for was to be close to the therapist as they both were split open down their abdomens so that their intestines would mingle warmly in living togetherness. Nevertheless, the realities, both of fulfillment of his needs and of the limitations on fulfilling his needs in the therapeutic relationship, were clear to Jim. These realities did in fact pose an obstacle to his maintaining the ideal of total fulfillment. However, this was an obstacle not to be overcome, but to be accepted as the basis for realistic growth and fulfillment in real life.

RESOLUTION AND CONCLUSION

At this point Jim had developed a steadily available sustaining introject based on his experience with his therapist. However, more work was needed in order to establish the self-introject relationship on a basis that closely enough related to the realities of life. This work involved the yearning for an idealized narcissistic togetherness, the second stage referred to above. Treatment centered on the grief stirred as Jim increasingly confronted the realities of life, including realities of the therapy relationship, which presented obstacles to fulfillment of the idealized qualities of holding, sustaining, soothing security that he yearned for. This process involved relinquishment of narcissistic

overvaluations of his mother, of his therapist, and of himself as object
of their caring. No aggression was involved because relinquishment
replaced the former mobilization of aggressive efforts to overcome
the obstacles. He worked through his grief with crying sadness,
nonmurderous anger, and progressive giving up of impossible yearnings as he found realistic fulfillments to replace them. His therapist's
role was to help him bear his disappointment and sadness by
empathically staying with him as he experienced these feelings and
by providing dynamic and genetic clarifications and interpretations
that helped him develop better perspective regarding them.

During this process Jim became preoccupied with interrelated
idealized holding introject formations based on good childhood times
with his mother and unrealistic beliefs about the therapist. He declared his love for the therapist. He wasn't concerned anymore about
the therapist's vacations because he knew that he kept him very much
in his thoughts. He fantasized their hugging in greeting when the
therapist returned, but never acted on his fantasy. At the same time
he reminisced tearfully about the passive bliss of being with his mother,
Jeannie. For example, for several weeks he had talked tearfully about
how beautiful life had sometimes been with her. She was everything
to him and he would do anything for her. He also spoke of the solid-
ity he felt in his relationship with the therapist. The therapist was, he
said, like the large oak trees that stood outside the office. In one hour,
he related a dream in which he was descending the stairs of an el-
evated streetcar station. There were several people on the ground
waiting for him, including the therapist and a woman. He noticed that
the stairs ended several feet above the sidewalk and that he was
expected to jump. The people could have helped by catching him,
but it was safe enough; they simply stood by watching. He was angry,
jumped anyway, and was alright. After telling the dream, he said he
had been wishing that the therapist would talk with him more. He felt
deprived, and he was angry about it. He felt jealous of other patients
and the therapist's family. He believed they all got something special
from him that Jim himself didn't get. He wanted to be like a man in a
recent movie who lived to be adored. He wanted all the therapist's
adoration. He wanted him to smile affectionately, touch him, clean
him all over, touch and clean every crevice of his body, like a mother
would her baby. He was jealous of people whom he fantasized the
therapist was close to sexually. The wonderful thing the therapist had
to give, he said, was like two golden pears on his chest. He yearned

for them so much and did not get them. He was furious about it, felt like destroying them. Then he turned sad; tears streamed down his cheeks. He felt badly about his anger because he knew what he wanted was unreasonable. The therapist commented that it was like his dream, that he wanted to be helped in jumping to the sidewalk even though he knew he actually didn't need help. His anger arose not because his need to be saved was ignored, but because he wasn't receiving something he so much yearned for. Jim agreed; that was the way he felt, that was what he was dreaming.

Here we can see simultaneously both his deep wish for idealized narcissistic togetherness as well as his beginning to reach toward a more mature relationship. A later hour illustrated the way Jim began to develop a more solid inner self that would eventually evolve to the point of mature self-sufficiency and more realistic use of relationships, i.e., the third stage of therapeutic development referred to earlier. In this process his hostility, anger, envy, and grief receded; no aggression was involved. Sadness, humor, and hope emerged. He said:

> I feel like I'm missing Jeannie, like I'm looking for her everywhere, and she ought to be all around, but she's not. [He looked mildly depressed and sad.] I miss her. I miss her, and you can't bring her back, and nobody can. It's like she died. [He began to laugh.] I wonder what the real Jeannie is like. The Jeannie I yearn for isn't the real one at all. It's some ideal Jeannie I'm wanting, someone very wonderful and very exciting. A Jeannie like that never really existed. [He grew sad, but retained his humor.] You know, the trouble is that I don't see people and places for what they really are, because I keep looking for Jeannie there. There are lots of girls I know but haven't ever appreciated because I haven't really related to them. I've missed out on them. I had a dream. All I remember is that there was a wonderful celebration for me, but I couldn't enjoy it because Jeannie wasn't there. It's like part of me has died, but it's not so much that I can't do okay without it. It's really as if she's been everywhere or is everywhere. She's part of me, and it's awfully hard to give her up. [Now with good humor, slightly hypomanic.] It feels like I can peel Jeannie off now, that it's like a layer of skin. And when I do, most of me is still left there, very solid.

In this hour Jim understood that his wish for the ideal Jeannie posed an obstacle to his having a real self of his own and living his own life in the real world. Unlike his earlier disposition, when he strove so mightily to overcome the obstacle which reality posed to possessing an idealized Jeannie-therapist of his fantasy, he came to view his idealized strivings as an obstacle to pursuing his real life, an obstacle for which he realized he had little or no need.

Jim's treatment continued for about two more years, during which his personal sense of identity solidified and his life with friends, a long-term lover, and his professional life as a university professor flourished. Some time after the end of treatment, his love relationship ended when his lover died of AIDS, and within a year it became evident that Jim himself had AIDS. He has dealt with his illness with remarkable courage and effectiveness, continues living a life he still enjoys, and has now survived his illness for sixteen years. Although for a brief time he needed help with antidepressant medication, at no time has he otherwise suffered any form of mental illness. He has never regressed to any form of the borderline condition for which he originally needed treatment.

AGGRESSION IN BORDERLINE ETIOLOGY

This case offers an opportunity to focus some of the differences between a therapeutic approach to borderline pathology predicated on the basis of instinctual drives and the approach based on a motivational perspective. Formulations that place the root of borderline pathology in some form of instinctual defect inevitably are caught in the dilemma as to whether the pathology can be basically attributed to an unusual titer of instinctual power or to a relative weakening or impairment of the resources of the ego to regulate, control, and modulate instinctual derivatives. Frequently, the borderline ego is pictured as helpless before the intensity of the onslaught of inner instinctual forces, so that to protect itself, the ego is forced into a position of helpless dependency or of omnipotent control (Geleerd, 1958). Such formulations frequently come out of an instinctual theory background and emphasize the continuity between borderline conditions and psychotic states. The underlying instinctual dynamics, with all their primitive force and primary process integration, seem to be postulated as given, and the ego is helplessly buffeted by these powerful internal forces.

The foremost proponent of the role of aggression conceived as instinctual drive in the etiology of borderline personality is Kernberg.

Drawing a contrast with his characteristic positions may help clarify some of the clinical and technical differences of an approach focused on motivation. Developmentally he has attributed borderline pathology to the developmental failure to adequately negotiate Mahler's (Mahler et al., 1975) separation-individuation process, particularly the rapprochement subphase. Further, he posits at the root of the pathology an excess of pregenital (oral) aggression, which prevents and interferes with effective integration of internalized object relations The predominance of primitive pregenital aggression strongly influences the nature of the oedipal conflict. There is a pathological condensation of pregenital and genital aims under the influence of these aggressive needs and, in consequence, a premature development of oedipal strivings (Kernberg, 1967, 1968).

The condensation of pregenital and genital libidinal aims, strongly contaminated by aggressive derivatives, results in residual instinctual conflicts which, together with unresolved issues of separation-individuation, influence the character of borderline transferences. Along similar lines, other authors have noted the chaotic and somewhat undifferentiated state of instinctualized energies giving rise to a sense of inner chaos. Particularly noteworthy in the evaluation of borderline patients is the manifestation of material from all phases of libidinal development, which presents a rather confused, mixed picture. This lack of instinctual phase dominance seems to reflect an interference with a normal processing of ego and id influences that allow the emergence of phallic trends in the oedipal situation. The bulk of the libido remains fixed in the oral and anal level, with little evidence of phallic maturation. Rosenfeld and Sprince (1963), for example, commented on this aspect of the borderline pathology in children:

> There seems to be a faulty relationship between the drives and the ego. At no stage does the ego give direction to the drives; neither does the ego supply the component drives with the special ego characteristics and coloring. It is as if the drives and ego develop independently and as if they belong to two different people. (p. 615)

In Jim's case, the motivational perspective, in contrast, would view the pattern of organization of his structural acquisitions and motivational themes as reflecting the vicissitudes of his developmental career and especially the complexities of his involved and troubled relationship with his mother. The problem would not lie in disruptive and unintegrated instinctual drives, but in the complex of motivational themes that were laid down progressively in his interaction primarily with his mother.

Kernberg describes the developmental process in terms of the interaction between instinctual vicissitudes and the structuralizing effects from the internalization of object relations. The condensation of pregenital and genital aims under the influence of aggressive impulses sets the stage for primarily oral-aggressive projection, particularly onto the mother, resulting in a paranoid distortion of early parental images. The projection of both oral- and anal-sadistic impulses turns the mother into a potentially dangerous, persecutory object. The father is also gradually contaminated by this aggressive projection, with a resulting amalgamated image of the father and mother as somehow dangerous and destructive. This leads to a concept of sexual relationships as dangerous and colored with aggressive and destructive themes. In an attempt to deny oral-dependency needs and to avoid the rage and fear related to them, there is a flight into premature genital strivings, which often miscarries because of the intensity of the aggression that contaminates the entire experience (Kernberg, 1967, 1968).

The earliest phase takes place prior to the differentiation of self and object and provides the ego core. This is followed by a stage of the consolidation of relatively undifferentiated self-object images, which are libidinally invested and carry a positive affective charge. At the same time, painful and frustrating experiences form a separate representation of an undifferentiated all-bad self-object representation. The all-good and all-bad images remain separated, with little or no separation between self and nonself. Pathological fixation at this level leaves the aggressively cathected images predominant and promotes a defensive refusion of the primitive all-good images in order to protect against excessive frustration and rage.

The next stage of development takes place after differentiation of self and object and results in splitting of both self and object images into all-good and all-bad alternatives. In the borderline personality, differentiation between self and object images is sufficient to allow for the establishment of integral ego boundaries and differentiation between self and others. But the predominance of primitive aggression prevents movement to a further stage in which self and object images may be integrated into concepts of self and others, embracing both good and bad characteristics. As Kernberg (1970b) commented:

> ... integration of libidinally-determined and aggressively-deter-
> mined self- and object-images fails to a great extent in borderline
> patients, mainly because of the pathological predominance of pre-
> genital aggression. The resulting lack of synthesis of contradictory
> self- and object-images interferes with the integration of the self-
> concept and with the establishing of "total" object relationships
> and object constancy. (p. 811)

The contamination of self and object images by aggression motivates
the defensive splitting from idealized good self and object images as
a means of avoiding intolerable anxiety and guilt. Thus, splitting is
the major defensive mechanism in borderline conditions and lies at
the root of ego weakness and other primitive defense mechanisms.
Ego weakness is reflected in the lack of impulse control, anxiety tolerance, and the capacity to sublimate. Borderline patients are able to
preserve reality testing, which distinguishes them from psychotics;
but also, because of splitting, they are relatively unable to use repression as an effective defense, a characteristic that distinguishes them
from the neuroses (Wilson, 1971).

Kernberg's theories have been criticized from a number of perspectives. His reliance on the differentiated role of libidinal and aggressive drives at a point early in development, before self-object
differentiation has taken place, has been strongly criticized (Meissner,
1984; Robbins, 1976). The metapsychological status of internalized
object relations (Meissner 1978, 1981a), particularly the location of
the pathological defect in the rapprochement phase of separation-
individuation (a position previously abandoned by Mahler herself
[Mahler, 1972, Mahler and Kaplan, 1977]), seems narrowly construed
(Meissner 1984).

The balance of constitutional as opposed to environmental factors is unclear in Kernberg's theory. It is clearly not exclusively a
theory of nature as opposed to nurture, but one has the impression
that constitutional factors play a clear-cut and decisive role. In this
sense, Kernberg's developmental theory strikes a somewhat different
pose from that of Mahler and her coworkers (Mahler et al., 1975). The
weighting in the direction of constitutional factors, specifically the
increased titer of primitive oral-aggressive impulses in Kernberg's
theory, has been detailed by Masterson and Rinsley (1975). The presence of such unneutralized primitive aggression produces a situation
in which there is a quantitative predominance of negative introjections,
which have further implications for the persistence of splitting and

the diminished capacity for constructive ego growth and the integration of self-concepts. Although Kernberg leaves room for the influence of early environmental frustration, the emphasis and the central role seems to be given over to a constitutionally determined heightened aggressive drive, which reflects his predominantly heredo-congenital view. Consequently, in his theory he pays little attention to the importance of maternal or interactional factors within the early mother-child exchange—an emphasis that sets his approach decisively off against the more specifically developmental approach of Mahler, not to mention more recent developmental perspectives (Stern, 1985). Both Mahler's and Stern's approaches, by way of contrast, emphasize the mother's libidinal availability and its role in eliciting the development of the child's intrapsychic structure (Mahler, 1968, 1971; Masterson and Rinsley, 1975; Stern, 1985).

If this more or less postulated and constitutionally given play of intensified aggression raises a suggestion of a kleinian motif in Kernberg's thinking, the suspicion is not without substance. Kernberg (1967) has commented:

> Pregenital aggression, especially oral aggression, plays a crucial role as part of this psychopathological constellation. The dynamic aspects of the borderline personality organization have been clarified by Melanie Klein and her coworkers. Her description of the intimate relationship between pregenital and especially oral conflicts, on the one hand, and oedipal conflicts, on the other, such as occur under the influence of excessive pregenital aggression, is relevant to the borderline personality organization. (p. 678)

But the kleinian influence extends beyond the constitutional given of a primary destructiveness, whether related to the postulation of a death instinct or not.[3] Kernberg further postulates that the primitive instincts, libidinal and aggressive, function as the specific organizing principles in the organization of the earliest psychic structures at a point before self-object differentiation has taken place. It is not clear whether these basic instincts or their affective expression serve the organizing function at this level, since Kernberg also suggests that it is the primitive experience of pleasure and unpleasure that serves this basic function. His formulation seems to suppose an early differentiation of aggressive as opposed to libidinal instincts and their primary defusion. It is the combination of this instinctual situation with the emerging experience of part-objects that provides the basis for Klein's paranoid-schizoid position. Thus, the central formulation of Kernberg's theory, the internalized object relation, seems to occur under the influence of these instinctual organizing principles prior to any differentiation between self and object—a formulation that seems to provide its own inherent difficulties.

Kernberg's clinical approach has also been criticized (Feinsilver, 1983). Authors who come to the therapeutic arena with an insistence on the holding environment and empathic acceptance tend to find Kernberg's emphasis on early confrontation and interpretation of transference distortions disturbing. From a motivational perspective, the early systematic interpretation of narcissistic transferences would be regarded as premature and counterproductive, and could be seen as reflecting the analyst's countertransference difficulties in dealing with the patient's transferences as they impinge on the analyst's own unresolved narcissism—as, for example, activation of unresolved grandiosity in the face of idealizing transferences, or envy of the patient's grandiosity aroused by the patient's mirroring transference. A motivational approach would prefer direction of the patient's attention to the sources and contexts, past and present, developmental and interpersonal, that gave and continue to give rise to his neurotic patterns of adjustment and interaction. The approach is less confrontational and more exploratory and investigative. Others have charged that the "oral rage" of Kernberg's borderlines may be an iatrogenic result of his intrusive transference interpretations that the narcissistically vulnerable patient experiences as threatening assaults. The resulting narcissistic rage justifies the rationale of Kernberg's approach. The approach through inquiry and exploration may be all the more telling in dealing with negative transference reactions in which aggressive motifs may dominate. He may thus continually create the monster his approach seeks to slay.

There is general clinical agreement that aggression plays a primary role in the borderline syndrome, particularly expressed in the ready mobilization of anger and the degree of primitive rage so often seen in such patients (H. Friedman, 1970; Gunderson and Singer, 1975; Meza, 1970). We can note that in large measure the so-called aggressive motifs in borderline conditions are expressed in affective terms, particularly of anger, rage, envy, jealousy, etc. The distinction we draw between aggression as motive and the associated affective states would imply that the actual role of aggression in these conditions is somewhat more mitigated than prevailing theories might suggest.

Anger, rage, and envy pervade Jim's case material, but these are not synonymous with aggression and can serve only to alert us to the possibility of aggressive dynamics.

The clinical facts argue unquestionably to the importance of the role of aggressive motivation in understanding borderline pathology, but they do not argue to the necessity of postulating a primary aggressive instinct or drive, nor do they force on us the theoretical conclusion that aggression is a constitutional given. Such has been the attitude expressed in early freudian and kleinian instinctual theory, but it may be that instinctual drives themselves can be conceptualized in terms of a developmental process in which certain constitutional givens are shaped and modified by the quality of interaction with significant objects, and that this process is better formulated in motivational terms (Loewald, 1971).

The appeal to instinctual factors as basic to the understanding of borderline conditions focuses on essentially economic-energic factors. The key issue then becomes the distribution, channeling, or transformation of basic energies, specifically aggression. This psychoeconomic concern is reflected in a preoccupation with disruptive states of hyperstimulation, modification of aggressive drive stimuli by fusion, and the need to protect nascent structure from overwhelming traumatic forces. We would argue that to the extent to which such factors are conceived as determining the pathology, therapeutic techniques directed at expressions of instinctual dynamics, as in the case of Kernberg's frontal and confrontational approach to transference manifestations, especially narcissistic and negative transference expressions, misplace the emphasis in the therapeutic interaction and risk diverting therapeutic effort from more meaningful exploration of motivational contexts.

These aspects come into clear relief in Jim's therapy. The experience of intense transference affects and yearning became the point of origin for exploring and gaining perspective on the crucial object relations and their history, especially in his relation with his mother. The intensity of his relation to the therapist and his frustrated dependency yearnings gave rise to intense, even murderous, rage and fantasies of maiming or killing the therapist. The meaning, context, and motivational bases of both the affects and their aggressive expression in fantasies of attacking, damaging, or destroying the therapist were opened up for exploration and inquiry. The therapist's task was to maintained his empathic stance of interested availability as a constant counterpoise not only to Jim's fears and terror of abandonment, but also to his wishes and fantasies of attacking and destroying the frustrating object in the person of his therapist. The ultimate revelation of the connection between these vicissitudes and the nature and quality of his relation to his mother and the complex motivational concerns and motifs they involved provided the foundation for Jim's latent ego resources to assert themselves and achieve a more mature and adaptive level of functioning. The basic proposition we are advocating is that these motivational themes and concerns are fundamental in determining the pathology. They provide an adequate basis for explaining Jim's psychic developmental history and the resulting personality structure and patterns of functioning that characterized his life adjustment.

Chapter 12

Aggression in the Analytic Process

TECHNICAL CONSIDERATIONS

AGGRESSION AS A CONDITION FOR ANALYTIC WORK

We have described our understanding of aggression as a normal and essential potential at the disposal of the self, assisting it to achieve completion of its psychically intended actions when those actions are impeded by an obstacle preventing them from attaining their aim, whether in private or in external reality. Internally, any aspect of an intended psychic activity, requiring participation of memory, cognition, wishfully cathected objects, and desired self-appraisals and satisfactions, may evoke opposition from the ego or superego to impede or prevent attaining the aim of the intended action. Such opposition itself can act as a stimulus capable of evoking intrapsychic aggression to overcome the obstacle. If the self finds a way of making the intended action acceptable, by employing defenses that bypass the ego's opposition (sublimation), or other defenses that mobilize the extra effort to overcome the ego's or superego's opposition (rationalization, etc.), the activity of the self will be able to reach its aim. If the intended activity remains unacceptable, the self, by way of its ego functions, may permanently repress or temporarily suppress the wishes to complete the action.

This schematic description simply attempts to illustrate the minute-to-minute intrapsychic processes that require the self to utilize aggression to order to achieve its basic aim of maintaining a viable psychic life in the face of external and internal conflictual circumstances. The normal and spontaneous use of intrapsychic aggression by the self is so continuous and subtle that most of the time we are unaware of ongoing preconscious and unconscious aggressive activity so indispensable for the integrity and functioning of the self-as-person. Similar spontaneous and barely noticed aggressive processes occur in everyday object relations and in dealing with external reality. When psychopathology is minimal, the utilization of aggression by the agent-self to accomplish its aims in multiple realms is not only effective and unobtrusive, but may carry with it the pleasure of being capable of action and of exercising mastery. In short, aggression, in its function in the formation of psychic defense and in the facilitating of the resources of the self to overcome obstacles posed to the achievement of goals, is basic to psychic life and ubiquitous in psychic functioning.

Aggression, as the motive eliciting the capability of the self to overcome obstacles, is indispensable for psychoanalytic treatment. The patient arrives with a vague sense of encountering significant obstacles within himself preventing him from achieving his life's goals; and in asking for treatment, he indicates that he intends to do what is more or less necessary to overcome his difficulties. His acceptance of analytic treatment and the conditions it imposes upon him implies consent to employing in some degree adequate psychic means to overcome the obstacles posed by his pathology. In making an agreement to work together in a therapeutic process, patient and analyst concur that the final task is to further the patient's ability to carry out his intentions to an appropriate completion, unimpeded by psychopathology. Thus a psychoanalytic treatment is based on the capacity of the patient's self to use aggression in the service of overcoming the intrapsychic obstacles posed to his life's aims by internal conflicts.

Obviously, this manner of thinking does not exhaust all the factors that are indispensable for successful treatment, such as transference, the real relationship, the alliance with the analyst, and the progressive articulation of affects and the description, naming, and interpretation of beliefs, wishes, and conscious and unconscious motives and intentions. It only asserts that psychoanalysis to be effective must count on the aggressive capacity of the patient to overcome his obstacles, internal and external. Some patients, such as Larry,[1] need analysis to overcome internal obstacles to be able to use their aggressive potential itself at the service of their own psychic life. In all patients, not just in cases such as Larry, the analytic process brings about a new freedom in the use of their aggressive potential to achieve their realistically appropriate aims. Such a freedom results from the analytic experiential separation of aggressive capacity from fantasized convictions and from negative affects that may have been linked to it, such as hostility, destructiveness, rage, omnipotence, and others.[2]

AUTONOMY AND RESPONSIBILITY

When aggression is conceptualized as a drive, the patient's autonomy suffers because a drive cannot be overcome—it can only be managed, tamed, or forced to submit to ego and superego regulation. Schwartz (1984), however, pointed out that even Freud expected greater autonomy and freedom from his patients than his theory of drives would allow: "When Freud wrote about actions directed toward conscious goals, he employed a teleological intentional causality which includes the 'deliberate.' He contrasted these more or less conscious 'pulls' from the future with 'pushes' from the past in the form of other varieties of intentional though non deliberate actions, namely, behaviors that follow from drives and unconscious wishes" (p. 558). Freud (1925) himself held his patients responsible for what they did and for the evil impulses in their dreams, showing that they were part of the patient's own being (p. 133), what we are calling the self, i.e., as the source of action, the self-as-agent. Thus, even within the conceptual context of a drive pushing from below, Freud nonetheless still considered the patient's autonomous responsibility essential for the effective carrying out of the treatment.

We understand aggression as a potential of the self, in its role as agent, that is, the person who is the source of all actions, conscious, preconscious, and unconscious. Our understanding converges with Freud's focus on the patient's responsibility and autonomy during the analytic process, in particular on his accountability as the agent of his own analysis and all of his actions and wishes. The analyst analyzes the patient as a self who is responsible for his agency and invites him to make sense of all of his experiences as his own. There is nothing driving the patient beyond the complexities of his own psyche, motives, beliefs, wishes, fantasies, memories, and modalities of relatedness in the context of the current realities of his life.

The analyst strives to help the patient acknowledge and exercise his autonomy during the analytic process. We understand autonomy in the same sense as Blum and Blum (1990), as the "capacity for dawning awareness of motive and intent, the ability to achieve an intended goal, converging with developing self-regulation" (p. 585). Acceptance of autonomy is *the* condition in analysis for the patient's progressive discovery of previously unconscious motives and goals that have become obstacles for self-regulation and the achievement of meaningful life objectives. Encouraging the patient to recognize his autonomy and inviting him to exercise it removes from the analytic process, as much as possible, the risk of the analyst himself becoming an obstacle to the discovery of the patient's inner world. When the analyst moves ahead of the patient's self-discoveries, he may create a major obstacle for the analysand by inviting either compliance or outright rejection of something he cannot accept as his own, something he is not ready to be responsible for.

Coen (1989) described a particular type of patient "who has marked intolerance of taking responsibility for his internal conflicts so as to confront them, analyze them, and change. . . . Responsibility for oneself and for what is within oneself is held to be terrifying— more than anyone can bear on his own" (p. 943). The motive for such terror is the conviction that assuming responsibility for hostile and destructive feelings is equivalent to killing the parents. According to our manner of understanding the analytic process, the patient's feared destructiveness is not aggression in the sense of a drive, but a fantasized conviction about the power of feelings that requires not only description and naming but, as Coen points out, that the patient himself confront (itself a form of aggressive overcoming of an obstacle) the illusion, the conviction that such feelings cannot be tolerated. The analysis can be carried to completion only when the patient can assume full responsibility for his wishes, feelings, thoughts, and actions, conscious and unconscious, including the aggressively motivated actions he carries out to achieve his aims.

To analyze him and make it possible for the patient to change, the analyst must count on the integrative power of the self. Freud (1919b) described it: "As we analyze it [the mind] and remove the resistances, it grows together; the great unity which we call his ego fits into itself all the instinctual impulses which before had been split off and held apart from it. The psychosynthesis is thus achieved during analytic treatment without our intervention, automatically and inevitably. We have created the conditions for it by breaking up the symptoms into their elements and by removing the resistances" (p. 161). Freud's "aggressive" technique of analyzing by removal of resistances helps the patient overcome the obstacles one by one, confidently trusting that the patient's ego (self-as-ego, as an integral function of the self-as-person and -as-agent) will create a new synthesis. There is no need for the analyst to foster a particular type of conflict resolution or outcome. Once the resistances (obstacles) are removed, the self knows what to do. For us, the aim of the analytic process is to assist the patient to use his own aggressive capacity to progressively remove the obstacles interfering with his psychic functioning and his life ambitions.

Our understanding of aggression as a capacity available to the self to overcome obstacles interfering with its intended actions allows us to define psychoanalysis as a process, in which the analyst continuously enhances the agency of the patient, facilitates his autonomy to explore his inner world, and promotes his assuming responsibility for all his actions, conscious and unconscious, as key elements in bringing about resolution of pathology and self-integration. By discarding the theory of aggression as a biological force that "drives" the patient, we are returning the full ownership of his pathology as well as of the cure of it to him. In brief, we help to enable him to take possession of himself as the responsible and authentic agent of his life.

THERAPEUTIC PROCESS

Our definition of the therapeutic aim of psychoanalysis differs substantially from other analytic approaches. The therapeutic aim of psychoanalysis has evolved along with analytic theory and with the appearance of new schools of analytic thought (Moore and Fine, 1990). Freud first aimed at connecting affect and representation that have been pathologically separated by trauma (Green, 1999). The connection permitted normal psychic processing to take place, "discharging" previously "strangulated affect." Around the turn of the century, making the unconscious conscious became Freud's prevailing therapeutic goal. In 1923, Freud's new structural concepts focused on the ego as the key therapeutic agent in helping the patient to understand the workings of his own mind. Klein favored the analysis of very early pathological structures, while object relations theorists brought into focus the organization of the self around object relations, and the correlative need to analyze the internal world of self and objects. Kohut reshaped those ideas in terms of the pathological structuralization of the self as a result of defective primary object mirroring. He made intra-analytic "transmuting internalizations" the core of his technique. Present-day intersubjective and relational schools believe in the therapeutic transformation of the subject by way of the relational interaction and exploration of shared subjective constructions of experience.

Our approach considers that all experiences, from infantile object relations and mirroring to present-day exchanges with other subjects, must be perceived, organized, and integrated as functional components of the self or be defended against and transformed into pathological intrapsychic processes by means of all three subagencies operating as substructures of the self, i.e., id, ego, and superego. The relational potentials, the fantasies and symbols, the beliefs and convictions, the habitual dispositions and defenses formed during processes of integration or defense are all under the effective guidance of the self-system. It is the self-as-agent, the total psychic person as source of action, who is the master in the psychic house. All transformational processes, from modification of feelings and relational stances to transformation of desires and construction of reality with others, must be processed through the self as the organizing agent of all experiences as well as the master using his aggressive potential to overcome obstacles to his integrity and intentions.

Pathology always results from the self's inability to overcome external or internal obstacles to the self's task of keeping developmental and relational needs and desires adequately satisfied. Pathology reflects the persistence of obstacles integrated in unconsciously disguised form into beliefs, fantasies, convictions, compulsive actions, acting out, somatizations, pathological relations, and other symptomatic manifestations, revealing that the self has failed to achieve some of its desired or intended goals. The analytic task consists in inviting and assisting such a beleaguered self to carry out an autonomous exploration of motives and to assume responsibility for its obscure participation in the unwanted pathology, in order to progressively and effectively overcome the persistent obstacles to satisfactory psychic functioning and effectiveness.

During the process of analytic work, we focus exclusively on the clinical material brought to light by the analytic process. The analyst attempts to find the meanings, contexts, conditions, genetic and present determinants, and transferential and nontransferential motives and stimulus conditions that would make understandable why the patient acts and reacts in the manner he does. There is no appeal to any metapsychological drive explanation. The understanding attempts only to make sense of the unique dynamic organization of the patient's actions and experience. This dynamic organization results from the complex convergence of motivational sources imbricated or intertwined to create an intricate fabric, in which some motivational sources of a given action may be developmentally and contextually mature in their pursuit of a specific satisfaction, while another motivational source may be gravely conflictual and inhibiting.

As an example, we might take the case of the scholar who finds deep satisfaction in the pursuit of knowledge, while her grandiosity, linked to the wish to impress and become her father's favorite, interferes continuously with the public presentation of her work to a collection of father-substitutes. In this case, the analytic task requires exploring as many motivational sources as necessary until the associative links uncover the unconscious motives that have become an obstacle to her otherwise mature and satisfying motivations to learn, to enjoy learning, and even to display herself as learned. This approach means that we do not pursue an analysis of "aggression" and its motives, but that we analyze the person in his or her broad motivational context, as presented by associations, to find in the array of motives those psychic processes, acting as obstacles, that transform human actions into pathological symptoms.

Our experience, as demonstrated clearly by our cases, most clearly by Mr. T,[3] shows that "aggressive" behaviors disappear as soon as the unconscious obstacles to fulfillment of his need—ones that called for pathological and inefficient means to overcome them (making women suffer)—are removed through the work of the analysis. When Mr. T relinquished his conviction that no woman would respond to him, when he finally experienced himself as listened to, understood, and accepted in analysis, and made sense of his wish to force women to respond to him, he no longer had any use for his sadistic behaviors. He could then accept himself as himself, thus obviating his need to force an external object to accept him. To achieve this goal, it was necessary to trace with him, in the transference and in his recollection of childhood experiences, the dynamic sources of his deep beliefs along with his defensive self-glorification and externalizations with all their affective richness. This revisiting of the past in memory and transference in the context of intensely experienced affects gave Mr. T the conviction Freud (1937) spoke about as essential to achieve permanent change.

The analyst endeavors to accomplish a series of tasks in dealing with the assumed obstacle. In listening to the patient's associative process, he attempts to describe the obstacle in the patient's mind to himself, to name it in ordinary and dynamic terms, and to see if there is a predictable context or pattern of stimulus conditions that would prompt aggressive moves against the obstacle, such as, for example, a break in associations when certain conditions obtain. It is not enough to become simply aware of what the obstacle may be. It is essential to contextualize it in the patient's past and present in order to understand what dynamic constellation gives it the character of an obstacle, and what in it gives the obstacle its specific quality as obstacle. In Mr. T's case, it was not merely that women did not respond to him, but that he could not *believe* that they wanted and appreciated him in their hearts. There was nothing any woman could do to change his belief. It was he who had to remove his own disbelief in the sincerity of women as the obstacle to any meaningful relation with a woman. The stimulus conditions for his aggression with women rested not so much in the woman as in the attitude he brought with him in meeting a partner. Whatever conditions she offered, from loving to challenging, could not modify his built-in conviction that the woman did not care for him as himself.

The patient's improvement, therefore, is effected not by transformation of a putative aggressive drive, but by an elaborate affective and motivational understanding of how some particular issue has become a psychic obstacle, and progressive transformation of the patient's experience that eventuates in the removal of the obstacle or its transformation into a non-obstacle. In ideal circumstances, it may be possible to trace, by way of the transference, associations, dreams, metaphors, and imagery, the genetic sources of some originally intended action, the obstacles it encountered, the patient's inability to overcome them, and the transformation of this failure into symptoms that repeat the original setback in disguised form. Rather than uncovering probable recollections, patient and analyst more frequently develop a meaningfully constructed narrative of the type of events that affected the patient by leaving behind significant obstacles to achieving desirable aims. Freud (1937) believed that "if the analysis is carried out correctly, we produce in him an assured conviction of the truth of the construction which achieves the same therapeutic result as a recaptured memory" (p. 266).

Mr. T offered graphic illustrations of such constructions which he created autonomously in the course of the analysis. We can condense several of his key constructions into the continuing narrative of overcoming his core internal obstacle: "Mother's rejection was compounded by my and her disrespect. I feel the full impact of the rejection. . . . My capacity to kill the people I love scares me. I did wish to murder her. . . . My relationship with my mother was a lie. I was not able to be the perfect child. I chose to put myself between my parents. I lied. I was inferior. I felt superior." Finally, he uncovered the key *unconscious conviction* that prompted him to try to "force" women to respond to him. He said: "If I couldn't conquer my mother, how could I conquer anybody else?" This recognition opened the possibility for him of carrying out the essential aggressive action needed to overcome his internal obstacle. He said: "If I accept that I lost my mother and she lost me, I can be free. Then, I can love a woman." His acceptance of oedipal defeat removed the obstacle of having to "force" his mother and any other woman to respond to him, leaving him free to enjoy mutual love and respect.

FORMS OF PATHOLOGY

Each of the patients we have presented had to experience—in the transference and working through of their conflicts—the stimulus conditions motivating the emergence of the aggression necessary to overcome their core obstacles to a freer psychic life. Each of them arrived at his or her core construction by many circuitous ways and by successive overcoming of a multitude of other obstacles in their inner world and in the transferential relationship with their analysts. Phobic patients seem least successful in fully overcoming their internal obstacle, defined as a lingering wish for passive protection. This type of resolution is compatible with our conceptualization of phobia (Meissner et al., 1987) as "the final result of a series of defensive maneuvers to overcome a situation in which incompatible needs or

wishes and their anticipatory fantasized actions can neither be resolved nor renounced" (p. 473). Frankie's[4] childhood phobia was organized around his need to overcome the obstacle posed by separation
from his mother that opposed and disrupted his passive longings for
her care. His treatment transformed the phobic fears into more muted
characterological obsessive doubts, thus effecting a compromise formation in overcoming his internal obstacle, permitting him to function effectively in reality while still maintaining an unconscious passive
longing for protection. Similarly, Paul[5] managed to overcome the intensity of his passive longings to remain a child under the care of
loving parents who expected him to go to medical school. He overcame his feelings of betrayal in their forcing him to become an adult
by partially surrendering his passive wishes and the rage and sadistic
impulses toward his otherwise beloved parents. He dutifully entered
medical school and completed his studies. But his aggressive efforts
to overcome the obstacle posed by his intense passive wishes transformed his symptoms from psychotic delusion into a pattern of characterological obsessive control and repression of his longings sufficient
to allow him to practice his profession, although with some restrictions.

Sadomasochistic pathology, as we have suggested (in chapter 9
above), is organized around several pathogenic factors, of which the
prevailing components are: (1) sadism, masochism, or both is present
in one or both parents; (2) the child identifies with that parent, and
ego and superego regulation of self-appraisal and self-esteem are
governed by constant conflict between personal desires and the internalized parent; (3) actual childhood experiences of devaluation and
humiliation and the concomitant affective reaction to it; (4) compensatory and revengeful conscious and unconscious fantasies; and (5)
intense affect-laden fantasies of finally convincing the parental object
to deliver the love and appreciation that has been denied. These
factors create a complex network of intertwined obstacles that can
never be dealt with in isolation but which must be slowly worked
through by removing obstacles, one after another, until a certain core
organization configured around the prevailing obstacle may appear,
as it did with Mr. T. Sometimes, as Coen (1989) points out, the core
difficulty constituting the primary obstacle is fear of feeling one's own
feelings, guided by the illusion that one may kill, even the analyst.
The core obstacle within this series of obstacles is omnipotence of
thought serving as a persistent narcissistic compensation. In many
cases, the constructions converging on describing and naming the

obstacle are not single but multiple. Each of them corresponds to a different aspect of the patient's experience, contributing to formation of a more general narrative embracing obstacles already overcome or yet to be overcome.

To illustrate, analysis of the complex mixed neurotic character pathology of a patient such as Larry[6] confronted a series of developmental and relational obstacles that had to become conscious and worked through as they emerged, some in isolation, some emerging simultaneously. In the end, however, his narrative could be organized around his pathological relation to his mother as a defective child who would not dare to use his potential as self-agent in his own behalf lest he would lose his privileged position with her as her secret partner and master. In the case of a borderline patient, such as Jim,[7] the patient presents a multitude of preoedipal issues that appear as insurmountable obstacles to any kind of meaningful life. Analyst and patient needed a very prolonged time to discern and identify his powerful longings for fusion and progressively trace them to an almost delusional idealization of his seductive and abandoning mother. In the end, the patient came to see that such very early and continued idealization of a possessive and rejecting mother, his intense longing for her and desperate aloneness with her, all combined to form the final obstacle he had to overcome, renounce, and then, freed of his burden, undertake pursuit of his own life.

These broad reflections aim at presenting the overall picture of completed analyses in which the crucial task consisted of helping the self-as-agent to elicit adequate aggression under proper motivating and stimulus conditions in order to overcome successive obstacles interfering with intended intrapsychic or external aims and goals. Understood in this manner, the objective of analysis consists in helping the patient create the necessary conditions for overcoming psychic or other obstacles. The analytic situation goes about this task by implementing several factors. The patient must become able to experience, recognize, name, and observe the moments in which obstacles, both in his life and in the analytic interaction, manifest themselves. The patient must be able to say: "This is what I am up against," and experience the ego-dystonic frustration posed by the obstacle. Under these conditions and guided also by the progressive elaboration of the transference (as both help and obstacle to work within analysis), the patient begins to feel the need to find a way of overcoming the internal obstacle in order to complete the action, be it to be able to love, to be free, to be a center of initiative, to leave behind a cumbersome object, to grow up, to tolerate one's feelings, or any other task that up to that point had seemed insurmountable. It should be obvious that, in offering this schematic representation of the analytic process, we intend only to illuminate the manner in which our understanding of aggression influences the conceptual and technical understanding of the patient's essential participation in analytic work.

AGGRESSION IN MAINTAINING THE ANALYTIC STANCE

The analyst cannot carry out his analytic task without using his own aggression to overcome internal obstacles interfering with his ability to hear the patient's communications, consciously and unconsciously, and respond to them as an analyst. Analytic education, specifically the training analysis and supervision, provides models for identification and internalization of psychoanalytic patterns of listening, behaving, and mental processing (Smith, 2001). Psychoanalytic competence (Makari and Shapiro, 1993) is the ability to employ a specific analytic mode of listening to make sense of the patient's discourse, implying that the analyst does not select an a priori meaning or draw quick conclusions before the material itself acquires a particular shape of descriptive and dynamic meaning. Analytic competence and its exercise makes strong demands on the analyst. He must suspend any other manner of listening in order to maintain his analytic listening stance, i.e., "withhold all conscious influences from his capacity to attend, and give himself over completely to his 'unconscious memory'" (S. Freud, 1912, p. 112). To achieve this stance the analyst frequently needs to put aside his private thoughts, feelings, and impulses that could distract him from his listening commitment.[8] To maintain his professional stance, the analyst not only needs aggression to overcome distracting mental activities, but also, paradoxically, to attend to them, not as personal issues, but as potentially dynamic resources to ascertain emotional and dynamic aspects of the patient's communications and experiences.

The transference and real relation between patient and analyst pose intense demands on the analyst by tempting him to abandon his commitment to maintaining the therapeutic alliance. Two of the cases described above contained moments in which the entangling of powerful and terrifying transferential feelings (in Larry's case) and tremendous longings for incorporation of the analyst (in the case of Jim), affected the real relationship and seriously threatened the patient's ability not only to maintain the alliance but to continue the analysis itself. Early in his treatment, Larry believed himself to be in the clutches of a powerful and controlling monster-analyst, a Nazi delighting in the sadistic submission and destruction of a helpless Jewish boy. The terror and intensity of his anxiety threatened the continuation of the analysis. The analyst used aggression to overcome the obstacles to maintaining their therapeutic relationship. He used his knowledge of the patient's history to interpret his terror and anxiety as transferential. He interpreted that the thoughts and feelings Larry perceived in the analyst were actually projections of his own fears. The real analyst was not as Larry saw him. The analyst could establish that, by virtue of Larry's own observing, he did not in fact know the analyst's thoughts. Finally, the analyst addressed the obstacle to maintaining the alliance by saying that Larry had little previous experience with cooperative relationships and that letting his feelings run their course without understanding them in the analysis could not serve his best interest. With this prelude the analyst was able to overcome the obstacle to their alliance by reminding Larry of their initial and ongoing commitment to collaborating as two adults in helping him with his problems.

Jim displaced his need for incorporation of the therapist and his rage at being denied satisfaction by consciously and defiantly cruising in a dangerous homosexual district where he indulged in fellatio, while declaring to himself and the therapist, "I'll take what I have coming." His risk of suffering actual physical harm was high. The therapist resorted to the still intact alliance to insist that his behavior was dangerous and that he had to stop it. The patient reacted with surprise that the doctor was so forceful in insisting that he remove himself from danger, but, in the end, he acquiesced and stopped his dangerous cruising. In these two instances, the analysts aggressively used their efforts to overcome transferential enactments in order to reinforce the alliance and preserve the psychical and physical safety of the analysand. In both cases, the analyst's aggression overcame the obstacles posed by the patient's dynamically motivated intense terror of the analyst and unbearable longings for psychic nurturance. Neither analyst understood the patient's feelings and behaviors to be aggressive acts directed against them as therapists or as persons, but as a powerful internal obstacle each patient needed to overcome to be able to maintain the analysis. The intensity of both patients' feelings interfered with their ability to benefit at that specific moment from interpretive work. The obstacle that could not be overcome at that point by dynamic understanding was transiently surmounted by the use of aggression within the alliance. The analyst's interventions served to borrow time enough for the patients to become more available for understanding of the motivational sources of their overwhelming feelings.

COUNTERTRANSFERENCE

The analyst's countertransference can also call for aggressively overcoming the obstacles that it may pose to maintaining his stance as the person responsible for the integrity of the analysis (Weinshel, 1984). The analytic process itself is a continuous task of overcoming obstacles posed by the patient to the requirement that he disclose his inner world to the analyst by allowing himself to freely associate. The transference onto the analyst of the revived imagos of earlier figures with their promises and threats, the affects originating in past real events and in deeply ingrained fantasized scenarios of defeat, harm, humiliation, shame, deprivation, or torture on the one hand, or the unremitting demand for satisfaction or for an assumed promised triumph that would not go unpunished on the other—all of these transferences mobilize resistances in the patient, resistances to facing and verbalizing what is in his mind. The analyst, in turn, cannot help but respond internally to the manner in which the analysand manifests his resistances or attempts to achieve transferential satisfaction. The patient's personal style of being in analysis, his intense affects, his insistent appeals to and accusations against the analyst about what he does or does not do, find echoes in the analyst's experience of himself as a person and as a professional, echoes which may take the form of countertransference.

    Countertransference as a concept has evolved from Freud's first formulation. Today it may be used in its narrow or broad meaning. Freud (1910) understood countertransference to be "a result of the patient's influence on his [the analyst's] unconscious feelings" and insisted that the analyst "shall recognize this counter-transference in himself and overcome it" (pp. 144–45). In this early conception, Freud saw the countertransference as a direct obstacle to analytic work. Segal (1977) pointed out that most countertransferential phenomena are unconscious and that we notice them only indirectly by mediation of unconscious derivatives. Carpy (1989) sees it as a more observable phenomenon and suggests that the analyst, when confronted with a strong transference, must allow himself to tolerate the countertransference, to allow himself "to experience the patient's projections in their full force, and yet be able to avoid acting them out in a gross way" (p. 289). Carpy believes that such tolerance of distressing feelings reassures the patient about his own panic because the analyst, in spite of the feelings, persists in doing his job.

Abend (1986) insisted on the inevitability of some countertransference reactions affecting the analyst's capability at least in minor ways and warned analysts against setting up a perfectionistic ego ideal for analytic functioning. Bouchard et al. (1995) see the countertransference as both an instrument and as a potential obstacle. While considering the classical unconscious transference as an obstacle and as a defense, they see the possibility of using an analytic reflective attitude that includes preconscious and conscious activity aimed at understanding the psychic process evoked in the analyst. They list four phases of such reflective activity in relation to the analyst's working through the countertransference for the benefit of the patient: "(1) during emergence, an inner reaction appears; (2) immersion, through a regressive exploration, leads to introjective identification; (3) integrative elaboration involves a shift in cathexis, more distance, and an organization of the regressed contents, while (4) an interpretation is forming in mind" (p. 717).

Each of these aspects of countertransference requires that the analyst, as Freud said from the beginning, overcome the obstacle it poses to the continuation and efficiency of the analytic work. To notice derivatives that will inform him about his countertransference, the analyst must overcome his own resistance to accepting whatever unpleasant feelings and related motives underlie the countertransference. To tolerate intense countertransferential experiences the analyst has to overcome the dislike we all have of painful feelings and the temptation to get rid of them. To establish a reflective way of handling countertransference feelings, the analyst must overcome the resistance to distressing regression. And, when the analyst has failed, as we all do, and has acted on some countertransferential matter, he must overcome the obstacle posed by the criticism of his ego ideal and his teachers of the past to recover the balance he needs to return to his normal analytic functioning. In any of these instances, the analyst must force himself to understand his inner processes through a self-analysis that more frequently than not brings into focus conflicted areas and painful memories from the analyst's own personal life. Such "forcing" of himself requires intrapsychic aggressive action to overcome the reluctance and resistances posed by the analyst's mind to exploring his distressing feelings and thoughts for the benefit of the analytic process, the final goal of all the analyst's actions. In brief, the analyst must frequently employ intrapsychic aggression to overcome the obstacles presented by his temptations and resistances to carrying out his analytic aim of fully understanding the patient's motivations and experiences.

The emergence of new understanding of the psychoanalytic field and situation and the influence of the kleinians, in particular of their concept of projective identification, has brought to light new aspects of the countertransference. Projective identification refers to the effect that the patient's disowned and projected fantasies and affects have on the analyst's psyche during the analysis. Projective identification may be conceptualized as a projected intrapsychic fantasy (Segal, 1964; Spillius, 1992) or as part of a broader interpersonal engagement. As early as the 1950s some British analysts such as Rosenfeld (1952), Money-Kyrle (1956) and Bion (1957, 1958, 1959, 1962a, b, 1970), elaborated on the interpersonal process involved in projective identification. The projected intolerable feelings are contained by the mother or the analyst, who are, in a certain manner, coerced to play the role assigned to them in the patient's fantasy. The containing analyst can then elaborate the accepted projection and help the patient reintroject the metabolized affect or fantasy (Ogden, 1979, 1982). Kohut (1971) and Goldberg (1979), starting from a very different theoretical stance, discussed the analyst's need to accept idealizing, merger, and mirror transferences to help the analysand to tolerate and work through his narcissistic deficits and imbalances.

Kleinians and self-psychologists introduced indirectly the interpersonal and interactional aspects of the transference-countertransference field. Joseph (1989) described that patients attempt to induce the analyst to act in the manner suggested by the projection. The analyst may experience the projection as alien to him or find in himself some psychic disposition that makes it feel as an internal urge (Gabbard, 1994). Sandler's (1976) concept of role responsiveness elaborates the second situation: "Very often the irrational response of the analyst, which his professional conscience leads him to see entirely as a blind spot of his own, may sometimes be usefully regarded as a compromise-formation between his own tendencies and his reflexive acceptance of the role which the patient is forcing on him" (p. 46). Sandler's description of "irrational responses" leads directly to the concept of analysis as interactional, intersubjective and co-constructed. Renik (1993), in turn, believes that countertransference enactment precedes countertransference awareness. The interaction itself brings out the possibility of understanding the analytic moment. Social-constructivists (Hoffman, 1991) assert that the intrapsychic and inter-personal realms of the analytic dyad cannot be teased apart and that transference and countertransference are joint creations of the ana-lytic pair. Intersubjectivists suggest that analysis involves intersubjective engagement. Bollas (1987), asserted: "In order to find the patient we must look for him within ourselves" (p. 202). Ogden (1994), para-phrasing Winnicott (1960), said" "There is no such thing as an analysand apart from the relationship with the analyst, and no such thing as an analyst apart from the relationship with the analysand" (p. 63). All these contributions have greatly enlarged the concept and theoriza-tion about the sources of the countertransference, its manifestations, and its technical use to further analytic progress.

Modern object relations theorists (Mitchell, 1988, 1993b; Aron, 1991; Hirsch, 1993, 1994; Tansey, 1994, and others) agree on the un-avoidable and useful presence of countertransference enactments in analysis. Mitchell (1988) believes that "[t]here is no way for the analyst to avoid his assigned roles and configurations within the analysand's relational world. The analyst's experience is necessarily shaped by the analysand's relational structures; he plays assigned roles even if he desperately tries to stand outside the patient's system and play no role at all" (p. 292).

The concept of countertransference, even when looked at from so many different theoretical angles, is becoming a point of conver-gence for such diverse theorists. Gabbard (1995) comments:

> The perspective that the countertransference represents a joint creation that involves contributions from both analyst and analysand is now endorsed by classical analysts, modern Kleinians, rela-tional theorists, and social constructivists. Although differences do exist, most contemporary analysts would agree that at times the patient actualizes an internal scenario within the analytic rela-tionship that results in the analyst's being drawn into playing a role scripted by the patient's internal world. The exact dimen-sions of this role, however, will be colored by the analyst's own

> subjectivity and the 'goodness of fit' between the patient's pro-
> jected contents and the analyst's internal representational
> world.(pp. 481–82)

How can our theory about the analyst's use of aggression during
analytic work be understood in the context of this expanded understanding of the countertransference? We return to Weinshel's (1984)
concept that the analyst is responsible for the integrity of analytic
work. The analyst's self is the agent of this task. Intrapsychic activities, intra-analytic exchanges, interpersonal communications,
intersubjective interpenetration, interactional events during analysis—
all of these require that the analyst overcome any internal or interpersonal obstacle that interferes with the emergent analyzable issues of
the moment. The enlarged concept of countertransference in the
intersubjective matrix of transference-countertransference makes the
analytic task seem daunting. It becomes obvious that without the
constant attentiveness of the analyst to his own internal obstacles to
carrying out his analytic task the process could easily derail or become superficial. To say it with the words of our understanding of
aggression, the analyst's attentiveness to the analytic process in his
patient, in himself, and between them requires his readiness to act
aggressively to bring to analytic focus—be it through self-analysis or
analysis of the process between patient and analyst—that which appears as an obstacle for the task.

The task becomes particularly difficult when transferential feelings of great intensity suggest or predict direct harm to the analyst or
to the patient himself. Mr. T described graphically how he was going
to rape his analyst; Jim risked his life, while Larry announced the
need to kill himself. These are difficult and delicate moments because
they require almost contradictory actions: first, a realistic assessment
of the actual risk involved with the unavoidable fear and horror they
inspire; second, toleration of the ongoing experience of these threats
and feelings in order to give the patient psychic time and space to
experience his own intentions, feelings, and desires—as much as is
required for the patient to gain some understanding of the motivations behind them. Here the analyst's aggression acts to overcome the
natural tendency of his mind to avoid the intense and painful feelings
summoned by these threats. This exercise of the analyst's own intrapsychic aggression makes it possible to tolerate the threatening expe-

rience and avoid any action other than the continued effort to find dynamic motives in the patient's menaces.

The analyst's manner of speaking may also require aggressive effort to overcome intrapsychic obstacles posed by his wish to express his countertransference anger to the patient rather than carry out the more appropriate analytic activity of analyzing motives and experiences. The obstacle here can reveal itself most frequently in the ironic, sarcastic, teasing, seductive, enticing, and other varieties of tone of voice that address the patient directly as posing an obstacle to analytic work and not as the person who is an analysand. The analyst always owes the patient an analytic stance, as formed in and through the alliance, enabling them to work together in such a way that, as Freud (1914) said, the patient's compulsion to repeat "is allowed to expand in almost complete freedom and in which it is expected to display to us everything in the way of pathogenic instincts that is hidden in the patient's mind" (p. 154).

In summary, the analyst's ability to keep to the analytic task, to maintain the goal of exclusively analyzing the patient's motives and experiences, requires constant aggressive and intentional overcoming of internal obstacles arising from singular or complex countertransferential reactions. This activity only refers to the intrapsychic aggression the analyst must apply to overcome the obstacle he encounters to remain only and simply an analyst. There is another type of aggression that is at the very core of his activity and aims as an analyst. We may call it technical aggression, an aggression which is continuously put to the service of assisting the analysand to overcome his pathogenic obstacles.

AGGRESSION AS TECHNIQUE

There is no aggression on the analyst's part that can remove psychic obstacles from the patient's mind. As Valenstein (1983) asserted, insight is not enough to accomplish psychic change: "Ultimately, the working through of insight is pivotally related to the function of action and to definitive changes in action patterns as they are consolidated into the action system" (p. 371). We would suggest further that for psychic change to occur, the patient needs to put in play aggressive psychic actions to overcome internal obstacles interfering with completion of his intended actions. The cumulative overcoming of successive obstacles in analysis and the emergence of previously inhibited or interfered-with psychic actions brings about, in the extended course of treatment, changes in behavior and the emergence of new or previously inhibited personal aims. Larry illustrates the vicissitudes of a patient whose pathology interfered with his capacity to use aggression to overcome both intrapsychic and external obstacles obstructing the path to his achieving personal and professional goals. His conviction that he had to cling to his mother as a defective child continuously interfered with his need to become his own man. The analytic process enabled him to retrieve, among other things, the ability to use his own aggression in its normal function of helping him overcome internal and external interferences in gaining a greater degree of separation from his mother and diminishing his maternal dependence, establishing a more stable level of personal autonomy, and achieving his goals as a man and a professional.

Day-to-day analytic work confronts the analyst with a multitude of simultaneous issues that cannot be dealt with all at the same time, yet none can be neglected. Transference and countertransference are always present and defenses never absent. Normal and pathogenic wishes emerge, are repressed, and reemerge. Affects are ubiquitous and words have as much power to reveal as they have to conceal the patient's subjective experiences. Recurrent real and screen childhood memories repeat the lamentations of past sufferings. Unconscious fantasies sustained by narcissistic and oedipal investment recur in many derivative forms. How is the analyst to find his way through this forest to trace the motivational sources behind such a vast array of psychic phenomena? Analytic technique requires a mode of listening that would allow the analyst to mentally conceptualize the nature of the patient's urgent need to communicate a particular type of affective predicament and the narrative vehicle he uses to do so. These predicaments are always related to basic psychic dangers: annihilation, abandonment, loss of love, narcissistic depletion or injury, oedipal defeat, fear of castration or destruction by an angry or a malignant object, fear of being possessed by or fused with an overpowering object.

Each analysand enters the analysis attempting to protect himself from one or other or some combination of these terrible dangers. We know that the danger lies in the patient's imagination or transference fantasy and is not real. But the patient's belief in their reality and the anxieties they evoke, as aspects of his psychic reality, create the stimulus conditions for the type of aggressive effort the patient will be called on to deploy if he is to avoid what he unconsciously or consciously predicts will happen to him in analysis. The opening phase of the analysis offers a unique opportunity to watch the patient as he sets up the scenario for transforming the anticipated danger into an actual event. Patients also come with a personal agenda for satisfaction of cherished, sometimes urgent yet unsatisfied wishes. In all these dangers and wishes, the narcissistic self-valuation is of the utmost importance. Paired issues of big/small, inferior/superior, powerless/powerful, masterful/impotent, respectable/laughable, lovable/unlovable, smart/ stupid, normal/defective, male/female color every interaction and add another affective dimension to these dangers and wishes. Each of these issues is loaded with intense affect, conscious or repressed, but always connected to historical interactions and the fantasies about them.

In describing all these psychic coordinates, our purpose is to propose a broad frame of reference permitting us to locate the type of obstacle the patient may be trying to overcome in displaying certain behaviors in analysis, whether transferential or nontransferential. There is no human action or experience that can escape these dangers and issues. Besides, they are the points of reference we all use on occasion to assess ourselves and imagine or seek to learn how others evaluate us. When we have to present ourselves to another, we must select certain of these coordinates in presenting ourselves to a new person. The coordinates we choose may reveal our psychic history and the elaboration we have made of it. Similarly, when the patient begins to work with us, he cannot help but choose unconsciously the issues and the dangers he would have to confront with us. What he unconsciously selects reveals the internal stimulus conditions for his affective reactions and beliefs, the motivational grid in which he finds himself embroiled. Correspondingly, we try to select our technical interventions on the basis of our understanding of the patient's state of mind.

Mr. T opened his analysis with a dream revealing how marginal he felt and how he never made any commitments. This dream set the stage for the entire analysis. His conviction about his being unable to obtain the responses he desired from others gave him the right to force them to recognize him. Soon the analyst became the object of his sarcastic and superior mockery and his sadistic description of how he would rape her to make her his plaything in payment for her not responding to him. The analyst soon came to understand that Mr. T's compensatory narcissism, expressed in his stance of power, grandiosity, superiority, and his sadistic humiliation of her as his analyst, were significant defensive maneuvers to ward off some unbearable pain that posed a major obstacle to maintaining his narcissistic equilibrium.

Based on this understanding, the analyst opted to give Mr. T maximal autonomy and to limit her technical interventions, thus facilitating and hopefully enhancing his own understanding of what he was experiencing and expressing. Her interpretations were few and limited, and even those only after extensive efforts to help him to carefully explore his feelings, thoughts, and wishes. This technical stance reflected the analyst's assessment that Mr. T's compelling need to be superior, to have power over the analyst, could and would have transformed any more active interventions into a major obstacle threatening his narcissistic fragility and would have further disturbed not only the alliance but Mr. T's progressive ability to become available for later interpretive work. His narcissism posed an obstacle to analytic work that could not be overcome directly. Rather, it was the analyst who had to overcome her habitual need to work in a more active manner. The analyst opted for a low-key technique, as a way of helping Mr. T experience in the analysis—through the analyst's careful attention to and respect for his words, actions, and efforts to control the analysis, no matter how gruesome—the feeling that whatever he was and did was accepted by the analyst with respect and constructive analytic listening.

In due course, he developed enough autonomy and self-regard be able to begin listening more receptively to some interpretations. This step forward was made more possible because the analyst did not regard any of his extremely hostile and destructive feelings, words, and actions to be expressions of an aggressive drive aiming at her destruction, but rather as affects connected to his transferential anticipations that posed such an obstacle for his analysis. If these anxieties were not effectively acknowledged, accepted, and responded to, he would feel intensely humiliated and rejected. Mr. T's extreme hostility and sadistic pleasure in humiliating the analyst were connected to motivations deriving from his unresolved oedipal failure and humiliation and the actual experiences of mutual rage and abuse between himself and his mother. The deepest motivational stratum harbored his conviction that he was unlovable and did not have in himself what it takes for a woman to respond to him. His destructive and hostile feelings toward the analyst were, in the end, a smokescreen covering the great humiliation of being impotent in his efforts to relate to a woman. The only aggression involved in his protracted display of hostility and sadism was his inefficient effort to overcome that most intractable internal narcissistic obstacle, the belief in his impotent, unloved, and unlovable condition. As soon as the analysis overcame this tremendous obstacle, Mr. T not only joined the analyst in the reconstruction of his neurotic development, but began to experience the tenderness and affection he did not know he had in him. The original childhood goal of loving and being loved had been restored and now became a possibility.

We base our clinical understanding of such dynamic moments in analysis firstly on the distinction of affects from aggression, and secondly on our notion of the posing of an obstacle to an intended action as the motivational stimulus for calling upon aggression as the capacity to employ the extra effort needed to complete the intended action. The complex and persistent linkage between intentions, motivations, and affects, dynamically connected as they are with development and the history of object related experiences, creates multiple possible configurations for understanding each analytic moment. The result of free association and analysis of defenses against it prepares for the emergence of more restricted scenarios progressively revealing their dynamic organization around specific perceptions and interpretations involved in the patient's experience of significant life events. The technical commitment of the analyst consists in using questions, clarifications, and finally interpretations to arrive progressively at the reconstruction of the type of events that have derailed the patient's psychic life in order to restore present-day ego-syntonic and reachable goals. To achieve this final objective, the theory of aggression we present offers a dynamic understanding of pathology as structured around the failure to achieve necessary biological, developmental, and object related aims and the psychic effects of such failure. In each analytic moment, we work to make explicit the motivational structure of the psychopathology as a key to making sense of affects, desires, fantasies, beliefs, and actions.

Affects can often provide a major key for understanding motivational structure. They can only be analyzed in vivo, when they are experienced in the analytic relationship. They serve multiple functions, from essential organizers of the person's feeling of being himself, to varied defenses, including those against other affects or those employed to cloud understanding of conflictual issues. We emphasize that affects are not expressions of an aggressive drive (see chapter 5), nor are they attributable to aggression even as a psychic capacity.

They are instead manifestations of experiences of particular dynamically motivated psychic moments, which are always structured, even if paradoxically (as in masochism), under the guidance of the pleasure principle.

In discussing the agent of aggressive action in chapter 4 above, we stated that aggression is not simply a biologically based drive in constant state of activity or discharge. Rather, it is a biologically grounded capacity requiring appropriate stimulus conditions to elicit activation or response. We also asserted that the motivational aspect of this model of aggression arises from conditions of activation, namely the need for activating stimuli, the goal-oriented or purposeful character of the response, and its inherent connection with wishes, desires, meaning, and intentions. The goal of aggression is to overcome a psychical or physical obstacle that interferes with intended action. We took pains to clarify the distinction between affects of the person during an aggressive action and the aggression itself. Affects are dependent upon the dynamic motivations that become the condition for the eliciting aggressive responses. The affects are always dynamically determined as part of the motivational context of the moment. Experienced or expressed rage or anger are not manifestations of aggression but of the person's stance in relation to insult, injury, or thwarting of wishes. The aggression that the offended individual may employ to remove the obstacle posed by the insult is the action of the total individual, the self-as-agent, not a postulated aggressive drive. This aggressive action, as discussed in chapter 5 whether consciously intended or unconsciously motivated, is always the intentional action of the self-as-agent. Motivation, consequently, is not meant to explain the causality of the action as such, but merely to account for the conditions in which the agent is aroused to action. Motives can be stated as the reasons for particular types of behavior. When Mr. T tortured women during his sexual encounters, his motivational configuration had him convinced that by making them suffer he could force them to see and love him. His actions, aimed at violently forcing a woman, were motivated by a desperate search for love.

Intentional behavior seeking to gain an objective, to reach a goal, to perform an action, is dependent upon eliciting conditions of the internal or external environment. We have in this understanding a major clue for analytic understanding and technique. We can ask: What internal conditions prevail within the patient's inner world? How does he understand the analytic situation at this moment as an eliciting condition for his feelings and intentions? How does the person of the analyst, as experienced by the patient, become a conditioning for his emerging wishes and intentions? How does his present-moment transference condition his wishes and his frustration? This type of questioning will show that even the patient's most destructive and hostile words and actions are not motivated by aggression as a drive, but by the contextual stimulus factors of the moment—internal, transferential, and real. The contextual motivational and stimulative aspects conditioning the analytic situation and the phenomenon of transference create an optimal situation for the revival of past stimulus contexts that have contributed to the patient's pathology. The revival makes it possible to gain understanding of those past contexts now in the exchanges and experiences with the analyst.

The transferential regressive revival of past contextual moments activating pathological affects and motivational derailments requires that the analyst help the patient understand himself in his compulsion to repeat past injuries in the present. The analyst's manner of conceiving how the pathology was structured makes all the difference in the world. If the pathology is understood as the result of an excessive amount of aggressive drive or of untamed aggressive force pushing the patient to act in a particular way, the attempt to cure must opt for either fusion of libido and aggression, or for ways of containing the manifestations and discharge of such "aggression" upon others and upon oneself. If the pathology is understood as the result of actual or internal obstacles posed to intended psychical actions preventing them from achieving completion, then the effort to cure consists in assisting the patient to retrieve in the present the uncompleted activity from the past and to assist him to remove the psychic obstacles interfering with it by mobilizing his own aggression (in the sense of aggression as we understand it).

Such was the case for each of our patients. Mr. T overcame his conviction that he was unlovable, and accepted that his mother did not belong to him and that he could not force her to do what he wanted her to do. Larry managed to see that there was life and people who would relate to him, if he renounced clinging to his mother as a defective child and stood up as a man with his own initiative, capable and finally able to use aggression to achieve his aims. Jim, after working through almost unbearable yearnings for fusion and bodily communion, came to see that he had used his greatly idealized mother as a skin for himself and realized what an obstacle his yearning for his mother had become to his living his own life.

Key to our technical approach is preservation of the patients' autonomy at all times, as the fundamental quality enabling them to use their own aggression to overcome their obstacles and to assume full responsibility for their psychic life. Each analytic pair carried out this style of working in a different manner. Mr. T took hold of the reins of his analysis, and even at the deepest moment of collaboration provided and reorganized the key insights. Larry and his analyst worked like a younger trainee and a respectful coach, but it was Larry who carried the ball. Jim did the best he could to literally incorporate and physically blend with the therapist, while the therapist remained continuously empathically available as an object that could be used to go beyond his fusion with his mother by resolving his need for fusion with his analyst, to the point that he was ready to shed his mother's skin.

Our technical approach makes the analyst an assistant to the patient during the analytic process. The analysand is the main actor and the person, ultimately autonomous and responsible, who is able to take charge of his or her life and future self-analysis. The aggression necessary to carry out this transformative process, directed to and involved in overcoming internal obstacles to achievement of essential psychical aims, is a fundamental requisite for successful analysis.

Endnotes

Chapter 1

1. The relation of aggression and affects is addressed in chapter 6.
2. The theoretical foundations for this theoretical revision are detailed in chapter 4.
3. The same charge had been variously argued by Guntrip (1969, 1973).

Chapter 2

1. This section complements the discussion of Freud's view of aggression in chapter 1.
2. The contributions of Parens (1979) will be included in chapter 7 on developmental issues.
3. Our approach has been characterized in these terms—see Schmidt-Hellerau (2002).
4. Our sense is that in these terms Winnicott is not paying attention to the distinction between action and aggression. The infant in utero may act or move, but there is no need to imagine his actions as aggressive, unless there is some obstacle to be overcome.
5. See our discussion of developmental aspects of Kohut's theory in chapter 7.
6. This aspect of Kohut's theory has something in common with our notion of aggression at the service of overcoming obstacles to intended actions.
7. For a review and critique of the Papez circuit and Maclean's findings, see Ledoux (1996).
8. The significance of these pathways for understanding patterns of emotional reactivity to aggressive motivation is considered further in chapter 6.
9. One should note that definition of such connections is complex and difficult to establish. The complexities of research on the somatic origins of affects, especially anxiety, given that affects can be both conscious and unconscious, are discussed by Wong (1999). See also LeDoux (1989, 1996) and Schore (1994). Neuroimaging studies have been especially helpful in documenting brain circuitry in emotions (Dolan, 2000).

10. Damasio (1999) also reports documenting different patterns of brain activation in different emotions by the use of PET-imaging, including differential patterns of brainstem activation. It seems that the amygdala, which is so involved in fear reactions, is little involved in happiness or disgust.

Chapter 3

1. These technical decisions were based on the understanding of Mr. T's provocations not as stemming from an aggressive drive, but from complex libidinal and narcissistic motivations.
2. Mr. T was convinced that no one, least of all a woman, would recognize him as he wished. This was the obstacle he continuously strove to overcome by "forcing" the woman, by painfully humiliating her, to give him the minimal acknowledgment that he was really there causing her pain.
3. To his surprise, the expected obstacle of a woman not recognizing him did not appear in the analysis.
4. See chapter 1.
5. See chapter 1 and chapters 9 and 12.

Chapter 4

1. See the discussion of some of these issues in Meissner (1981b) and criticisms of Schafer's action language approach in Meissner (1979a, b)
2. See the further discussion of Parens's contribution to the development of aggression in chapter 7.
3. The issues of the relationship between the economic principle and Freud's energic model, and the distinction and divorce of economic considerations from energic factors, are discussed in detail in Meissner (1995a, b, c).
4. This is *not* an argument for computer modeling of the mind—the point of the analogy is only that such a sophisticated informational processing system does not run without a power source.
5. This way of putting the matter diverges from Rubinstein's (1967) analysis of the energy-structure connection. He speaks of effector structures, perceptual structures, structures related to anticipation, and motive and motive-like structures. His view of structures as powered by psychic energy seems to retain the classic view of energy, rather than seeing it as merely the inherent capacity of these structures to perform their appropriate functions. This would pertain especially to motive structures.
6. It should go without saying that the performances of work by these functions are actions. Moving my arm is an action, as are thinking, imagining, fantasizing, feeling, dreaming, desiring, hoping, loving, even defending. This perspective harkens back to Schafer's (1976) "action language," but it does not share Schafer's metapsychology, particularly his abandonment of the structural theory. See the discussion of action language in Meissner (1979a, b) and the formulation of the self-as-agent in psychoanalysis (Meissner, 1993). This contextual understanding is related to the ensuing discussion.
7. See the last paragraph of chapter 1.

8. It should be noted that these specifications of the self as the source of agency do not exclude unconscious action or unconscious motivation. Unconscious fantasizing, for example, is an action whose source is in the self, even though it remain unconscious. The self remains autonomous in that it is the self-determining source of its own action and is not driven causally by any other source. Determination of the action of the self is in motivational terms, not causal (Meissner, 1999a, b).

9. As discussed previously in this chapter.

Chapter 5

1. The point has been argued by Toulmin (1954) to the effect that Freud was not investigating efficient causes of behavior but motives for action, that motives are not causes, and that the causes for behavior are explained by neurophysiology, motives by psychology. In our view, however, keeping within the confines of a psychological theory, the cause of behavior is to be sought in the self-as-agent, not exclusively in the neurophysiology, but in conjunction. The self is a body self whose actions are in some sense physical even when they are also classified as psychological. See the discussion of the self in the body in Meissner (1997, 1998a, b, c).

2. The phrase makes the putative integration of cause and motive clear—but in our view forces are causal, appetite motivational.

3. Humans do not have an exclusive claim on curiosity—exploratory behavior is well known in animal species.

4. As Holt (1976) also pointed out, the concept of wish as a motivational term distinguishes psychoanalysis from other nondynamic psychologies and underlines the purposive nature of human action.

5. Satisfaction is cast in terms of the pleasure principle—more in terms of goal-attainment than sensory pleasureful experience. See Meissner (1995b).

6. See the discussion of this connection in Meissner (1995b). Some authors also distinguish wishes from hopes on the grounds that hopes include a real intentionality; see Lynch (1965).

7. Brenner (1979) regards wishes as forms of drive derivation that can operate in conjunction with ego and superego functions to respond to internal and external stimulus conditions and give meaning to the drive articulated as wish. In this formulation, the ego becomes the executor of wish-fulfillment. Oour argument differs somewhat in that wish may arise from a variety of need states but need not imply derivation from a drive, and my appeal to the self-as-agent does not bypass the ego, since the ego functions as a component subsystem of the self: ego may be the executor of wish-fulfillment, but both ego-action and wish are functions of the self. Ego and self are not opposed in terms of agency; see Meissner (1993, 2000c).

8. This is not to say that when the eliciting conditions involve both sexual interest and a need to overcome an obstacle to fulfilling that need, both libidinal and aggressive motives cannot be integrated in stimulating a proportional response.

9. Other theoretical efforts to encompass these aspects of psychic functioning have dealt with the inherent tensions by resorting, for example, to concepts of neutralization (Hartmann) or compromise formation (Brenner). Neither resolution escapes the inherent difficulties of drive theory. Whether neutralized or drive-derived, actions draw their causal potential from the drives as opposed to the

self-as-agent. Hartmann had to compromise this derivation by appeal to conflict-free capacities in the ego, and Brenner to our understanding does not satisfactorily account for the agency of the compromising component. Interpretations of compromise and drive-derivation as departures from Freud's instinctual theory seem to ignore the obvious.

10. Question: Is there any difference between such dispositional factors and drive-derivative formations (Brenner, 1979)? We would suggest that such internal factors derive from a variety of sources related to response readiness: hormonal, nutritional, and other physiological variables, to name a few. Factors related to fatigue or even biorhythms are also relevant. In hunger, as previously discussed, the lack of food creates a state of physiological need that can dispose to action, but has nothing to do necessarily with drives. If one were to postulate a "hunger drive," we would have to question what that meant, other than an inducible physiological state and not an instinctual drive as understood psychoanalytically. Sexual needs, however, can also serve as dispositions, but the same argument would apply—are they physiologically induced need states or drives? Brenner's drive derivatives would seem to imply a necessary connection with drives, even if, as derivatives, they are put to other uses.

11. We can ascribe reasons for knee-jerks and blinks, but they are reasons we ascribe externally to rationalize the behavior, they are not the reasons of the subject. My knee reflex responds when tapped, but I do not intend to extend my knee.

12. The term "libidinal" in such usage connotes the affective and appetitive nature of the desire as descriptive attributes; it need not designate a drive as would be the case in the classic frame of reference.

13. See the further discussion of this perspective in Meissner (1992, 1996a, b, 2003).

Chapter 6

1. The original German does not say "thoughts" but "*zur richtigen Erganzung*," that is, "correct completion" of the complex (Freud, 1900, p. 464).
2. See chapters 7, 9, 10, 11, and 12.
3. Mr T was discussed in chapter 3.

Chapter 7

1. In chapter 2.
2. It seems doubtful that the self could be "destroyed." Psychic structures, by definition, are endurable formations.
3. This formulation is congruent with Rochlin's (1973) earlier view of aggression in the service of narcissistic self-protection. See also Greenspan's (1991) comments in this regard and the discussion by Mayes and Cohen (1993).
4. See also the representative study of Mayes and Cohen (1993) in support of the role of aggression in facilitating separation and individuation.
5. Winnicott's views on aggression are also discussed in chapter 2.

Chapter 8

1. The dream seems to utilize the imagery of the magic staff (caduceus), capable of protecting its bearer in classical times. In early times, the caduceus was a branch with intertwined twigs. In a later development the twigs became snakes. The caduceus was a symbol of the Greek god Hermes (Guirand, 1968), and was used by Asclepius as the symbol of the physician; it is still used as a symbol of the health sciences. Hermes, the messenger of the gods, carried it with him as a protection against the many dangers the world poses to travelers (Rose, 1971). For Paul, the symbol condenses his ambivalence as a physician and as a young man about to go out into the WORLD, and his need for safety and protection. It also conveys the fear of his penis and its magical destructive power.

Chapter 9

1. This chapter is a modified version of Buie et al. (1996).
2. This discussion is complementary to the more ample discussion of the points of comparison and differentiation between our theory of aggression and more traditional and other contemporary approaches in chapter 2 above.
3. A more ample discussion of the points of comparison and differentiation between our theory of aggression and more traditional and other contemporary approaches can be found in Rizzuto et al. (1993).
4. These formulations pertained primarily to transference derivatives, but obviously the question of the distribution of power and authority in the analytic relation is more complex.
5. His pathology is practically a perversion because all objects are incidental to his need to prove to himself his value as a man by sadistically overpowering women or others.
6, It can be noted that in these instances his aggression was accompanied by affects of rage, whereas in window peeking the aggressive act involved no conscious rage, but did bring him the feeling of mastery and triumph.

Chapter 10

1. During this period, the analyst was on call in a hospital and had to be reachable at all times. Larry understood this, but was nonetheless furious about it.

Chapter 11

1. See Buie and Adler (1972) and Meissner (1988) on the role of confrontation in the treatment of borderline patients.
2. See Buie and Adler (1982–83) for further discussion of the role of evocative memory in the treatment of borderline patients.
3. The basics of the kleinian position have been discussed in chapter 2.

Chapter 12

1. Discussed in chapter 10.
2. See chapter 6.
3. Discussed in chapter 3.
4. The case of Frankie is discussed in chapter 7.
5. The case of Paul is discussed in chapter 8.
6. The case of Larry is presented in chapter 10.
7. The case of Jim is discussed in chapter 11.
8. This form of analytic listening stance diverges from that espoused by Ogden (1997) in his use of reverie. The direction of the analyst's listening focus in reverie is internal, the analyst listening to himself rather than to the patient. The analytic stance leaves room for both forms of listening (Meissner, 2000a), and a given analyst may prefer one or the other, or find ways of combining them. It should be recognized, however, that they are divergent, that to the extent that one listens in a more objective mode, his listening is less subjective, and vice versa. Properly understood, both approaches would be consistent with a meaningful therapeutic alliance (Meissner, 1996b). The point for our discussion is that a subjective focus, as in the use of reverie, would not seem to require aggressive effort of the analyst in maintaining such a listening posture.

References

Abend, S. (1986). Countertransference, empathy, and the analytic ideal: The impact of life stresses on analytic capability. *Psychoanalytic Quarterly,* 55: 563–75.

Aguayo, J. (2002) Reassessing the clinical affinity between Melanie Klein and D. W. Winnicott: 1935–1951: Klein's unpublished "Notes on baby" in historical context. *International Journal of Psychoanalysis,* 83: 1133–52.

Ainsworth, M. D. (1969). Object relations, dependency and attachment: A theoretical review of the infant–mother relationship. *Child Development,* 40: 969–1025.

Ainsworth, M. D., Blehar, M. C., Waters, E., and Walls, S. (1978). *Patterns of Attachment: A Psychological Study of the Strange Situation.* Hillsdale, NJ: Lawrence Erlbaum.

Armony, J. L., and LeDoux, J. E. (2000). How danger is encoded: toward a systems, cellular, and computational understanding of cognitive-emotional interactions in fear. In M. S. Gazzaniga (ed.), *The New Cognitive Neurosciences.* Cambridge, MA: MIT Press, 1067–79.

Arnetoli, C. (2002). Empathic networks: Symbolic and subsymbolic representations in the intersubjective field. *Psychoanalytic Inquiry,* 22: 740–65.

Arnold, M. B. (1960). *Emotion and Personality.* 2 vols. New York: Columbia University Press.

Aron, L. (1991). The patient's experience of the analyst's subjectivity. *Psychoanalytic Dialogues,* 1: 29–51.

Badalamenti, A. F. (1985). Energy and psychical pain. *Journal of Religion and Health,* 24: 316–42.

Basch, M. F. (1979). An operational definition of the "self." Paper presented at the Boston Psychoanalytic Society and Institute, November 16, 1979.

Benjamin, J. (1995). *Like Subjects. Love Objects.* New Haven, CT: Yale University Press.

Berliner, B. (1940). Libido and reality in masochism. *Psychoanalytic Quarterly,* 9: 322–33.

———. (1947). On some psychodynamics of masochism. *Psychoanalytic Quarterly,* 16: 459–71.

———. (1958). The role of object relations in moral masochism. *Psychoanalytic Quarterly,* 27, 38–56.

Bernstein, I. (1962) Dreams and masturbation in an adolescent boy. *Journal of the American Psychoanalytic Association,* 10: 289–302.

Bion, W. R. (1955). Language and the schizophrenic. In M. Klein et al. (ed.), *New Directions in Psychoanalysis.* London: Tavistock, 220–39.

279

————. (1957). Differentiation of the psychotic from the non-psychotic personalities. *International Journal of Psychoanalysis*, 38: 266–75.

————. (1958). Our arrogance. International Journal of Psychoanalysis, 39: 144–46.

————. (1959). Attacks on linking. *International Journal of Psychoanalysis*, 40: 308–15.

————. (1962a). The psycho-analytic study of thinking, II. A theory of thinking. *International Journal of Psychoanalysis*, 43: 306–10.

————. (1962b). *Learning from Experience*. In Seven Servants: Four Works by Wilfred R. Bion. New York: Aronson, 1977.

————. (1970). *Attention and Interpretation*. In Seven Servants. New York: Aronson, 1977.

Blum, H. P. (1995) The clinical value of daydreams and a note on their role in character analysis. In E. S. Person, P. Fonagy, P., and S. A. Figueira (eds.), *On Freud's "Creative Writers and Day-Dreaming."* New Haven, CT: Yale University Press, 39–52.

Blum, E. J., and Blum, H. P. (1990) The development of autonomy and superego precursors. *International Journal of Psychoanalysis,* 71: 585–95.

Bollas, C. (1987). *The Shadow of the Object: Psychoanalysis of the Unthought Known*. New York: Columbia University Press.

Bornstein, B. (1949). The analysis of a phobic child. Some problems of theory and technique in child analysis. *Psychoanalytic Study of the Child*, 3/4: 181–226.

Bouchard, M.–A., Normandin, L., and Séguin, M.–H. (1995). Countertransference as instrument and obstacle: A comprehensive and descriptive framework. *Psychoanalytic Quarterly,* 64: 717–45.

Boyer, B. (1986). Technical aspects of treating the regressed patient. *Contemporary Psychoanalysis,* 22: 25–44.

————. (1989). Countertransference and technique in working with the regressed patient. *International Journal of Psychoanalysis,* 70: 701–14.

Brenner, C. (1959). The masochistic character. *Journal of the American Psychoanalytic Association*, 7: 197–226.

Brenner, C. (1974). On the nature and development of affects: A unified theory. *Psychoanalytic Quarterly*, 43: 532–56.

————. (1975). Affects and psychic conflict. *Psychoanalytic Quarterly*, 44: 5–28.

————. (1979). The components of psychic conflict and its consequences in mental life. *Psychoanalytic Quarterly*, 48: 547–67.

————. (1982). *The Mind in Conflict*. New York: International Universities Press.

Breuer, J., and Freud, S. (1893–95). Studies on hysteria. *Standard Edition,* 2.

Buie, D., and Adler., G. (1972) The uses of confrontation with borderline patients. *International Journal of Psychoanalytic Psychotherapy*, 1: 90–108.

————. (1982–83). The definitive treatment of the borderline patient. *International Journal of Psychoanalytic Psychotherapy*, 9: 51–87.

Buie, D. H., Meissner, W. W., Rizzuto, A.–M., and Sashin, J. (1983). Aggression in the psychoanalytic situation. *International Review of Psychoanalysis,* 10: 159–70.

Buie, D. H., Meissner, W. W., and Rizzuto, A.–M. (1996). The role of aggression in sado-masochism. *Canadian Journal of Psychoanalysis*, 4: 1–28.

Carpy, D. V. (1989). Tolerating the countertransference: A mutative process. *International Journal of Psychoanalysis*, 70: 287–94.

Chessick, R. D. (1977). *Intensive Psychotherapy of the Borderline Patient*. New York: Jason Aronson.

Coen, S. J. (1989). Intolerance of responsibility for internal conflict. *Journal of the American Psychoanalytic Association*, 37: 943–64.

Compton, A. (1983). The current status of the psychoanalytic theory of instinctual drives. I. Drive concept, classification, and development. *Psychoanalytic Quarterly,* 52: 364–401.

Condry, J., and Condry, S. (1976). Sex differences: a study of the eye of the beholder. *Child Development,* 47: 812–819.

Damasio, A.R. (1994). *Descartes' Error: Emotion, Reason and the Human Brain.* New York: Putnam.

———. (1999). *The Feeling of What Happens: Body and Emotion in the Making of Consciousness.* New York: Harcourt.

Davidson, R. J. (2000) The neuroscience of affective style. In M. S. Gazzaniga (ed.), *The New Cognitive Neurosciences.* Cambridge, MA: MIT Press, 1149–59.

Dolan, R. J. (2000) Emotional processing in the human brain revealed through functional neuroimaging. In M. S. Gazzaniga (ed.), *The New Cognitive Neurosciences.* Cambridge, MA: MIT Press, 1115–31.

Emde, R. N. (1993). Epilogue: A beginning—research approaches and expanding horizons for psychoanalysis. *Journal of the American Psychoanalytic Association,* 41 (Suppl.): 411–24.

Epstein, L. (1979). Countertransference with borderline patients. In L. Epstein and A. Feiner (eds.), *Countertransference.* New York: Jason Aronson.

Erikson, E. H. (1950). *Childhood and Society.* Rev. ed. New York: Norton, 1963.

———. (1959). *Identity and the Life Cycle.* New York: International Universities Press [Psychological Issues, Monograph 1].

Fairbairn, W. R. D. (1952). *Psychoanalytic Studies of the Personality.* London: Routledge and Kegan Paul.

———. (1963) Synopsis of an object–relations theory of the personality. *International Journal of Psychoanalysis,* 44: 224–25.

Feinsilver, D. B. (1983). Reality, transitional relatedness, and containment in the borderline. *Contemporary Psychoanalysis,* 19: 537–69.

Fenichel, O. (1944). Remarks on the common phobias. In *The Collected Papers of Otto Fenichel.* New York: Norton, 1954, 278–87.

Flescher, J. (1955). A dualistic viewpoint on anxiety. *Journal of the American Psychoanalytic Association,* 3: 415–46.

Fonagy, P., Moran, G. S., and Target, M. (1993). Aggression and the psychological self. *International Journal of Psychoanalysis,* 74: 471–85.

Fonagy, P., and Target, M. (2002). Early intervention and the development of self-regulation. *Psychoanalytic Inquiry,* 22: 307–35.

Fosshage, J. L. (1998). On aggression: Its forms and functions. *Psychoanalytic Inquiry,* 18: 45–54.

Freud, A. (1936). *The Ego and the Mechanisms of Defense.* New York: International Universities Press, 1946. Also in *The Writings of Anna Freud.* Vol. 2. New York: International Universities Press, 1966.

———. (1965). *Normality and Pathology in Childhood: Assessments of Development.* In *The Writings of Anna Freud.* Vol. 6. New York: International Universities Press.

———. (1972). Comments on aggression. *International Journal of Psychoanalysis,* 53: 163–71.

———. (1977). Fears, anxieties, and phobic phenomena. *Psychoanalytic Study of the Child,* 32: 85–90.

Freud, S. (1900). The interpretation of dreams. *Standard Edition,* 4 and 5.

———. (1905a). Fragment of an analysis of a case of hysteria. *Standard Edition,* 7: 1–122.

———. (1905b). Three essays on the theory of sexuality. *Standard Edition,* 7: 123–245.

———. (1909). Analysis of a phobia in a five-year-old boy. *Standard Edition,* 10: 1–149.

———. (1910). The future prospects of psycho-analytic therapy. *Standard Edition,* 11: 139–51.

———. (1912). Recommendations to physicians practicing psycho-analysis. *Standard Edition,* 12: 109–20.

————. (1914). Remembering, repeating and working through. *Standard Edition,* 12: 145–56.

————. (1915). Instincts and their vicissitudes. *Standard Edition,* 14: 109–40.

————. (1916). Some character types met with in psychoanalytic work. I. The "exceptions." *Standard Edition,* 14: 309–15.

————. (1918). From the history of an infantile neurosis. *Standard Edition,* 17: 1–123.

————. (1919a). "A child is being beaten": A contribution to the study of the origin of sexual perversion. *Standard Edition,* 17: 175–204.

————. (1919b). Lines of advance in psycho-analytic therapy. *Standard Edition,* 17: 157–68.

————. (1920). Beyond the pleasure principle. *Standard Edition,* 18: 1–64.

————. (1923). The ego and the id. *Standard Edition,* 19: 1–66.

————. (1924). The economic problem of masochism. *Standard Edition,* 19: 159–70.

————. (1925). Some additional notes on dream-interpretation as a whole. *Standard Edition,* 19: 123–38.

————. (1926). Inhibitions, symptoms and anxiety. *Standard Edition,* 20: 75–175.

————. (1930). Civilization and its discontents. *Standard Edition,* 21: 57–145.

————. (1931). Libidinal types. *Standard Edition,* 21: 215–20.

————. (1933a). New introductory lectures on psycho-analysis. *Standard Edition,* 22: 1–182.

————. (1933b). Why war? *Standard Edition,* 22: 195–215.

————. (1937). Constructions in analysis. *Standard Edition,* 23: 255–69.

Friedman, H. J. (1970). Dr. Friedman replies (Correspondence). *American Journal of Psychiatry,* 126: 1677.

Friedman, L. (1995). Main meaning and motivation. *Psychoanalytic Inquiry,* 15: 437–60.

Gabbard, G. O. (1989). On "doing nothing" in the psychoanalytic treatment of the refractory borderline patient. *International Journal of Psychoanalysis,* 70: 527–34.

————. (1991). Technical approaches to transference hate in the analysis of borderline patients. *International Journal of Psychoanalysis,* 72: 625–37.

————. (1994). Commentary on papers by Tansey, Hirsch, and Davies. *Psychoanalytic Dialogues,* 4: 203-213.

————. (1995). Countertransference: The emerging common ground. *International Journal of Psychoanalysis,* 76: 475–85

Galenson, E., and Fields, B. (1989). Gender disturbance in a three-and-one-half-year-old boy. In S. Dowling and A. Rothstein, A. (eds.), *The Significance of Infant Observational Research for Clinical Work with Children, Adolescents, and Adults.* Madison, CT: International Universities Press, 39–51.

Gedo, J. E. (1982). On black bile and other humours. *Psychoanalytic Inquiry,* 2: 181–91.

————. (1995). On the psychobiology of motivation. *Psychoanalytic Inquiry,* 15: 470–80.

Geleerd, E. (1958). Borderline states in childhood and adolescence. *Psychoanalytic Study of the Child,* 13: 279–95.

Giovacchini, P. L. (1975). Various aspects of the psychoanalytic process. In P. L. Giovacchini (ed.), *Tactics and Techniques of Psychoanalytic Therapy.* Vol. 2. New York: Jason Aronson, 5–94.

Girard, R. (1986). *The Scapegoat.* Baltimore: Johns Hopkins University Press.

Glasser, M. (1986). Identification and its vicissitudes as observed in the perversions. *International Journal of Psychoanalysis,* 67: 9–18.

Goldberg, A. (1979). *The Psychology of the Self. A Casebook.* New York: International Universities Press.

Goleman, D. (1995). *Emotional Intelligence.* New York: Bantam.

Green, A. (1999). *The Fabric of Affect in the Psychoanalytic Discourse.* New York: Routledge.

————. (2001). *Life Narcissism, Death Narcissism.* London: Free Association Books.

Greenspan, S. I. (1975). *A Consideration of Some Learning Variables in the Context of*

Psychoanalytic Theory: Toward a Psychoanalytic Learning Perspective. New York: International Universities Press [Psychological Issues, Monograph 33].

———. (1991). The development of the ego: insights from clinical work with infants and young children. In T. Shapiro (ed.), *The Concept of Structure in Psychoanalysis.* Madison, CT: International Universities Press, 3–55.

Grossman, W. I. (1991). Pain, aggression, fantasy, and the concepts of sadomasochism. *Psychoanalytic Quarterly,* 60: 22–52.

Grotstein, J. S. (1982). The analysis of a borderline patient. In P. L. Giovacchini and B. Boyer, B. (eds.), *Technical Factors in the Treatment of Severely Disturbed Patients.* New York: Jason Aronson, 261–88.

Guirand, F. (1968). Greek mythology. In *New Larousse Encyclopedia of Mythology.* New York: Prometheus Press, 85–198.

Gunderson, J. G., and Singer, M. T. (1975). Defining borderline patients: An overview. *American Journal of Psychiatry,* 132: 1–10.

Gunther, M. S. (1980). Aggression, self-psychology, and the concept of health. In A. Goldberg (ed.), *Advances in Self Psychology.* New York: International Universities Press, 167–92.

Guntrip, H. (1969). *Schizoid Phenomena, Object Relations and the Self.* New York: International Universities Press.

———. (1973). *Psychoanalytic Theory, Therapy, and the Self.* New York: Basic Books.

Hamilton, V. (1996). *The Analyst's Preconscious.* Hillsdale, NJ: Analytic Press.

Harris, A. (1998). Aggression: Pleasures and dangers. *Psychoanalytic Inquiry,* 18: 31–44.

Hartmann, H. (1939). *Ego Psychology and the Problem of Adaptation.* New York: International Universities Press, 1958.

———. (1948). Comments on the psychoanalytic theory of instinctual drives. In *Essays on Ego Psychology: Selected Problems in Psychoanalytic Theory.* New York: International Universities Press, 1964, 69–89.

———. (1950). Comments on the psychoanalytic theory of the ego. In *Essays on Ego Psychology: Selected Problems in Psychoanalytic Theory.* New York: International Universities Press, 1964, 113–41.

———. (1952). The mutual influences in the development of ego and id. In *Essays on Ego Psychology: Selected Problems in Psychoanalytic Theory.* New York: International Universities Press, 1964, 155–81.

———. (1955). Notes on the theory of sublimation. In *Essays on Ego Psychology: Selected Problems in Psychoanalytic Theory.* New York: International Universities Press, 1964, 215–40.

———. (1964a). *Essays on Ego Psychology: Selected Problems in Psychoanalytic Theory.* New York: International Universities Press.

———. (1964b). Introduction. In *Essays on Ego Psychology: Selected Problems in Psychoanalytic Theory.* New York: International Universities Press, ix–xv.

Hartmann, H., Kris, E., and Loewenstein, R. M. (1949). Notes on the theory of aggression. *Psychoanalytic Study of the Child,* 49: 293–312.

Heimann, P., and Isaacs, S. (1970). Regression. In M. Klein et al., *Developments in Psycho-Analysis.* London: Hogarth Press, International Psycho-Analytical Library, 169–97.

Hendrick, I. (1942). Instinct and the ego during infancy. *Psychoanalytic Quarterly,* 11: 33–58.

———. (1943a). The discussion of the "instinct to master." *Psychoanalytic Quarterly,* 12: 561–65.

———. (1943b). Work and the pleasure principle. *Psychoanalytic Quarterly,* 12: 311–329.

Hesse, E., and Main, M. (1999). Second generation effects of unresolved trauma in nonmaltreating parents: dissociated, frightened, and threatening parental behavior. *Psychoanalytic Inquiry,* 19: 481–540.

Hirsch, I. (1993). Countertransference enactments and some issues related to external factors in the analyst's life. *Psychoanalytic Dialogues,* 3: 343–66

———. (1994). Countertransference love and theoretical models. *Psychoanalytic Dialogues,* 4: 171–92

Hoffman, I. (1991). Reply to Benjamin. *Psychoanalytic Dialogues,* 1: 535–44

———. (1996). The intimate and ironic authority of the psychoanalyst's presence. *Psychoanalytic Quarterly,* 65: 102–36.

Holt, R. R. (1976). Drive or wish? A reconsideration of the psychoanalytic theory of motivation. In M. M. Gill and P. S. Holzman (eds.), *Psychology versus Metapsychology: Psychoanalytic Essays in Honor of George S. Klein.* New York: International Universities Press, 158–97 [Psychological Issues, Monograph 36].

Jacobs, T. J. (1991). *The Use of the Self: Countertransference and Communication in the Analytic Situation.* Madison, CT: International Universities Press.

Joseph, B. (1989). Psychic equilibrium and psychic change. In M. Feldman and E. B. Spillius (eds.), *Selected Papers of Betty Joseph.* London and New York: Routledge.

Kernberg, O. (1966), Structural derivatives of object relations. *International Journal of Psychoanalysis,* 47: 236–53.

———. (1967). Borderline personality organization. *Journal of the American Psychoanalytic Association,* 15: 641–85.

———. (1968). The treatment of patients with borderline personality organization. *International Journal of Psychoanalysis,* 49: 600–19.

———. (1970a). Factors in the psychoanalytic treatment of narcissistic personalities. *Journal of the American Psychoanalytic Association,* 18: 51–85.

———. (1970b). A psychoanalytic classification of character pathology. *Journal of the American Psychoanalytic Association,* 18: 800–22.

———. (1971). Prognostic considerations regarding borderline personality organization. *Journal of the American Psychoanalytic Association,* 19: 595–635.

———. (1975). *Borderline Conditions and Pathological Narcissism.* New York: Aronson.

———. (1982). Self, ego, affects, and drives. *Journal of the American Psychoanalytic Association,* 30: 893–918.

———. (1984). *Severe Personality Disorders: Psychotherapeutic Strategies.* New Haven, CT: Yale University Press.

———. (1991). Sadomasochism, sexual excitement, and perversion. *Journal of the American Psychoanalytic Association,* 39: 333–62.

Kihlstrom, J. F. (1987). The cognitive unconscious. *Science,* 237: 1445–52.

Klein, G. S. (1967). Peremptory ideation: structure and force in motivated ideas. In R. R. Holt (ed.), *Motives and Thought: Psychoanalytic Essays in Honor of David Rapaport.* New York: International Universities Press, 80–128 [Psychological Issues, Monograph 18/19].

———. (1969). Freud's two theories of sexuality. In M. M. Gill and P. S. Holzman (eds.), *Psychology versus Metapsychology: Psychoanalytic Essays in Honor of George S. Klein.* New York: International Universities Press, 1976, 14–70 [Psychological Issues, Monograph 36].

———. (1970). Two theories or one? In *Psychoanalytic Theory: An Exploration of Essentials.* New York: International Universities Press, 1975, 41–71.

———. (1975). *Psychoanalytic Theory: An Exploration of Essentials.* New York: International Universities Press.

Klein, M. (1945). The Oedipus complex in the light of early anxieties. In *Contributions to Psychoanalysis 1921–1945.* New York: McGraw-Hill, 1964, 339–90.

———. (1970). Some theoretical conclusions about the emotional life of the infant. In M. Klein et al., *Developments in Psycho-Analysis.* London: Hogarth Press, International Psycho-Analytical Library, 198–236.

————. (1975a). *Envy and Gratitude and Other Works, 1946–1963.* New York: Delacorte Press.

————. (1975b). *Love, Guilt and Reparation and Other Works, 1921–1945.* New York: Delacorte Press.

Knapp, P.H. (1966). Libido: A latter–day look. *Journal of Nervous and Mental Disease,* 142: 395–417.

Kohut, H. (1971). *The Analysis of the Self.* New York: International Universities Press.

————. (1972). Thoughts on narcissism and narcissistic rage. *Psychoanalytic Study of the Child,* 27: 360–400. Reprinted in P. Ornstein (ed.), *The Search for the Self: Selected Writings of Heinz Kohut: 1950–1978.* Vol. 3. New York: International Universities Press, 1978, 615–58.

————. (1977). *The Restoration of the Self.* New York: International University Press.

————. (1980). Reflections on "Advances in Self Psychology." In A. Goldberg (ed.), *Advances in Self Psychology.* New York: International Universities Press, 473–554.

Kraft-Ebing, R. von (1886). *Psychopathia Sexualis: A Medico-Forensic Study.* New York: Putnam, 1965.

Kris, A. O. (1984). The conflicts of ambivalence. *Psychoanalytic Study of the Child,* 39: 213–34.

Kuhn, T. S. (1970). *The Structure of Scientific Revolutions.* Enlarged edition. Chicago: University of Chicago Press.

Lacan, J. (1992). *The Seminar of Jacques Lacan. Book VII: The Ethics of Psychoanalysis 1959–1960.* New York: Norton.

Laplanche, J., and Pontalis, J.–B. (1973) *The Language of Psychoanalysis.* New York: Norton.

LeDoux, J. E. (1987). Emotion. In F. Plum (ed.), *Handbook of Physiology. 1. The Nervous System. Vol. V: Higher Functions of the Brain.* Bethesda, MD: American Physiological Society, 419–59.

————. (1989). Cognitive-emotional interactions in the brain. *Cognition and Emotion,* 3: 267–89.

————. (1996). *The Emotional Brain: The Mysterious Underpinnings of Emotional Life.* New York: Simon and Schuster.

————. (2002). *Synaptic Self: How Our Brains Become Who We Are.* New York: Viking Penguin.

Levy, D. (1972). Oppositional syndromes and oppositional behavior. In S. I. Harrison and J. F. McDermott (eds.), *Childhood Psychopathology.* New York: International Universities Press, 340–359.

Lichtenberg, J. D. (1982). Frames of reference for viewing aggression. *Psychoanalytic Inquiry,* 2: 213–31.

————. (1989). *Psychoanalysis and Motivation.* Hillsdale, NJ: Analytic Press.

Little, M. (1966) Transference in borderline states. *International Journal of Psychoanalysis,* 47: 476–85.

Loewald, H. W. (1962) Internalization, separation, mourning, and the superego. In *Papers on Psychoanalysis.* New Haven: Yale University Press, 1980, 257–76.

————. (1971) On motivation and instinct theory. In *Papers on Psychoanalysis.* New Haven, CT: Yale University Press, 1980, 102–37.

Lynch, S. J., W.F. (1965). *Images of Hope: Imagination as Healer of the Hopeless.* Baltimore, MD: Helicon.

MacLean, P. D. (1955). The limbic system ("visceral brain") and emotional behavior. *Archives of Neurology and Psychiatry,* 73: 130–34.

————. (1990). *The Triune Brain in Evolution: Role in Paleocerebral Functions.* New York: Plenum.

Mahler, M. S. (1968) *On Human Symbiosis and the Vicissitudes of Individuation. Vol 1: Infantile Psychosis.* New York: International Universities Press.

————. (1971). A study of the separation-individuation process and its possible application to borderline phenomena the psychoanalytic situation. *Psychoanalytic Study of
the Child*, 26: 403–24.

————. (1972). The rapprochement subphase of the separation-individuation process.
Psychoanalytic Quarterly, 41: 487–506.

Mahler, M.S. , and Kaplan, L. (1977). Developmental aspects in the assessment of narcissistic and so-called borderline personalities. In P. Hartocollis (ed.), *Borderline Personality Disorder: The Concept, the Syndrome, the Patient*. New York: International
Universities Press, 71–85.

Mahler, M. S., Pine, F., and Bergman, A (1975). *The Psychological Birth of the Human
Infant: Symbiosis and Individuation*. New York: Basic Books.

Makari, G., and Shapiro, T. (1993). On psychoanalytic listening: Language and unconscious communication. *Journal of the American Psychoanalytic Association*, 41: 991–
1020.

Maleson, F. G. (1984). The multiple meanings of masochism in psychoanalytic discourse.
Journal of the American Psychoanalytic Association, 32: 325–56.

Masterson, J. F., and Rinsley, D. B. (1975). The borderline syndrome: The role of the
mother in the genesis and psychic structure of the borderline personality. *International Journal of Psychoanalysis*, 56: 163–77.

Mayes, L. C., and Cohen, D. J. (1993). The social matrix of aggression: Enactments and
representations of loving and hating in the first years of life. *Psychoanalytic Study of
the Child*, 48: 145–69.

McDevitt, J. B. (1983). The emergence of hostile aggression and its defensive and adaptive modifications during the separation-individuation process. *Journal of the American Psychoanalytic Association*, 31 (Suppl.): 273–300.

McIntosh, D. (1993). Cathexes and their objects in the thought of Sigmund Freud. *Journal
of the American Psychoanalytic Association*, 41: 679–709.

Meers, D. (1982). Object relations and Beyond the Pleasure Principle revisited. *Psychoanalytic Inquiry*, 2: 233–54.

Meissner, S. J., W. W. (1978). *The Paranoid Process*. New York: Jason Aronson.

————. (1979a). Critique of concepts and therapy in the action language approach to
psychoanalysis. *International Journal of Psychoanalysis*, 60: 291–310.

————. (1979b). Methodological critique of the action language in psychoanalysis. *Journal of the American Psychoanalytic Association*, 27: 79–105.

————. (1981a). *Internalization in Psychoanalysis*. New York: International Universities
Press. [Psychological Issues, Monograph 50].

————. (1981b). Metapsychology—who needs it? *Journal of the American Psychoanalytic Association*, 29: 921–38.

————. (1984). *The Borderline Spectrum: Differential Diagnosis and Developmental Issues*. New York: Jason Aronson.

————. (1986). Can psychoanalysis find its self? *Journal of the American Psychoanalytic
Association*, 34: 379–400.

————. (1988). *Treatment of Patients in the Borderline Spectrum*. Northvale, NJ: Jason
Aronson.

————. (1989). The viewpoint of a devil's advocate. In S. Dowling and A. Rothstein
(eds.), *The Significance of Infant Observational Research for Clinical Work with Children, Adolescents, and Adults*. Madison, CT: International Universities Press, 175–94.

————. (1992). The concept of the therapeutic alliance. *Journal of the American Psychoanalytic Association*, 40: 1059–87.

————. (1993). The self-as-agent in psychoanalysis. *Psychoanalysis and Contemporary
Thought*, 16: 459–95.

———. (1995a). The economic principle in psychoanalysis. I. Economics and energetics. *Psychoanalysis and Contemporary Thought*, 18: 197–226.

———. (1995b). The economic principle in psychoanalysis. II. Regulatory principles. *Psychoanalysis and Contemporary Thought*, 18: 227–59.

———. (1995c). The economic principle in psychoanalysis. III. Motivational principles. *Psychoanalysis and Contemporary Thought*, 18: 261–92.

———. (1996a). The self-as-object in psychoanalysis. *Psychoanalysis and Contemporary Thought*, 19: 425–59.

———. (1996b). *The Therapeutic Alliance*. New Haven, CT: Yale University Press.

———. (1996c). The therapeutic alliance and the real relationship in the analytic process. In L. E. Lifson (ed.), *Understanding Therapeutic Action: Psychodynamic Concepts of Cure*. Hillsdale, NJ: Analytic Press, 21–39.

———. (1997). The self and the body: I. The body self and the body image. *Psychoanalysis and Contemporary Thought*, 20(4): 419–48.

———. (1998a). The self and the body: II. The embodied self—self vs. nonself. *Psychoanalysis and Contemporary Thought*, 21(1): 85–111.

———. (1998b). The self and the body: III. The body image in clinical perspective. *Psychoanalysis and Contemporary Thought*, 21(1): 113–46.

———. (1998c). The self and the body: IV. The body on the couch. *Psychoanalysis and Contemporary Thought*, 21(2): 277–300.

———. (1999a). The dynamic principle in psychoanalysis. I. The classic theory reconsidered. *Psychoanalysis and Contemporary Thought*, 22: 3–40.

———. (1999b). The dynamic principle in psychoanalysis. II. Toward a revised theory of motivation. *Psychoanalysis and Contemporary Thought*, 22: 41–83.

———. (1999c). Notes on the therapeutic role of the alliance. *Psychoanalytic Review*, 86: 1–33.

———. (1999d). The self-as-subject in psychoanalysis. I. The nature of subjectivity. *Psychoanalysis and Contemporary Thought*, 22: 155–201.

———. (1999e). The self-as-subject in psychoanalysis. II. The subject in analysis. *Psychoanalysis and Contemporary Thought*, 22: 383–428.

———. (2000a). On analytic Listening. *Psychoanalytic Quarterly*, 69: 317–67.

———. (2000b). The many faces of analytic interaction. *Psychoanalytic Psychology*, 17: 512–46.

———. (2000c). The self-as-person in psychoanalysis. *Psychoanalysis and Contemporary Thought*, 23: 479–523.

———. (2000d). The self-as-relational in psychoanalysis: I. Relational aspects of the self. *Psychoanalysis and Contemporary Thought*, 23: 177–204.

———. (2000e). The self-as-relational in psychoanalysis: II. The self as related within the analytic process. *Psychoanalysis and Contemporary Thought*, 23: 205–47.

———. (2000f). The self as structural. *Psychoanalysis and Contemporary Thought*, 23: 373–416.

———. (2000g). The structural principle in psychoanalysis: I. The meaning of structure. *Psychoanalysis and Contemporary Thought*, 23(3): 283–330.

———. (2000h). The structural principle in psychoanalysis: II. Structure formation and structural change. *Psychoanalysis and Contemporary Thought*, 23(3): 331–71.

———. (2003). *The Therapeutic Alliance: A Vital Element in Clinical Practice*. Northvale, NJ: Jason Aronson.

Meissner, S. J., W. W., Rizzuto, A.-M., Sashin, J., and Buie, D. H. (1987). A view of aggression in phobic states. *Psychoanalytic Quarterly*, 56: 452–76.

Menaker, E. (1942). The masochistic factor in the psychoanalytic situation. *Psychoanalytic Quarterly*, 11: 171–86.

———. (1953). Masochism—a defense reaction of the ego. *Psychoanalytic Quarterly*, 22: 205–20.

Meza, C. (1970). Anger—a key to the borderline patient. (Correspondence). *American Journal of Psychiatry*, 126: 1676-77.

Mitchell, S. A. (1988). *Relational Concepts in Psychoanalysis*. Cambridge, MA: Harvard University Press.

———. (1993a). Aggression and the endangered self. *Psychoanalytic Quarterly*, 62: 351–82.

———. (1993b). *Hope and Dread in Psychoanalysis*. New York: Basic Books.

———. (1995). Commentary on "Contemporary structural psychoanalysis and relational psychoanalysis." *Psychoanalytic Psychology*, 12: 575–82.

Money-Kyrle, R. E. (1956). Normal counter-transference and some of its deviations. *International Journal of Psychoanalysis*, 37: 360–66.

Moore, B. E., & Fine, B. D. (eds.) (1990). *Psychoanalytic Terms and Concepts*. New Haven and London: American Psychoanalytic Association and Yale University Press.

Moran, F. M. (1993). *Subject and Agency in Psychoanalysis: Which Is to Be Master?* New York: New York University Press.

Muller, J. P., and Richardson, W. J. (1982). *Lacan and Language: A Reader's Guide to Écrits*. New York: International Universities Press.

Ochonisky, J., David, M., and Frismand, J. (1974). Des grands principes aux grands sentiments (Freud: de l'énergie psychique à la dynamique pulsionelle). *L'Evolution Psychiatrique*, 39: 813–32.

Ogden, T. H. (1979). On projective identification. *International Journal of Psychoanalysis*, 60: 357–73.

———. (1982). *Projective Identification and Psychotherapeutic Technique*. New York: Jason Aronson.

———. (1994) *Subjects of Analysis*. Northvale, NJ: Jason Aronson.

———. (1997). Reverie and interpretation. *Psychoanalytic Quarterly*, 66: 567–95.

Ornstein, A. (1998). Response to the discussants: The fate of narcissistic rage in psychotherapy. *Psychoanalytic Inquiry*, 18: 107–19.

Ornstein, P. (1978). Introduction: The evolution of Heinz Kohut's psychoanalytic psychology of the self. In P. Ornstein (ed.), *The Search for the Self: Selected Writings of Heinz Kohut: 1950–1978*. Vol. 1. New York: International Universities Press, 1–106.

Parens, H. (1979). *The Development of Aggression in Early Childhood*. New York: Aronson.

———. (1982). A response. *Psychoanalytic Inquiry*, 2: 283–20.

———. (1997). The unique pathogenicity of sexual abuse. *Psychoanalytic Inquiry*, 17: 250–66.

Pollock, L., & Slavin, J. H. (1988). The struggle for recognition: Disruption and reintegration in the experience of agency. *Psychoanalytic Dialogues*, 8: 857–73.

Rapaport, D. (1960a). On the psychoanalytic theory of motivation. In M. M. Gill (ed.), *The Collected Papers of David Rapaport*. New York: Basic Books, 1967, 853–915.

———. (1960b). *The Structure of Psychoanalytic Theory*. New York: International Universities Press [Psychological Issues, Monograph 6].

Reik, T. (1941). *Masochism in Modern Man*. New York: Farrar and Rinehart.

Renik, O. (1993). Techniques in the light of the analyst's irraducible subjectivity. *Psychoanalytic Quarterly*, 62: 553–71.

———. (1995). The ideal of the anonymous analysts and the problem of the self-disclosure. *Psychoanalytic Quarterly*, 64: 466–95.

Ritvo, S. (1965). Correlation of a childhood and adult neurosis: Based on the adult analysis of a reported childhood case. Paper presented at the 24th Congress of the International Psycho-Analytical Association, Amsterdam, July.

Rizzuto, A.-M., Sashin, J. I., Buie, D. H., and Meissner, S. J., W. W. (1993). A revised theory of aggression. *Psychoanalytic Review,* 80: 29–54.

Robbins, M. D. (1976). Borderline personality organization: The need for a new theory. *Journal of the American Psychoanalytic Association,* 24: 831–53.

Rochlin, G. (1973). *Man's Aggression: The Defense of the Self.* Boston: Gambit.

Rose, H. J. (1971). Caduceus. In *Encyclopaedia Britannica.* Vol. 4. Chicago: William Benton, 566.

Rosenblatt, A. D., and Thickstun, J. T. (1970). A study of the concept of psychic energy. *International Journal of Psychoanalysis,* 51: 265–78.

———. (1977). Energy, information, and motivation: A revision of psychoanalytic theory. *Journal of the American Psychoanalytic Association,* 25: 537–58.

Rosenfeld, H. A. (1952). Notes on the psycho-analysis of the superego conflict of an acute schizophrenic patient. *International Journal of Psychoanalysis,* 31: 111–31

Rosenfled, S. K., and Sprince, M. P. (1963). An attempt to formulate the meaning of the concept "borderline." *Psychoanalytic Study of the Child,* 18: 603–35.

Rothstein, A. (1979). Oedipal conflicts in narcissistic personality disorders. *International Journal of Psychoanalysis,* 60: 189–99.

Rubinstein, B. B. (1967). Explanation and mere description: A metascientific examination of certain aspects of the psychoanalytic theory of motivation. In R. R. Holt (ed.), *Motives and Thought: Psychoanalytic Essays in Honor of David Rapaport.* New York: International Universities Press, 20–77 [Psychological Issues, Monograph 18/19].

Rustin, J. (1997). Infancy, agency, and intersubjectivity: A view of therapeutic action. *Psychoanalytic Dialogues,* 7: 43–62.

Sandler, J., and Sandler, A.-M. (1994). Comments on the conceptualisation of clinical facts in psychoanalysis. *International Journal of Psychoanalysis,* 75: 995–1010.

Schafer, R. (1976). *A New Language for Psychoanalysis.* New Haven, CT: Yale University Press.

———. (1997a). *The Contemporary Kleinians of London.* Madison, CT: International Universities Press.

———. (1997b). *Tradition and Change in Psychoanalysis.* Madison, CT: International Universities Press.

Schmidt-Hellerau, C. (2002). Why aggression? Metapsychological, clinical and technical considerations. *International Journal of Psychoanalysis,* 83: 1269–89.

Schore, A. N. (1994). *Affect Regulation and the Origin of the Self: The Neurobiology of Emotional Development.* Hillsdale, NJ: Lawrence Erlbaum.

———. (2002). Advances in neuropsychoanalysis, attachment theory, and trauma research: implications for self psychology. *Psychoanalytic Inquiry,* 22: 433–84.

———. (1966). *The Id and the Regulatory Principles of Mental Functioning.* New York: International Universities Press.

Schwartz, W. (1984). The two concepts of action and responsibility in psychoanalysis. *Journal of the American Psychoanalytic Association,* 32: 557–572.

Searles, H. (1986). *My Work with Borderline Patients.* Northvale, NJ: Jason Aronson.

Segal, H. (1964). *Introduction to the Work of Melanie Klein.* New York: Basic Books.

———. (1977). Countertransference. *International Journal of Psychoanalytic Psychotherapy,* 6: 81–87.

Shane, M., and Shane, E. (1982). The strands of aggression: A confluence of data. *Psychoanalytic Inquiry,* 2: 263–81.

Sherby, L. B. (1989). Love and hate in the treatment of borderline patients. *Contemporary Psychoanalysis,* 25: 574–591.

Smith, H. F. (2001). Hearing voices: The fate of the analyst's identifications. *Journal of the American Psychoanalytic Association,* 49: 781–812.

Spillius, E. B. (1992). Clinical experiences of projective identification. In R. Anderson (ed.), *Clinical Lectures on Klein and Bion*. London and New York: Tavistock/Routledge, 59–73.

Spitz, R.A. (1957). *No and Yes: On the Genesis of Human Communication*. New York: International Universities Press.

Stechler, G. (1985). The study of infants engenders thinking. *Psychoanalytic Inquiry*, 5: 531–41.

———. (1986). Gender and the self: developmental aspects. *Annual of Psychoanalysis*, 14: 345–55.

———. (1987). Clinical applications of a psychoanalytic systems model of assertion and aggression. *Psychoanalytic Inquiry*, 7: 348–63.

Stechler, G., and Halton, A. (1987). The emergence of assertion and aggression during infancy: a psychoanalytic systems approach. *Journal of the American Psychoanalytic Association*, 35: 821–38.

Stern, D. N. (1985). *The Interpersonal World of the Infant*. New York: Basic Books.

Stoller, R. J. (1979). *Sexual Excitement: Dynamics of Erotic Life*. New York: Pantheon.

Stone, L. (1971). Reflections on the psychoanalytic concept of aggression. *Psychoanalytic Quarterly*, 40: 195–244.

Tähkä, V. (1988) On the early formation of the mind. II. From differentiation to self and object constancy. *Psychoanalytic Study of the Child*, 43: 101–34.

Tansey, M. (1994) Sexual attraction and phobic dread in the countertransference. *Psychoanalytic Dialogues*, 4: 139–52

Tomkins, S. S. (1962). *Affect, Imagery, Consciousness*. Vol. 1. New York: Springer.

———. (1970). Affects as the primary motivational system. In M. B. Arnold (ed.), *Feelings and Emotions: The Loyola Symposium*. New York: Academic Press, 101–10.

Toulmin, S. (1954). The logical status of psychoanalysis. In M. Macdonald (ed.), *Philosophy and Analysis*. New York: Philosophical Library.

Twemlow, S. W. (2000). The roots of violence: converging psychoanalytic explanatory models for power struggles and violence in schools. *Psychoanalytic Quarterly*, 69: 741–85.

Tyson, R. L. (1994) Neurotic negativism and negation in the psychoanalytic situation. *Psychoanalytic Study of the Child*, 49: 293–312.

Valenstein, A. F. (1962) Affects, emotional reliving, and insight in the psycho-analytic process. *International Journal of Psychoanalysis*, 43: 315–24.

———. (1983) Working through and resistance to change: Insight and the action system. *Journal of the American Psychoanalytic Association*, 31 (Suppl.): 353–73.

Weinshel, E. M. (1984). Some observations on the psychoanalytic process. *Psychoanalytic Quarterly*, 53: 63–92.

White, R. W. (1959). Motivation reconsidered: The concept of competence. *Psychological Review*, 66: 297–333.

———. (1963). *Ego and Reality in Psychoanalytic Theory: A Proposal Regarding Independent Ego Energies*. New York: International Universities Press [Psychological Issues, Monograph 11].

Wilson, C. P. (1971). On the limits of the effectiveness of psychoanalysis: Early ego and somatic disturbances. *Journal of the American Psychoanalytic Association*, 19: 552–64.

Winnicott, D. W. (1958a). Aggression in relation to emotional development. In *Collected Papers: Through Paediatrics to Psycho-analysis*. London: Tavistock Publications, 204–28.

———. (1958b). Hate in the countertransference. In *Collected Papers: Through Paediatrics to Psycho-analysis*. London: Tavistock Publications, 194–203.

————. (1960). The theory of the parent-infant relationship. In *The Maturational Processes and the Facilitating Environment.* New York: International Universities Press, 1965, 37–55.

————. (1969). The use of an object and relating through identifications. In *Playing and Reality.* New York: Basic Books, 1971, 86–94.

————. (1984). *Deprivation and Delinquency.* Edited by C. Winnicott, R. Shepherd, and M. Davis. London: Tavistock.

————. (1986). Aggression, guilt and reparation. In *Home Is Where We Start From.* New York: Norton, 80–89.

Wong, P. S. (1999). Anxiety, signal anxiety, and unconscious anticipation: Neuroscientific evidence for an unconscious signal function in humans. *Journal of the American Psychoanalytic Association,* 47: 817–41.

Index